The Philosophy of Schooling

Robin Barrow

READER IN PHILOSOPHY OF EDUCATION,
UNIVERSITY OF LEICESTER

Wheatsheaf
Books

A MEMBER OF THE HARVESTER PRESS GROUP

First published in Great Britain in 1981 by
WHEATSHEAF BOOKS LTD
A MEMBER OF THE HARVESTER PRESS GROUP
Publisher: John Spiers
Director of Publications: Edward Elgar
16 Ship Street, Brighton, Sussex

W16127 (2) £3.95. 981

© Robin Barrow, 1981

British Library Cataloguing in Publication Data
Barrow, Robin
    The philosophy of schooling.
    1. Education—Philosophy
    I. Title
    370.1
    ISBN 0-7108-0105-X
    ISBN 0-7108-0100-9 Pbk

Photoset in Great Britain by
Rowland Phototypesetting Ltd
Bury St Edmunds, Suffolk
and printed by
St Edmundsbury Press,
Bury St Edmunds, Suffolk

Contents

For G.B., who taught me more than he realises,
though no doubt less than he wished.

"Take, for example, the kind of issue which is talked about a good deal nowadays—education and industry. That subject cannot be considered without first asking how far it is the responsibility of, say, the schools to prepare pupils for industry, or to meet the needs of the economy. How far, too, should colleges, universities and polytechnics concentrate on economically and socially useful courses?"

Fred Jarvis, General Secretary, National Union of Teachers, Britain.

Mother: "Head Master, what do you prepare your boys for?"
Head Master: "Death, Madam, death."

Dr Alington, Headmaster of Eton College.

"When the school introduces and trains each child of society into membership within such a little community, saturating him with the spirit of service and providing him with the instruments of effective self-direction, we shall have the deepest and best guarantee of a larger society which is worthy, lovely and harmonious."

John Dewey, American philosopher.

Preface

All three quotations on the opposite page recognise the need to look into the question of the relationship between school and society. I do not mean the question of how they do relate, but the question of how they ought to relate. Should they feed the factories of tomorrow, prepare us for life and death, make society a better place or what? These are fit questions for philosophers to examine.

Philosophy is an abstract activity which consists essentially of thinking things through and can therefore be carried out well enough in the privacy of a study or while walking in a wood. But nothing is more noxious than the misconception that philosophy is impractical. What could be more important for practice than a clear understanding of, and an informed response to, such fundamental questions as these?

Square brackets enclose material that might interrupt the flow of the argument, either by being rather difficult or by going beyond the immediate point, or that is dealt with more fully elsewhere in the book.

Italics are used for a term or phrase being introduced and explained for the first time (and occasionally the second). They are also used for foreign words and phrases, and, occasionally, for emphasis.

The standard dictionary referred to is The Penguin English Dictionary.

1 Philosophy: its Nature and Point

Some years ago I wrote an introduction to philosophy of education. One reviewer, while rather grudgingly conceding that he thought it well enough done, raised the question of whether there was any need for it to have been done at all.[1] Did we, he wondered, really need another introduction to this subject? Since that time a few more have appeared, so the need for yet another one might seem to be highly questionable. I am therefore going to start this one by explaining why, however inadequately it may be done, the main thing is that it should be done at all. This will enable me to introduce the question of what philosophy involves by drawing attention to a few of its peculiarities.

There is a widespread tendency to think that introductions by their very nature cannot (or perhaps should not) be contentious, and that therefore they will not vary a great deal. They are bound to cover the same sort of area as each other, in much the same sort of way, and therefore we can stick with those we already have, at least until some rare revolution in the field makes them obsolete. This may well be the case with a subject such as, say, physics. But it is not the case with philosophy. For in philosophy there is room for a great deal of argument about its nature: what it is and what form it should take. Whereas, generally speaking, French and English physicists do not have fundamentally different ideas of what physics is, French and English philosophers certainly do have different conceptions of philosophy. Indeed, quite often two colleagues in the same department may have radically different views on the nature of philosophy. Even at an introductory level one unavoidably takes one kind of stance rather than others, and that gives us one reason why, ideally, we want several introductions to philosophy of education, to represent the many different views of the subject that there are. A second and obvious reason, which, unlike the first, would apply in any field, is that different readers will prefer different styles and approaches. There is, for example, a striking difference between the view of those who think that time spent on explaining what philosophy is, is time wasted, and who consequently jump headlong into doing some philosophy (e.g. James Gribble, *Introduction to Philosophy of Education*), and my view that there is nothing more important than getting people to appreciate the distinctive nature of the subject before getting immersed in it. Yet such people and I may have more or less similar conceptions of philosophy.

Thirdly, it is often very hard to distinguish between the introductory text and the learned article in terms of quality and excellence in philosophy. There is, for example, much more of value, erudition and importance in John Hospers' *Human Conduct*, a comprehensive and well-constructed introduction to ethics, than there is in a good many articles published in the leading philosophical journals. This is because the quality of philosophy has to be assessed far more by reference to the way in which it is done or proceeds than to its conclusions or the production of original ideas. Philosophy is more concerned to make advances in our understanding by refining our grasp of what we already have some knowledge of, than to generate completely new knowledge. So a basic introductory account of a familiar theory such as the moral or ethical (I use the words interchangeably) theory of intuitionism might be more enlightening, more penetrating and more valuable than a more ambitious attempt, even a quite reasonable attempt, to present an entirely original ethical theory. Sir Alfred Ayer, now a distinguished elder statesman amongst philosophers, first came to prominence with a little book called *Language, Truth and Logic*, which certainly did introduce a number of (then) startling and revolutionary ideas. But in the end, although to some extent his fame rests on that book, what makes him a very good philosopher is not the fact that he produced such an arresting theory or set of ideas, but that he argues with extraordinary lucidity and clarity. Indeed, later in this book I shall argue, as would most people, that what Ayer originally had to say about ethics was palpably inadequate as a final statement on the subject. But that does not mean that his presentation of his view was not illuminating and stimulating, or that he was not a good philosopher.

The point is that philosophy is an activity; it is something you do rather than a body of subject matter you study. Doing philosophy means philosophising, and your competence is measured for the most part in how well you are doing it rather than in what you come up with at the end of it. As a matter of fact, philosophising in some shape or form is very easy and is almost certainly something you already do, as will shortly become clear. The object of a book like this is to help people do it well, which is an acquired art, by attuning the philosophical ear more finely, by helping the reader to increase his sensitivity to the sort of points that interest the philosopher and by improving his facility in handling them.

Fourthly, introductory philosophical texts are extremely important in practical terms, because, philosophy being what it is, it is more important that everybody should develop some competence at it, than that a few should be very good at it. By and large, the value of all citizens having a basic grasp of something like chemistry has probably been overrated, although our way of life makes us heavily reliant on top level scientific expertise. The situation is more or less reversed with philosophy: top level philosophers, while they may alter the face of philosophy for academics in some respect, do not make a significant impact directly on society through their philosophy, nor should one expect them to. What matters, however, is that familiar insights in philosophy should be disseminated far more widely. In fact philosophy has crucial practical importance on a very wide scale, as will become clear throughout this book, and it is a sad indictment of academic philosophers that, with honourable exceptions, they have managed to bury this truth.

There are four reasons then, three of which arise out of the particular nature of philosophy, for concluding that in principle we should welcome many introductions to philosophy: there are a variety of conceptions of the subject, different approaches or styles will suit different people, work of quality and insights are to be found as readily at this level as in more advanced monographs or learned journals, and, from a practical point of view, the introductory level is the crucially important one in this subject.

In addition I have a fifth, personal, reason for wanting to write another introductory text and that is that with increased reflection made possible by the passing of time my views have changed or been modified in various ways. I have a much clearer conception of what I take philosophy to be, for one thing. In fact the only view that remains quite unchanged is not a philosophical one, but one about writing books like this; it is that, though the emphasis of an introduction to philosophy should be on enabling people to philosophise better or to become more familiar with the art of philosophising, that is no reason for such an introduction to avoid getting its hands dirty and taking a stand in relation to real issues. Accordingly this book makes its attempt to introduce the reader to the art of philosophising by using that art to pinpoint and answer some fundamental questions relating to schooling.

2 THE NATURE OF PHILOSOPHY

So far I have merely made a few comments *about* philosophy. Now let me clarify what I take it to be or consist in. If you look up "philosophy" in the dictionary you will not get a lot of help, because the definitions given there do not really coincide with what contemporary academic philosophers mean by the term. Thus the dictionary offers as one definition "the study of ultimate nature of existence"; well, maybe some academic philosophers think that at the end of the day that's what it's all about, but to most of us it is not even clear what that means, let alone how it relates to what we actually do. Another definition provided by my dictionary is "any specified system of thought" on matters such as reality, knowledge and goodness. This is quite a common sense in everyday use, as exemplified by people saying things like "my philosophy of life is this". But although I shall make further reference to this sense at the end of the chapter, at this stage it is rather misleading; on the whole, academic philosophy is not concerned to create systems of thought. Thirdly, the dictionary refers to "resignation", which reminds one of expressions such as "He took the blow philosophically", meaning that he didn't make a song and dance about it. But again, perhaps unfortunately, professional philosophers are not necessarily any more stoical or philosophical in this sense than anybody else. Almost the only clue the dictionary provides to the sense "philosophy" has for the practising academic is a reference to the study confining itself to matters "discoverable by human reasoning". For philosophy in the sense we shall be concerned with is essentially bound up with reasoning. We can start, then, by making the point that no empirical inquiry as such is philosophical. Philosophy may make reference to physical facts in a number of ways, but the business of philosophising is exclusively a business of reasoning.

I define philosophy as "the examination of logic and meaning" and will now expand on that definition. Nobody need be frightened by the perhaps portentous sound of the phrase "examination of logic". It is possible to study logic as a branch of philosophy and that may be quite a technical and stringent business. But it is necessary to distinguish between the *study of logic* and a general *concern with logic*, which is a feature of all philosophising. The study of logic involves an interest in formulating and classifying rules of logic, rather as an etymologist is concerned to pinpoint and classify the derivations of words, or a lepidopterist to classify butterflies. The student of logic learns of such things as the law of the excluded middle, the law of non-contradiction or the fallacy of illicit progress. He learns these labels or names, he learns what these laws (or fallacies) are, and he learns what pattern they follow; hence he is able to classify arguments in terms of observing or failing to observe them, and he recognises instances of them when they crop up. Studying logic involves trying to understand the basic principles of logic rather than trying to be logical about anything in particular. In *symbolic logic* a language of signs is developed to represent the basic phrases and rules; *formal logic* proceeds verbally, but in a strict and technical way; *informal logic*, as its name implies, involves a classification more in terms of everyday language.

No doubt studying logic in one of these forms may have some important repercussions on one's ability to think in a logical manner and to recognise illogical argument where one sees it; but it is not a sufficient condition of being logical, nor is it a necessary condition. The fact that you have studied logic does not in itself mean that you are bound to be logical (so it isn't sufficient) and you can be logical without studying logic (so it isn't necessary). It is being logical rather than studying logic that is an essential part of philosophising. In saying that philosophy is partly an examination of logic, I mean that the philosopher's attention should always be on whether an argument is logical, as opposed to any of the other things it might also be such as elegant, amusing, rhetorical, clever, persuasive or intimidating. When your ear is philosophically attuned, you are able to shut out all such other considerations and discern only the harmonious flow of the logical or the discordant crash of a lapse in logic.

I stress this point because, still to my surprise, I encounter many students new to philosophy who react to certain authors by saying things such as "I don't like his style", "This appeals to me" or "He's a reactionary fascist", none of which should be of any immediate concern. The question for the philosopher is: is the argument that I have before me logical? That is to say, does the argument that I have before me proceed from its premises coherently, clearly and without contradiction or obvious omission; is it, as the dictionary definition of "logical" has it, "in conformity with the laws of correct reasoning"? (To return to a previous point, note that it is possible to be able to judge whether an argument is in conformity with the laws of reasoning, without being able to tabulate and name such laws in the abstract.)

Although keeping an eye on logic does not necessitate the study of logic as such, it does rapidly and inevitably lead one to raise questions about what in particular instances is logical. An important part of the philosopher's task is to be continually probing and querying whether steps are logical. For example, the philosopher contemplating the question of God's existence might well be driven to ask himself what *kind* of evidence would constitute a good reason for believing in his existence. (e.g. Is it logical to treat the appearance of design in the universe as evidence?) The moral philosopher might question the validity of trying to base evaluative conclusions on exclusively factual premises. (e.g. Is it logical to draw the conclusion that the classless society is good from the mere fact, if it is a fact, that it is inevitably coming?)

In short doing philosophy, being a philosopher or philosophising, involves minimally both a concern that all reasoning, whether one's own or another's, should be logical in the broad sense of rational, and that it should be assessed from that point of view, and also, intermittently, a more specific attempt to consider what would constitute good reasons or logical steps in particular kinds of case.

One factor that may very obviously affect whether what somebody says is logical is what they mean by key terms in their argument. Whether it is coherent and sensible to claim that all knowledge is relative or that God exists depends to some extent upon what is meant by "knowledge" "relative" "God" and "existence". Concern with *meaning*, the other part of my definition, lies at the heart of philosophy, and this requires slightly more comment than did the concern with logic.

The word "meaning" itself has many meanings. It can be used as a synonym for "portends", as in the question "What do those clouds mean?"; it can be used as a synonym for "intend" ("I mean to get you"), as a synonym for "necessitate" ("This means war") or even as a synonym for "is a synonym for". ("Beanz means Heinz", if it means anything, means that "Beans" and "Heinz Beans" are interchangeable.) Its most common use, however, is probably to refer to something like a dictionary definition, as when we say that "table" means "a piece of furniture with a flat top supported on legs at a convenient height for use by a seated person". When you ask what a word means you might conceivably be asking for its *denotation*, which is to say instances or examples of what it refers to (i.e. "House" denotes the place I live, the place you live, No. 10 Downing Street, the White House, etc.). But philosophers at any rate, and probably you most of the time, are far more likely to be interested in its *descriptive meaning* and *emotive meaning*.

The descriptive meaning of a word, which is sometimes also called the *designation* of a word, is typically what the dictionary gives: a list of the characteristics that something has to have to be a house, a table or whatever. So the definition of "table" quoted above tells you what "table" means in the sense of giving you the designation or the descriptive meaning of the word "table". The emotive meaning of a word or sentence is embodied in its capacity to evoke or express feelings. This capacity arises out of what is usually termed the *connotation* (i.e. the overtones or associative ideas) of a word. Thus "snake" designates or means descriptively "a long legless serpent". It denotes each and every snake there is. For many of us the word connotes something revolting and slimy (even though snakes, as it happens, are not slimy). To call somebody a snake consequently serves to express and arouse feelings of revulsion; that function is the emotive meaning of the utterance "You snake". (Students of logic sometimes use the term "connote" in the way that the rest of us use "designate".)

Probably the most important point to appreciate at this stage is that some utterances, for example "hullo" and "push off", only have emotive meaning. This gives rise to the interesting suggestion that a great deal more of our language, particularly in areas like moral and religious discourse, though it is presumed to have descriptive meaning, may not in fact do so. It may turn out to be essentially or even purely emotive. [See below, Chapter Five.]

We come now to a most important issue: the distinction between words and concepts. And the first thing to take to heart is that there *is* a distinction. Strictly speaking, and in the interests of precision and communication we should speak strictly, a concept is a general notion or idea, an abstraction that represents or signifies the unifying principle of various distinct particulars. You grasp or have the concept of redness when you appreciate the idea of the red colour common to all red things; you have the concept of colour when you grasp the idea that there is something common to all coloured things, despite some of them being of a different colour; you have a concept of justice when you go beyond thinking in terms of particular acts and classify them together in respect of some common feature which in your view is what makes them just. It follows that you cannot have a concept of concrete particulars such as this pen or that man. You can, of course, have an image of this pen or that man—a mental picture or a thought relating to them. But the concept of pen must by definition be abstract and general: the concept of a pen is the notion of what constitutes penness, what makes pens pens or what is common to all pens. A phrase such as "my concept of Ronald Reagan" therefore amounts to a misuse of language; one should rather talk of one's picture or one's idea of Ronald Reagan.

It is always dangerous to talk of misuse of language, since

today's misuse is tomorrow's orthodoxy, but it is important here, because to understand philosophy you need to appreciate the distinction between concepts, as defined, and words. It should be obvious, now that it is clear what a concept is, that they are distinct, but they are obviously also closely related. We, being verbal thinkers, identify or refer to our concepts by means of words. "Red" is the word that picks out the concept of redness. But clearly they are not identical. Sometimes one word may be variously used to refer to more than one concept on different occasions. The word "brownie" may sometimes denote what are otherwise called "fairies" (as in Britain) and sometimes what is otherwise known as a species of cake (as in the USA). Equally, one concept may have more than one word to refer to it, as "fairy" and "brownie" may both refer to the same thing, or as the English word "black" and the French word "noir" do. Indeed a person might have a concept and not have a word to label it: one might recognise the common element of plumage on birds, but not know that word or any other suitable public word. (An important convention to be aware of, and one that has already been observed in this chapter, is that of using inverted commas when one wishes to refer to the word and none when one wishes to refer to the concept. Thus "black" has five letters, and black is my favourite colour.)

One thing that almost all philosophers are interested in is the meaning of words. When we hear somebody say that creativity is an important objective in education, the philosophically tuned ear pricks up, and we want to ask what sense of "creativity" the speaker has in mind. Anybody with half an eye on what is going on knows that people use the word in widely differing senses (not just of different things or people), and whether we can agree that it is an important objective may depend on which sense is being employed. Similarly, if I am accused of attempting to indoctrinate my students, my immediate reaction would be one of denial. That is because what I understand by the word "indoctrination" is something that I regard as objectionable and that as a matter of fact I do not engage in. But it might well turn out that what the word "indoctrination" means to my critic is something different from what I take it to mean. [For detailed examination of the concepts of creativity and indoctrination see below this chapter and Chapters Two and Five.]

But—and here we come to the single most important paragraph in this book—examining different senses of words such as "indoctrination" and "creativity", which I shall call *verbal analysis*, is distinct from what I shall call *conceptual analysis*. And, although verbal analysis is of importance to the philosopher, as it must be to anyone who wants to communicate with understanding, it is not in itself sufficient for the philosopher. *Philosophical analysis* must include conceptual analysis in addition to preliminary verbal analysis. What constitutes conceptual analysis is a thorough, precise, and detailed unpacking or explication of a concept (i.e. general idea or unifying principle), which nine times out of ten will mean a more detailed exploration of one particular usage of a word. Thus, to stick with our examples, let us assume that you answer my verbal inquiry as to what you mean by "creativity" or what sense of "creativity" you have in mind, by saying that a feeling of effective surprise is the hallmark of the creative act. I now know what sense you give to the word; I can distinguish this sense from, say, its use as a synonym for self-expression or lateral thinking. But now I find that I have difficulty in fully grasping this particular sense: what exactly is a feeling of effective surprise? How do I know whether I am experiencing it? Who is supposed to experience it? Tell me more. It is in raising these sorts of questions, and trying to focus more clearly on what is actually involved in the notion of a feeling of effective surprise, that we embark upon conceptual analysis, for we are now trying to understand a particular conception, as referred to in one particular use of the word. Doing the same sort of thing with the indoctrination example, we note again first the need for verbal analysis—the need to answer questions like how and why is he using the word "indoctrination", which, let us suppose, gets this answer: "He is using the word both emotively and descriptively. He is hoping to provoke you and turn others against you, but he is still saying something descriptive. In this case the designation of the word is more or less 'intentionally closing somebody else's mind on a matter'". There we have a definition, one sense of the word singled out; and there the verbal analysis stops. Now begins conceptual analysis as we try to gain a more detailed understanding of the notions of intention and closing the mind which are an integral part of this conception of indoctrination.

We can now answer the frequently-raised question: "What is the difference between a dictionary definition and conceptual analysis?" The answer is largely one of degree. A dictionary usually gives a more detailed synonym (though not always; sometimes it describes the function of the word, especially if, like "good", it has no agreed designation). Conceptual analysis begins, can only begin, when you know the meaning of the word in the sense of having a verbal definition such as the dictionary may give, but do not fully grasp the significance and implications of that definition. It follows that there is by no means always any call for conceptual analysis. Sometimes it could take place but would be trivial, as would be the case if somebody, on being told that "biscuit" means "a kind of crisp dry bread, more or less hard" were to raise questions about whether shortbread counted as a biscuit or not, or how hard "more or less hard" was. These would be genuine conceptul questions, exactly on a par with asking whether "intentionally closing the mind" is compatible with sincerely thinking you are not doing so. The difference is that the latter is a more important question. Sometimes conceptual analysis simply isn't called for. When you know that a bachelor is an unmarried man of marriageable age, you have a clear grasp of the concept.

One final preliminary about concepts. There is a common but mistaken tendency to equate vague concepts with general ones and precise ones with specific ones. But a concept may be vague and general, vague and specific, precise and specific or precise and general. Animal is a more general concept than duck, but no more vague in the sense of hazy or confused. While the Boojum in Lewis Carroll's *Hunting of the Snark* is, though specific like duck, remarkably vague or unclear. Philosophy is concerned to clarify all concepts, general and specific; it does not automatically refuse to countenance general concepts although, as we shall see later, they are less informative.

It should now be clear what conceptual analysis is and how it differs from verbal analysis. I do not want to lay down the law about what people who call themselves philosophers must do, nor do I want to pretend that in practice verbal and conceptual analysis can be kept quite separate. I merely want to stress that there are two distinguishable activities—considering various senses of a word and giving more detailed consideration to a particular sense —and to emphasise this distinction by giving each activity a distinct label.

But now a closely-related issue has to be raised. There is a school of thought which thinks that the appropriate strategy for engaging in conceptual analysis is by means of a study of *ordinary language usage*. So, if we want to explicate the concept of happiness, the way to proceed on this view is to inquire into the sort of locutions or utterances that are commonly to be found amongst language users. We have to ask questions like: "Do people say 'I thought I was happy but I wasn't' or 'He feels happy, but he's not', or 'Pigs are happy animals'?" The answers to such questions are used to draw up a picture of what it makes sense to say concerning happiness and what it does not. This view is generally termed the ordinary language view and leads to such epigrammatic utterances as "meaning is use". It is a school of thought to be treated with extreme caution, if not rejected outright.

The objections to it, as thus baldly stated, are as follows. Firstly, there is the problem of what counts as ordinary usage. If this means all actual usage, then conceptual analysis becomes an empirical business and philosophers could not do it, as they persist in maintaining they can, while sitting at home in their studies. If on the other hand ordinary usage does not mean all actual usage, we have the problem of determining what is ordinary usage. Is the use of "happy" in reference to pigs ordinary or not? One could find a way out of this by interpreting "ordinary" to mean "frequent" or "usual", but any such strategy would be arbitrary and still involve either the problem of judgement or the problem of empiricism. That is to say either the activity becomes the empirical one of tabulating a set of uses; or it becomes one of judging whether some actual usages count, without any apparent criteria for making the judgement. Secondly, whatever is meant by ordinary language, it is highly likely that the findings will sometimes be contradictory: some people will talk as if pigs can be happy, others will find that way of talking strange. Thirdly, it is absurd to suggest that the test of whether it makes sense to say that pigs are happy is whether ordinary people do say it, since this makes it impossible to have a view not generally held. If, for example, I suddenly awake to the new thought that animals too might be capable of experiencing happiness, this cannot be true, for what "happy" means is partly defined in terms of it not applying to animals. Fourthly, one might add the intuitive feeling that when one deliberates over the question of whether shortbread should count as a biscuit, whether and in what sense intending to close the mind is compatible with sincere avowal that one isn't, or whether happiness seems the kind of thing one might legitimately attribute to pigs, it simply isn't the case that we are interested in how people may talk. Our manner of talk will give expression to our way of thinking, and *that might be mistaken.*

The above considerations make it clear beyond a doubt that no crude version of ordinary language philosophy is acceptable, and that the claim that "meaning is use" may be true of words but has no obvious application to concepts. There is, besides, the more important point that if you take philosophy to be co-extensive with ordinary language philosophy, you leave something undone which could have been done. Never mind how English language speakers tend to use the word "love", there remains the question of what precisely I mean by love, what exactly I am getting at—of articulating my conception, if I have one that is clear, and of clarifying it, if it is hazy and vague. That is a vital task, and that is what I understand by conceptual analysis.

What I am arguing for does not preclude an interest in ordinary language, but it goes beyond it and refuses to be dominated by it. At the level of methodology it seems very sensible to take account of ordinary language: it may be suggestive, give one ideas and provide a path to set out on; but one may want to leave that path. The fact that people say, if they do (and *a fortiori* think it makes sense to say), "I thought I was happy but I wasn't" is worth thinking about. It shows that one aspect of their conception of happiness is that it is possible to think one is happy and yet not be so. But (*a*) they may be mistaken, even on their own terms, because it might be logically incoherent given other aspects of their view of happiness to make the claim, and (*b*) I do not have to share their conception, and my interest is in my conception, not in the largely factual question of what other people's conceptions are. The philosopher's job is not to report the conceptions of others, but to root out incoherence and refine conceptions, especially his own. In clarifying my concept of happiness (or anything else), I present a more perfect conception to the world, for the quality of conceptions lies in their internal coherence and clarity. No amount of people saying "X feels happy but he is not" proves that it makes sense to say it, just as no amount of people saying that Athene sprang fully armed from the head of Zeus proves that it makes sense. We need then to distinguish a *linguistic test* and an *intelligibility test*. Frequent in philosophical literature are phrases like "we would not say such and such". These phrases can be interpreted either as appeals to usage (i.e. straightforward claims about how words are used) or as disguised appeals to intelligibility (i.e. a way of saying "surely you, reader, don't regard it as intelligible to say . . ."). The former has its place, as I've already admitted. But the latter is the crucial one. Language use may guide, but it may be gainsaid. The philosopher's task is, by means of introspection and guided by usage, to explore concepts and to reveal what is entailed and to lay it out in the open; his main task is to clarify hazy concepts. In the end it is a very personal matter. I can't finally clarify your concepts, since I don't have them. I clarify a conception. You decide whether it is of interest to you, and whether you want to give it the same label or name as I do.

A very understandable and frequent question about conceptual analysis is this: "How do I know if and when my analysis is correct? *If* it is just a case of looking inside my mind, what are the criteria of success?" It's a good question. But there's a straight-forward answer, which is that there are four criteria. Firstly, you may be internally incoherent or unclear. In explicating your conception of education, for instance, you might say that education is of the whole man. But that would merely replace one conceptual problem with many, for the notion of the whole man, though it sounds well enough, is far from clear or obviously coherent. Secondly, you may be inconsistent. You might say that education is of the whole man, and then say that emotions don't come into it. But on the face of it this is contradictory since, whatever con-stitutes the whole man, it must surely include his emotional side. Thirdly, you may fail to see entailments or implications which, were you to see them, you would not accept. Fourthly, you may fail to note that a consequence of your conception is a clash with certain other opinions you hold. These, as far as I know, are the only criteria for assessing conceptual analysis. They are, therefore, the only legitimate terms in which to mark a philosophy essay (concerned with analysis).

"So, if I write a clear, coherent, internally consistent account of my idea of education which squares with my other beliefs and the implications of which I discern and accept, I cannot be wrong?" No, you cannot be wrong. You can be marvelled at, you can be idiosyncratic, you can have a conception shared by no-one else, you can have a conception that would be given a different label by other people. You can look something of an idiot. But you cannot be wrong. "But that means that if we have a seminar on democracy, we're just talking about different things. Your conception, her conception, his conception, my conception." Well, yes, it may do. But that in itself may be a realisation of the utmost importance— that we *are* talking about different things and there are different things to be talked about, call them what you will. We may have to learn to live with the fact that what you understand by "democracy" is not what I understand by it. Besides, it does not always turn out that we are talking about different things. The situation is not always so anarchic. The truth is that conceptions once articulated and refined don't often vary much between people, partly because the four criteria mentioned set some limits, and partly because we acquire our concepts through a public language that both moulds and standardises conceptions. There is really little as misconceived as the mythical argument between the philosopher claiming he's looking for education in the true sense, and the sociologist saying there are only socially determined meanings. What there are, are, firstly, concepts, which by their nature are what they are and not another thing, whether anybody is entertaining them or has thought of them or not. (The concept of colour does not cease to exist, because people cease to have it in their minds). Secondly, there are ideas, as entertained by people, and thirdly there are words publicly ascribed to concepts. (There may also be words privately ascribed to concepts). What we are interested in achieving is a state of affairs where words are systematically applied to clear conceptions, and those conceptions are entertained as ideas. The words people *use*, the ideas they *have* (that is to say the concepts they actually entertain or recognise) obviously are to some extent influenced by social factors. But concepts themselves, by definition, are beyond such influence. Roundness is roundness is roundness is roundness, no matter what the state of the world.

When it comes to discussion about a concept, therefore, the task of each disputant, to a large extent, is to act as exemplar of one attempting to give a clear account of his own conception. But there are nonetheless points of contact between disputants: one can point out inconsistencies or ambiguities and any inadequacy in respect of the four criteria mentioned in what the other person says. But if what is said is clear and coherent there is nothing more to be said by the other person except I do or do not care about this.

Now that we know what philosophy is, a few more remarks can be made about it. It should be clear why I said above that philosophy is something that everybody does and is already familiar with; you have almost certainly had occasion to vet your own or other people's arguments from the point of view of logic (as distinct from the point of view of pleasure, scoring points or even truth). You must surely have had occasion to wonder what *kind* of reason would be relevant to determining some issue, as distinct from wondering whether some particular reason does determine an issue. (That is to say most of us at one time or another have wondered not just whether our liberal democratic society is morally acceptable but what kind of reasoning would settle an issue like that anyway.) And there must have been times when you've confessed to yourself, if to nobody else, that though you keep using some word like "love" your conception of love is not all that it might be. You perhaps are confident that it denotes experiences like your present one, but what does it designate? What are you saying when you claim to be in love? Still more frequently you must have wondered what somebody else means by phrases like "the metaphysics of maths" "the reality behind reality" or "the dialectic of life" and whether they have any clear idea of what they are talking about or are just mouthing words, making much sound and little sense. Almost certainly, as I say, you can philosophise. The hard part is to do it better, which means more rigorously, more relentlessly and more thoroughly.

I call philosophy an art because it involves judgement and sensitivity as much as skills and technique. No doubt any activity will benefit from a degree of sensitivity, but attuning the philosophic ear partly means acquiring a certain sensitivity—the sort of sensitivity that recognises that pursuing the biscuit question is not really important or, more generally, judges when it is and when it is not appropriate to raise various questions. There is obviously no single skill of philosophising as there is of waggling your ears, and it is not to be defined in terms of subject matter as so many subjects are; you can philosophise about any subject from science to strip-tease or from history to hamburgers (although often judgement will tell you the task is trivial). This is why it is known as a *second-order* subject or discipline. It can be applied to the foundations of any other subject, for there are always philosophical questions to be asked about the basis of a discipline, questions about the meaning of its fundamental concepts and the logic of its procedures. (Science, for instance, relies heavily on induction. But the question of whether inductive reasoning is valid as a form of reasoning is obviously a philosophical rather than a scientific question). Other hallmarks of philosophy to be noted are its rigour, generality and abstract nature. If you are going to philosophise about something—let us say, the nature of beauty— this means that you are going to go all the way in probing the meaning and logic of claims about beauty—and going all the way, with single minded concern, means that you must be rigorous even to the point of what seems to the outsider pedantry. The activity is abstract and general because it is not concerned with particular concrete instances such as whether this painting is beautiful, that man is kind, this is God's home on earth or this shows that, but with the abstract and general matters of which these are merely instances. (i.e. What is meant by beauty? what is involved in kindness in the abstract? what is meant by God's home? does this kind of thing constitute evidence for that kind of conclusion?)

People sometimes wonder about the apparent absurdity and unreality of examples used by philosophers and their refusal to be bound by seemingly well known points of fact. We allow ourselves this freedom because we are concerned with points of principle and not particular cases. We are not concerned with whether this particular act or product is creative, but with what it would have to be, what conditions it would have to meet, to be creative; not with whether this school is facing a particular problem, but whether this sort of thing counts as a problem or whether a problem of this sort is of educational importance. We say things to ourselves such as, "Suppose a man were to throw mud at a wall, would he be creative?" not because we think it probable that many men will throw mud at walls, or that if they do they will be thought creative, but to test logical possibilities. Very often we push examples to the extreme in order to force ourselves to face up to unlikely considerations and to remove ourselves from irrelevant associations involved in more realistic examples. We challenge the ground rules that others take for granted and, indeed, that have to be taken for granted most of the time, if we are to carry on in the normal way of life. That is why, though it can be done conservatively or by people who happen to be conservative thinkers, philosophy is essentially radical. It leaves nothing as it is, for it replaces acquiescence with either understanding or frank perplexity. A philosopher might happen to end up committed to a set of conservative beliefs. But if he does, insofar as he is a philosopher and not just claiming to be one, he must be presumed to have committed himself to them only after trying to turn them and all other beliefs inside out and upside down, in an attempt to gain a fuller understanding of them and to establish their relative plausibility.

3 THE POINT AND DANGERS OF PHILOSOPHISING

The point, purpose and value of philosophy should be self-evident now that it is clear what it is, just as nobody who understands what is involved in being rational could coherently declare that he saw no point in rationality. By philosophising we aim to improve the quality of our thinking and our discussion, so that, provided our premises are well-founded and we do not ignore relevant factors, we may arrive at true conclusions. The premises themselves, of course, may also be scrutinised in turn for their coherence and plausibility. Nothing is more extraordinary then (nor, as I said above, more an indictment of academic philosophy), than that philosophy is widely thought of as being a subject irrelevant to practical concerns, or as not being of much use or value from the point of view of social welfare. The point of philosophy is to rid our minds of hazy generalisations, ambiguous slogans, inarticulate ideas and half-truths, and to enable us to detect and demolish them in the reasoning of others, and then, in their place, to cultivate the thinking and communicating of precise, discriminatory, clearly expounded truths or steps in reasoning. It is to enable us to resist and see through the catch-phrase, the advertisement playing on our emotions, package-deal thinking or ideology, unnecessarily or meaningless coined jargon, and gimmickry. It is to render us sceptical of all that is not presented to us simply and clearly. For there is no truth so profound that it cannot be presented in a simple and clear way (provided that we allow that the occasional need for technical terms may make what is said unfamiliar rather than abstruse). If you cannot express your ideas clearly, in nine cases out of ten that is because you haven't got a clear grasp of them. [Not, of course, in all cases. See below Chapter Four.]

Philosophy is in fact indispensable. Of course the cynic will say that it takes a philosopher to say that and that no doubt the sociologist holds much the same opinion of sociology. No doubt he does, and no doubt the cynic has a small point: we do have a predisposition to value our particular interests. But to assume that, because a philosopher is known to have a vested interest in saying that philosophy is indispensable, what he says is not true or can be ignored, is to provide an instance of precisely the fallacious sort of reasoning that philosophy is out to destroy. Whatever my personal stake in this, it remains quite clear that philosophy *is* of supreme importance, unless you do not value precise thinking. Those who deny its value will invariably turn out to be those who do not understand its nature. Those, for example, who think that "it's all about words" or who confuse it with the history of ideas or who assume that it is confined to the study of values—all of which are notable and valuable activities themselves no doubt, but which do not constitute adequate accounts of philosophy.

I'm saying all this with cheerful belligerence, because it's time to get tough. Politesse is all very well, but nonsense is nonsense and should be exposed as such and not deferentially respected as "a point of view" or protected on the grounds that it is a rare species the survival of which is in danger. (There is of course a pedagogical problem here, and not only for philosophy. When one is in some kind of teaching position, very often one is more respectful of poor argument and unsound opinion than one should be from the point of view of reason alone, on grounds such as those of encouragement, caution or even humility. Here I am granting myself freedom from any restraints other than those of reason, since I am not addressing myself to particular individuals or particular cherished opinions.)

One error that it is important to expose is the false but popular assumption that certain truth is the exclusive reward of the empirical search, and that speculation and logical reasoning off the field of battle must be less revealing about the real world. This is clearly not the case; in social affairs at least empirical research almost always means generalisation arrived at by means of observation or report at secondhand. Even well-done research of this kind must be tentative—a great deal more tentative than some of the findings of philosophy. It is far more certain that no bachelor is married than it is that bachelors are less happy than married men, though both claims have been made with equal confidence. Nor is philosophical research any the less about the real world (indeed we need some philosophising to clarify what the real world is—again, there's a widespread and clumsy assumption that only the physical world is real). Take for example the indubitable philosophical truths that morality and religion are logically autonomous, that the fact that something is the case is not sufficient to show that it is good that it is, that emotions differ from mere feelings in having a cognitive element, that indoctrination and education as commonly understood are logically incompatible —these are of considerable practical importance and are manifestly about the real world whatever precisely is meant by that phrase.

The trouble is that travelling by the philosophical road is obviously going to be a slow, painstaking business; it requires stamina and discipline that many people lack and it requires that one recognise inadequacies in one's thinking which it is hard to admit to. The fact remains that it is logically inconceivable that good empirical research should take place without good philosophising. For no research can be revealing and reliable that is not set up with precise discrimination and conceptual clarity and carried through in a logically coherent manner. It is worth repeating here that verbal definition is not the same thing as conceptual clarity: saying "What I mean by a 'progressive teacher' is a blue-eyed one" or "What I mean by a 'progressive teacher' is a metaphysical monster" is, in either case, to provide a definition. But the first, though perfectly clear, is too general to allow of anything much in the way of revealing research, while the latter doesn't, on further reflection, appear to mean anything. [See below for a more detailed examination of this point, Chapter Six.]

If you care to think about it you will appreciate that nothing could be more indubitable a fact than that precision of ideas is crucial for illuminating thought, research or discussion, and furthermore that what is usually confused with indubitable fact, namely empirically supported or based factual *claims*, can never be quite certainly fact. Any empirical research is always dependent to some extent on the perceiver—how he sees and organises the material he is concerned with—and any empirical finding must always be provisional, since it can never be the product of exhaustive research. Whereas the truths of mathematics and logic have a permanence quite beyond the touch of man. Another important point that arises directly out of what has been said is this: anybody could in principle do empirical work of any sort well, provided that he were neither physically handicapped nor conceptually lacking; but someone who lacks conceptual finesse cannot, except by chance, do good empirical work. None of this is designed to be hostile to the sciences, though some readers are bound to huff and puff and feel that it is. But I am not referring to the rival merits of actual accredited philosophers and empiricists, and I am not talking about the track record of the various disciplines. I am making a quite undeniable logical observation: it follows from what is meant by philosophy that philosophising is a necessary condition of any respectable academic research. A good sociologist must have something of the good philosopher in him. If he has not, he cannot be a good sociologist. And the same must be true, at the highest level, of the good historian, the good physicist or the good psychologist.

Despite this, there are of course dangers in studying philosophy as an academic discipline. One is that one may refuse to commit oneself on issues on the grounds that any positive view would be premature. In principle such grounds are generally correct: we don't, for example, *know* for certain whether abortion is morally acceptable or not. A dogmatic view is unwarranted. Yet action of some sort is inevitable (and it should be remembered that in cases like this inaction is itself a form of action). But there is little doubt, I'm afraid, that philosophers often find not so much that they want to sit on a fence as that they are stuck on one. Another danger is that one may begin to play the game for its own sake: one may become finickity about precise definition or exact logic when they are indeed lacking but are not perhaps necessary to the occasion. This is one area where those who do and those who don't understand philosophy may equally give it a bad name. The man who, when accused of brawling with someone on the floor of a bar, says "it all depends what you mean by brawling" is abusing the techniques of philosophy. Of course what he says is correct. It is also unnecessary and out of place. Knowing when it is appropriate to insist on philosophising is largely a matter of judgement and comes with experience and familiarity. The main danger, however, remains that of misconceiving the nature of the beast, and on that I have now said enough.

4 MEASURING PROGRESS IN PHILOSOPHY

We have already talked about judging or estimating success in conceptual analysis, but there is a wider problem of measuring progress in studying philosophy, since whereas in most subjects you learn more as you proceed, in philosophy in a sense you unlearn as you proceed, and that can be psychologically difficult to come to grips with. Pertinent to this issue and part of the rich mythology of philosophy is the story of Socrates. He was a Greek living in Athens during the second half of the fifth century B.C. That was perhaps the most glorious age the city ever experienced, despite the fact that it culminated in a crushing military defeat at the hands of the dour, totalitarian state of Sparta. Socrates was a stonemason by trade, but there's not much evidence that he practised his trade; rather, apart from fulfilling his obligations as a citizen on military service, jury service, a stint on the council and such like, he seems to have spent most of his time stationed in the market place, under a plane tree, at a friend's house or anywhere else in his beloved city where he could ruminate on basic questions about the make up of the universe and how men ought to live their lives. The nature of justice, the nature of beauty, the possibility of teaching people to be good, the best way to organise a state—these were the kinds of issue that absorbed him and his small but devoted circle of friends and admirers. But the story ends on a rather different note, for finally his fellow citizens, perhaps unduly fractious and nervous after the defeat by Sparta, decided that they had had enough of all this seeking after truth and asking of awkward questions. Socrates was brought to trial on a charge of not believing in the city's Gods and corrupting the minds of the young. A subversive, in fact.

Socrates himself wrote nothing during his lifetime, but one of his followers, Plato, devoted most of his own life to writing dialogues involving Socrates and various other people which may be supposed to give a good idea of the sort of things that interested Socrates and his views about them. One slightly unusual piece produced by Plato was what purports to be Socrates' defence speech at his trial (the *Apology*, as it is called, after the Greek word for defence). It tells a thought-provoking story.

When Socrates was a young man a friend of his travelled to the priestess at Delphi. This priestess was regarded with the utmost seriousness and veneration by all Greeks as an oracular mouthpiece. Few would dare to challenge or scorn her pronouncements. In reply to the question "Who is the wisest of all the Greeks?" she apparently replied with the then scarcely heard of name, Socrates.

When this was reported to Socrates himself he was, he tells us, extremely puzzled. How could he, a humble, inexperienced stone-mason be the wisest of men? Thereupon he decided to set out and examine the wisdom of other men to see if he could gain some understanding of what the oracle meant. He first associated with politicians and other successful public figures. But the more clearly he studied what they thought and said, the more he came to the disturbing conclusion that actually, behind the fine words and rhetoric, they were not really saying anything; they thought themselves great intellects, yet didn't know what they were talking about. Next he turned to the poets and playwrights, the in-telligentsia, so to speak, and found much the same thing: people thinking they knew a lot about matters they didn't really under-stand at all. Finally he turned to the tradesmen and craftsmen and found that these people at least knew something—namely their own trade; but once again, beyond that they were both profoundly ignorant and unaware of that ignorance. Then it dawned on him: the Delphic priestess regarded him as wisest of all not because he knew much more than everybody else (which he didn't), but because he knew how little he knew. He understood his own deep ignorance.

This story has a crucial bearing on philosophy. In the first place Plato proceeded to turn it into the basis of an article of faith to the effect that philosophising cannot begin until one arrives at a state of frankly acknowledged awe in the face of the universe. Secondly, and more generally, it is quite true that successful philosophising does depend upon at any rate suspending one's everyday beliefs. If you see no problem, no mystery, you will not see the point of many leading questions in philosophy. When the philosopher asks "What is God?" he does not expect a routine ecclesiastical answer; he means to challenge the received or normal answer. Equally, in order to ask such a question, he has to take it seriously, even if his own private assumption happens to be that talk of God arises purely and simply out of psychological needs. Similarly when the philosopher asks "How do I know I am here?" "What is justice?" or "What is education?" he is not operating at the everyday level, which would make most of the questions fairly ridiculous. He is effectively saying "To hell with your routine answers; let's start right from the beginning. There's a lot here that needs explaining and which is not satisfactorily covered by everyday responses." And there is a vital corollary: because we are probing at a level below everyday responses, we quite often unsettle more than we settle. Progress in philosophy is not always measured by finding answers or by ironing out perplexities. Sometimes the mere fact of seeing problems where you didn't before, of becoming more uncertain, is progress—not because in all things uncertainty is good, but because some things are uncertain to us and it is a great error to classify as clear and certain what we do not fully understand. There are, for example, plenty of people who, if you ask them what schools should do, will reply quickly, clearly and concisely. But such a prompt response does not necessarily show them to be bright, alert and wise. It might on the contrary show them to be very foolish, for it might be felt that what schools should do is a vast complex question to which no right-minded person would claim to have a simple straightforward answer.

Another point implied by the story of Socrates is that philosophy will have no truck with that most insidious of things, *group-think*. What I mean by "group-think" has a number of other possible titles such as "ideological thinking", "party thinking" or "received opinion". What I am referring to is a wholesale commitment to a package-deal or a system of thought. Now of course lots of ideas are interconnected, and anyway it would be a human impossibility to hold them all in isolation, unorganised and unarranged. But what can be avoided is a predetermined manner of cataloguing, interpreting and explaining. By all means consider a phenomenon or a situation and explain it or account for it in terms that happen to be Marxist, Catholic, behaviourist, feminist or whatever. But what must be avoided is insisting on looking at everything *as* a Marxist, a Catholic or what have you. It cannot be good reasoning to approach all issues as a Marxist (even if such an approach happens to throw up some feasible solutions to some problems), because to approach matters in that way is to beg questions. Of course, if you are a Marxist, you can account for everything in Marxist terms (and the same goes for Catholicism, fatalism, behaviourism, etc.); but if that is all you are willing to do, you never entertain the possibility that your account may be not just implausible but ridiculous. Possibly all of us are as a matter of fact limited by one conceptual framework or another—one way of looking at things—but that's no excuse for voluntarily limiting ourselves yet further. There can be no good thinking about matters where there is a prior commitment to a particular ideological view of the world. And philosophy is concerned with good thinking. To say in response to the problem of evil, "Well, I'm a Catholic, here's our answer . . ." or in response to an economic decline, "Well that was inevitable, because, as Marx said, . . ." is not thinking at all. It is repeating a view or parroting another's claim.

We must briefly note one attempt to counter the above, not by denying its truth, but by suggesting that philosophy too is a species of group-think and the philosopher himself equally ideologically bound. This argument however does not work, for it is based on an ambiguity in the word "ideological". Of course philosophers as a breed have an "ideology" if that means something loose like "something they believe in". Indeed they do; they have a belief in philosophy. They value good and clear reasoning (as incidentally most other people, whether philosophers or not and even if committed to some ideology in a more restricted sense, would claim to do). But if we take "ideology" in the narrower and more common sense to mean something like "an interrelated set of ideas having repercussions for how one lives one's life", they do not. It is ideological thinking in the second sense that is to be resisted. Switch it about how you will, use what words you want, there is a difference between belief in the value of good reason and con-ceptual clarity, which is formal and procedural, and belief in a substantive set of opinions. There is a difference of kind between the premise "We must follow reason", which leaves open the question of what the path of reason is and where it leads, and the premise "We must follow Marxism", which tells you what is reasonable and what path to take.

You measure progress in philosophy by assessing your ability to state your position or express your argument clearly and co-herently, and to recognise how little you know. Nobody who thinks that there are easy answers has made much progress. This may be a depressing thought, but it is the nature of the world and our place in it that is to blame.

5 THE PHILOSOPHY OF EDUCATION AND THE PHILOSOPHY OF SCHOOLING

The philosophy of education really comes into its own as a distinctive branch of philosophy with the work of men such as Richard Peters and Israel Scheffler in the 1950s. Prior to that philosophers had naturally often taken an interest in education. Some, as early as Plato and as prominent as John Dewey in America, had even devoted serious philosophical attention to educational issues, though more often, as in the case of John Locke and Immanuel Kant, philosophers seemed to set aside their philosophising and to revert to less disciplined speculation when they considered education. Furthermore, and coming up to date a bit, teacher training usually involved philosophy courses well before the impact of Peters and Scheffler. But these generally took the form of the history of educational ideas or (particularly in America) identifying specific schools of thought in philosophy, such as pragmatism, existentialism or idealism and exploring the educational implications. (This latter approach makes philosophical study ideological, of course, in the way that I have pointed out it need not be. Looking at education as an existentialist is no different *in kind* from looking at it as a Marxist.) One way of summarising the situation is to consider the types of textbook available in the broad area of educational philosophy prior to say, 1960. They fall into four groups. Philosophical treatises on the grand scale that took education seriously (Plato's *Republic*; Rousseau's *Emile*), educational views set forward by people who happen to have been philosophers (Locke and Kant), histories of educational ideas (Curtis and Boultwood, Rusk), and general philosophy books selecting material and concentrating on issues likely to be of some pertinence to education (Arnaud Reid, O'Connor). In other words, two types that were philosophical but in which education was not a crucial factor, and two that were evidently concerned with education but were scarcely philosophical in the sense explained above.

What was distinctive and important about the twist given in the fifties was that henceforward a tradition of familiarising students with some broad ideas about education was to be replaced by a rigorous look at the coherence of such ideas, never mind so much where they came from, and scrutiny of educational concepts and the logic of educational debate. At the same time as the focal point switched from general views of education to specific issues within education, the approach shifted emphasis from passive imbibing of opinion to critical consideration of it. At the centre of the programme, of course, had to be the question "What exactly constitutes education?" Through attempts to answer that, an ever widening circle of related concepts arose and a series of stepping stones into other areas of philosophy such as ethics, epistemology, religion and aesthetics was created. (For example, if it is argued that education involves developing intelligence and the creative faculty, we now have to consider what exactly they are. Consideration of the former might well lead us into epistemology and examining the concept of creativity could well take us into the domain of aesthetics.)

A great deal of philosophy of education in the last decade or so has seemed insubstantial to many. This is largely because its practitioners have failed to distinguish the conceptual from the verbal and have (to revert to an earlier example) shown a certain lack of judgement in situations like that of the biscuit and the shortbread. It has too often been assumed that any ambiguous word must represent a vexed concept, and that we can therefore proceed to ask questions about the use of the word which are bound to be philosophically interesting. But neither of these assumptions are necessarily warranted. There are certainly verbal ambiguities in a term like "play". It is used in slightly different ways by different people and one needs to know in a given context which sense is being employed. But there are no conceptual problems in any of the senses, as there are conceptual problems in notions like those of determinism, God or justice. And we do not profit much by reading articles cataloguing different senses of play. All that we need to know is what particular people mean by it in particular contexts.

Perhaps it should also be said that one weakness of philosophy of education recently has been the unexpected and undesired way in which the ideas and thoughts provoked by the new approach have become for some a new orthodoxy, to be rote learned in just the uncritical manner that had previously been accorded to the ideas of a Plato, a Quintilian or a Comenius.

For our purposes we may take it that philosophy of education is generally understood by its practitioners at this time to be no more than a question of philosophising in the manner described about the central claims and concepts that crop up in the sphere of education. It certainly does not imply the study of overall views or programmes of education. It is not only concerned with evaluative claims. And it is not ultimately concerned with words. It is concerned with casting a critical and rigorous eye on all claims (wherever and however they emanate) and potentially or actually hazy concepts. Many questions that arise in philosophy of education may, of course, arise also in other branches of philosophy, but that is not problematic in any way.

As far as I am concerned this conception of philosophy of education is quite coherent, and philosophy of education in this sense is a valuable subject, quite aptly named. Why, then, it may be asked, entitle this book *The Philosophy of Schooling*? The same cynic that we encountered above will reply that it is called the *Philosophy of Schooling* in order to differentiate it from other introductions to the philosophy of education with which it has to compete in the open market. And once again the cynic has a point. I do want to differentiate between this and other introductions to the philosophy of education. The point that the cynic may miss is that the differentiation is justified, because I believe that the area of professional concern to philosophers of education ought to be explicitly widened to include a number of things that do not fall within the province of education as such.

Much of Peters' early work was devoted to clarifying the concept of education itself, and he argued, in broad outline, that educating people, as opposed to training them, indoctrinating them or socialising them, had nothing to do with equipping them to take on particular jobs, preparing them for industry or meeting the needs of the economy, and therefore was improperly criticised when it failed to meet such aims; rather it was to be seen as the deliberate attempt to initiate people into worthwhile knowledge for its own sake. Now I think, as we shall see in more detail in the next chapter, that this is more or less correct. But, if it is, then there can be no doubt that much of what actually goes on in schools at the moment is not educational. (Indeed for a while a popular examination question in British Colleges of Education took the form "Is it true that most people leave school uneducated?") We must be careful to distinguish between things that do not themselves amount to or constitute education but which may nonetheless contribute to it, as for example picking up reading skills, and things that have nothing to do with it at all. Nonetheless, if education is about initiation into worthwhile knowledge for its own sake and educated people are people with breadth of understanding covering certain logically basic disciplines, a lot of school practice was and is either irrelevant to education or even counterproductive.

Wide acceptance of Peters' reasonably specific and clear characterisation of education has led much philosophy of education, quite unconsciously, astray. For nothing is more common in philosophy of education than to hear people objecting to things solely on the grounds that they are not educational. Superficially that seems quite proper; after all, we are philosophers of education, concerned about education; is it not our bounden duty to fight against practices that are thought of as educational when they are not, just as moral philosophers should expose as humbug practice which falsely poses as moral? Well, yes, it is our bounden duty, given the role we have cast ourselves in. But are we wise to insist that we are philosophers of education and hence to persist in assessing all activities in school in terms of education, when it is by no means clear that schools should only or even predominantly concern themselves with education (or even, in some cases, such as parts of the third world, concern themselves with it at all)? For, as people such as Illich, Reimer and Freire have recently emphasised, as things are, schools are attempting to do all sorts of things that are quite distinct from education, such as offer training in various skills, socialise, and simply occupy children's time and keep them off the streets. And a moment's thought is enough to remind most of us that we do not really believe schools ought only to provide education. At any rate we want freedom to examine the claims of other non-educational schooling practices. The point of my title, the point of renaming philosophy of education "philosophy of schooling" (though I am not very hopeful that it will nor worried about whether it does catch on in general) is not purely verbal. It is to replot the area of our concern. It is to say: let us philosophise about the wider area of schooling rather than merely the narrower field of education. Let us take an interest in all that schools do or might do and consequently recognise that the observation that some practice is not educational is not necessarily an argument against it as far as the practice of teachers goes. (If some practice is actually anti-educational, as opposed to simply not educational, it might be unacceptable for that reason.)

Thus, to take an illustration of the general point, I would entirely agree with the following three propositions that any philosopher of education might put forward: "Socialisation is not the same thing as education"; "vocational education is in many contexts a contradiction in terms"; and "physical training is not educational". But it does not follow that socialisation is not an important and justifiable aspect of schooling; it does not follow that what is badly labelled as "vocational education" is not worthy of respect or not appropriate in schools; and it does not follow that to justify physical training we have to strain our brain (and our credulity) to bolster it with intellectual or academic components and call it physical education. I want to devote the same kind of neutral philosophical attention to these wider issues of schooling as has been lavished on the narrower field of education, defending some practices, objecting to others, seeing where further conceptual clarity is needed, where clearer argument is needed, and, generally, asking what schooling is about. The change of name is designed to make this clear.

Besides emphasising a wider remit and ruling out the "it's not educational" ploy as an automatic disqualification for practice in schools, I hope to shift the emphasis, as compared with other introductions to educational philosophy, slightly away from conceptual analysis and towards argument. I mean by that only that I have not planned the book in terms of concepts as is often done, and of course I hope to avoid the error, referred to above, of asuming that every abstract word poses a conceptual problem and therefore requires a rundown or shakedown. For example, in the next chapter, I talk about both education and socialisation. The latter seems to be a simple notion so far as meaning goes, so I simply state my understanding of the term and busy myself with the questions of its legitimacy and importance. The former on the other hand seems to deserve conceptual analysis: any definition is likely to require careful elucidation.

Those who are unfamiliar with philosophy sometimes, and naturally enough, wonder how a book written in the context of one country can be applicable to that of another—specifically how a book such as this written in the context of Britain (which itself supports more distinct educational systems than most people realise) can be relevant to the rather different circumstances of such places as America, Canada and Australia (not to mention their internal distinctions). Familiarity with the nature of the discipline reveals the answer. Although any sensible philosopher of education (or any other kind of philosopher) will have his eye firmly on the particular practices of the various parts of the world he is interested in, and will object to philosophising or any other kind of theorising indulged in without any concern for what is actually going on, the fact remains that philosophy itself is not concerned with the particularities of one culturally bound situation or another. It is not concerned to establish what is happening here and now, so much as to map out what is conceivable, what is ideal and what is necessarily the case or logically entailed by agreed premises, and to do it all clearly. Being concerned, not with what different people happen to do in the name of education, but with clarifying conceptions of education, it can perfectly well cross cultural boundaries: my conception of education may be a great deal closer to that of someone in Massachusetts than to that of my next door neighbour in Manchester. Logical aspects by their very nature cross geographical boundaries: bachelorhood entails absence of wife, and contradictions are still contradictions, whether you're in Sydney or Quebec. It is perhaps true that the wider one's sphere of vision, for instance if one contemplates schooling rather than education, the more variation in proposals one might expect from people with different backgrounds: education, if it *is* what I understand by education, should look much the same everywhere in the world if it is taking place, but schooling taken as a whole is more likely to take different appearances in different locations, while still being recognisable as schooling. This is simply because schooling is a broader concept; ducks of whatever sort are pretty much the same the world over, but animals take many different forms in different parts of the world. Besides, possible legitimate differences in schooling practice in different cultures are less troubling to us than might at first appear. For our task is neither to catalogue what schools *are* doing nor to draw up *detailed* programmes of what they ought to do. Rather it is to pin-point and clarify *the sorts of things* that schools *should* do, and the sorts of things they should do will generally be similar. The detailed programmes or the specific means of doing these things become different as a result of combining different circumstances with the same basic principles. So final decisions on matters like bussing, reverse discrimination, use of educational measurement techniques or sexism might conceivably differ in different settings. But the principles involved, that have to be thoroughly understood and examined in any context, remain the same.

Another closely related worry that some people have is that philosophy gives no answers. Now as a matter of fact this worry is unfounded. Philosophy gives answers all the time, but only to philosophical questions and not to any and every question. However, if you recall the point of the story about Socrates, it is understandable that people should feel that philosophy creates doubt and open-mindedness where once there was certainty. What does have some truth and what explains some students' feelings of frustration is that philosophy as such (i.e. in and of itself alone) does not give final answers to matters of practical fact. This is scarcely surprising since, as we've just seen, philosophy is not about matters of practical fact. So it is somewhat odd that people who would probably never think of criticising the natural sciences on the grounds that they fail to solve aesthetic problems, should nonetheless criticise philosophy for not doing more than answering philosophical questions. Nonetheless the complaint is made; the frustration is real. All one can do is point out that philosophy is not about *why* people do things or *how* to do them, but about clarifying ideas and arguments. It follows obviously enough that philosophy alone can never give you the answer to practical problems ("Why did this happen?" "What should I do now?" "What is the most efficient way to do it?") because there's always more required for answering such questions than merely clarity and coherence of thought about them. At the same time the latter are almost always an indispensable part of a good answer to practical questions, and quite often the answer to such a question becomes immediately obvious once one has given such thought to it. What and how we should teach our children cannot be determined by philosophy alone, but having a clear and coherent grasp of what you take schooling to be about and what is involved in the idea of educating them takes you a long and necessary part of the way.

Finally I should point out that the way in which I conceive

philosophy and the way in which I have written this book means that what is said in subsequent chapters adds up to a philosophy of schooling in the quite different sense (referred to above) of a theory of schooling. Despite the quite correct observation that there is a distinction between the now out-of-fashion tendency to study philosophies of schooling or education in the sense of speculative theories, and the usual contemporary practice of studying philosophy of schooling or education in the sense of the logic and meaning of educational discourse, it occurs to me that more of an open marriage between the two could be most productive, diminishing what some see as the sterility of the latter and increasing the rigour of the former.

Accordingly, in doing my philosophising, I have tried to shape the whole into a clear plan and to make a set of interrelated positive proposals. At the same time these proposals are not just asserted, but are presented with detailed attention to unequivocal verbal expression, conceptual depth and clarity and overall coherence of reasoning. Since this is designed as an introduction I am also concerned throughout to draw attention to the manner in which I am proceeding.

The plan of the book is straightforward. The first question that must be asked is "What are schools for?" Questions don't have to be difficult to understand or to answer, in order to be important. I don't think this one is either, but it is important, since, without a clear view of the point and purpose of schooling we have no yardstick against which to measure anything. I argue that schools should be concerned with education, but also with several other things. The concept of education requires analysis and my analysis in turn leads me to consider the notion of thinking, and also to suggest that emotional development, worthy as it may be and important in the wider context of schooling, has little or nothing to do with education.

Then there are various organisational questions to be raised about schools. Not factual ones about how they *are* organised, but theoretical and speculative ones about who ought, in principle, to carry what responsibility. I argue for a state-imposed common core curriculum, detailed implementation of which should be left to the control of individual schools. That immediately raises the question of the decision-making process within a school, and I next examine the question of the role of the head teacher or school principal and the desirability of democratic staff leadership. Finally in this section the slightly different kind of question of teachers' neutrality in teaching controversial or contentious material is raised.

Though each set of questions collected together by chapter is important and though they are interconnected, the fourth set, pertaining to what the content of the curriculum should be, seems to me the most important for theorists to consider. I begin by arguing for a range of academic study in the name of education, and then add further studies justified by the wider concerns of schooling. Following that I concentrate on certain selected candidates for curriculum time. A special chapter is devoted to the claims of moral and religious education.

The final chapter raises some questions both about research into teaching styles and methods, and about certain approaches to teaching themselves. Not the least important aspect of the chapter, however, is to offer a final illustration of the way in which a philosophical dimension is deeply embedded even in so seemingly empirical an area, and thereby to stress the practical importance of philosophy.

2   Schooling: its Nature and Point

The etymology of the word "school" is interesting. It derives from the Latin "schola" which in turn comes from the Greek "σχολή" (schole). Originally "σχολή" meant "leisure". The typically Greek love of argument led to a shift in meaning to "the employment of leisure for disputation", then to "lecture" and then to "school" in something like the sense of the Latin "schola" and of course our own "school". The basic sense of "school" today is "an establishment in which boys or girls or both receive instruction" or, more generally, "an institution in which instruction of any kind is given (whether to children or adults)." The various other uses of the word, as for example in "the school of Biology" or "a school of thought" seem in accord with that fundamental sense. The verb "to school" has long since covered a range of activities including "to send to school", "to chastise", "to educate", "to train", "to discipline" and "to instruct". In short, "schooling" is a general term that implies little more than the imparting of some lesson to others by some means or other, while the word "school" adds only the implication of a location set aside for the purpose. (Incidentally, compulsory attendance, though generally required, is surely not part of the meaning of "school".) There is no real conceptual problem about the notion of a school as far as I can see—nothing, that is to say, about the above dictionary definition that is obscure or hard to grasp. What there is instead is the quite straightforward question of what purpose we want schools to serve.

This is therefore an appropriate point at which to consider the view that there is no adequate rationale for schooling, and that any purposes schools might happen to serve would be better served without them. That is the view of deschoolers such as Ivan Illich and Everett Reimer.[1] Their argument is that schools try to do too many things which inhibit each other, and that by their institutional nature they distort and teach us various undesirable lessons rather than what they intend. They implant in us undue deference to authority and to the professional, they make us childlike, they make us define merit in terms of academic qualifications, and they teach us to value competition. In addition they involve paraphernalia that is dislikeable and restricting such as examinations, graded classes and knowledge alienated from real life. The deschoolers' alternative strategy involves setting up what they call learning webs or networks of things and people in place of schools; informal, but organised groupings of resources and ways of putting people in touch with them and each other.

Without question some of these observations are well-founded and some of these value judgements persuasive. For instance, schooling does contribute towards our tendency to define merit in terms of certificates of achievement and that surely is, in itself, undesirable. More generally, schooling is a dangerous business, and in the wrong hands or out of control may become a sinister business. It is also worth pointing out that while matters are not particularly sinister, they may be all the more insidious, since they more easily escape attention. So one is grateful to the individuals concerned for pointing out and laying stress on some of the dangers inherent in the very practice of schooling. Nor, I think, would anyone object to their alternative proposals as an ideal. The questions are whether, in their eagerness to draw attention to some real dangers, they have not missed some of the advantages of schooling, failed to see that some of the disadvantages they discern could be ironed out within a system of schooling, and proposed equally or more dangerous alternatives. The answer to the last is, I am sure, that they have, though here necessarily we can only speculate. It seems plain enough to me that the likely result of deschooling Western democracies, while they remain in other respects much as they are, would be an even greater rift between groups or classes and a failure on the part of many more than at present to gain the sort of advantages that all parties to the dispute want them to gain (in broad terms, knowledge, skills, interests, sources of enjoyment and socially acceptable ways of behaving). Deschooling could not succeed as the first step in a cultural revolution; it would inevitably be counterproductive, leaving the individual even more at the mercy of the values and ideas that the school system to some extent embodies. The paraphernalia of assessment and evaluation [see below, Chapter Six] are not a necessary adjunct of schooling, so objecting to them, even if warranted, would not be sufficient to discredit schooling. And some of the things that schools do could be campaigned against without dismantling the whole system. The central question therefore has to be, notwithstanding the legitimate criticisms of the very idea of schooling, are there things that we think sufficiently important to make them the concern of a massive state directed effort?[2]

Presumably, if there is a case for schooling at all, it must rest on the broad argument that there are certain things we want children to acquire, or be provided with, which cannot be or cannot reliably be, or cannot as well be provided at home or by the social environment generally, even if the latter were to be rejigged in various ways. In the past that has certainly been the line of argument used to justify schooling: certain things are best learned from the master professional. Just as, in order to become a carpenter, one apprenticed oneself to the master carpenter, so, for instruction in such things as reading and writing one entrusted oneself, or was entrusted, to the local schoolmaster. (Nowadays, of course, as likely as not the carpenter too functions within the school.) The justification for schooling must be along some such lines as that it provides valuable instruction (or learning environments to use dreadful educationalese, which I only do here to avoid seeming to beg any questions) well, economically and fairly to all. What we have to ask is whether the various things schools may claim to provide, such as education, socialisation and vocational courses, are indeed valuable and are best provided in this manner.

But first we must consider an attempt to by-pass that longer route by suggesting that, if schools would only teach what is relevant, that alone would constitute justification enough for their existence. The proposal that schooling should be relevant and/or useful and/or geared to reality is obviously neither absurd nor false. It is, however, remarkably unhelpful. All three words have strong evaluative connotations or are rich in emotive meaning. Relevance, usefulness and realism are more or less self-evidently good things. It would be very curious to claim that one was in favour of irrelevance or uselessness. If somebody insisted nonetheless that he was, it would be a safe bet that he had found a use for so-called uselessness or seen some relevance in seeming irrelevance. The problem is that, although we know what these words mean ("relevance" means "pertinent", "useful" means "serviceable", and "real" means "actually existing"), whether things are relevant, real or useful is not a simple matter of fact, but a matter of judgement, involving personal tastes, values and perceptions, not to mention reference to a particular context. To insist that schooling should be relevant is like insisting that one's architecture should be aesthetically pleasing. Of course, of course . . . but our agreement that architecture should be pleasing does not help us very much to decide between particular submissions from architects, because whether a building *is* pleasing to the eye is a further question, depending on individual judgement, situation and purpose. In the same way, whether a particular schooling is relevant depends on who is making the judgement, from what perspective and with what end in view. Relevance is not a property that things possess, as they may possess the property of being square. Whether something has relevance depends upon answers to the further questions of to whom and for what. It is of relevance to one who wants to understand engineering to study physics. It is not of relevance to one who neither cares about nor needs to understand science for any further purpose. Furthermore, while, if something is irrelevant in some particular respect, that *may* be a criticism of it, it equally well might not be, for it might be irrelevant now but prove to have relevance later. Reading poetry did not have much relevance to me or my purposes as a child, but that study has turned out to be of great relevance to the way I enjoy spending some of my time now. (Maybe it was relevant to influencing the way in which I enjoy spending some of my time now, but that's a further question.)

Similarly, whether things are useful or not is not a matter to be decided by considering them in the abstract; it depends to a large extent on what your needs, wishes and circumstances happen to be. My carpentry skills, acquired at school and thought by some to be more obviously useful than piano-playing skills, have proved to be of little use to me, while my piano lessons have proved extremely useful.

Reality is perhaps the most insidious of the three words, for it seems more reasonable to claim that some things are real and some are not, no matter who you are or what the circumstances, than it does to make a similar claim about relevance and usefulness. But although common sense says that there is a real world which is to be distinguished from false or imaginary ones, it is over-simple to talk of reality exclusively in terms of everyday experience. Dreams are real enough as dreams. One danger of asking for schooling to be realistic is that "realistic" may be interpreted solely in terms of the here and now or what is the case, and thus become an intensely conservative concept serving always to keep things as they are. At the moment it is realistic to assume that there will be many unemployed in Britain in the next ten years. Should schools be governed by that consideration? It is realistic to assume that a certain percentage of our children will turn out to be criminals. Should we accept and encourage that? Realism forces us to acknowledge that children differ in background and performance; should schools acknowledge this real difference and accept it as an unalterable given? The real world of many children is relatively disadvantaged and poor; should we accept that and teach them to accept reality (their reality)? A second danger is that people tend to interpret real in such a way as to emphasise the working side of life at the expense of leisure interests. Ballet and science fiction are thought of as less real than plumbing and mechanics, even though there is no obvious sense in which they are. The fact is that the term "real" is equivocal. It may mean "actually existing or occurring", in which case more things are real than is sometimes admitted (e.g. ballet, prostitution and dreams), and it is not at all clear why being real is necessarily good or should be a guide to our practice in schools; after all, in this sense everything that is is real, including poor schooling. It may mean "relevant or useful", in which case we face the problems mentioned above. It may mean "genuine", in which case we need to discuss not what "genuine" means so much as what the criteria are in different areas for being genuine; what for example, is genuine schooling? (That of course is the very question that bringing in terms like "real" was supposed to answer.) It may mean "natural", but that will merely throw us back to the beginning, for "natural" is no less equivocal a term than "real" and could mean, at least, each of the things we have pointed out that "real" could mean.[3] One seemingly slightly more determinate suggestion would be that a "real schooling" is one that is geared to the demands of the everyday world. But in fact such an apparently straightforward claim gives rise to most of the problems noted. What aspects of the everyday world? (Sexual fantasies as well as ways of earning a living?) If "everyday" is interpreted in relatively mundane and practical terms, do we accept that schooling should concern itself exclusively with social utility? Such a suggestion, furthermore, totally ignores the point that the everyday world we prepare children for is not an inescapable given. To a considerable extent what turns out to be real life for them in the future depends on what we do now, including what we do by way of schooling them; if you only teach people how to earn a living, you effectively circumscribe their reality; if you help them to appreciate ballet, ballet too becomes a part of their reality.

All the above may be conceded, but somebody might now argue that what is meant is that schooling should *seem* relevant to the children concerned. If that is taken to mean that whether what we provide actually has any relevance to any specified purpose is neither here nor there, then surely nobody could seriously propose it. But if the assumption is that whatever seems relevant must also necessarily have relevance, it is false (except in the very limited sense that what seems relevant to the individual must be relevant to his immediate interest). Estimates of relevance can only be made with reference to an objective or purpose, and people may make mistakes in their calculations. There is no obvious reason why anybody (least of all young children) should be the best judge of what is relevant to their immediate needs, let alone what is relevant to them in the long term. A third possibility is that what is meant is that schooling should both be and seem relevant to children. By contrast with the first two proposals this seems an entirely sensible suggestion, but it is not of much practical help, since it takes us back to the beginning in leaving unanswered the question of to whom and for what schooling should have and seem to have this relevance. It also ignores the question of what should have priority, if, as must sometimes happen, we cannot achieve both relevance in fact and seeming relevance to the child.

The truth is that, though we all agree that schooling should be in some respects relevant, useful and realistic, such claims are unclear, involve no practical guidance at all and are too often narrowly and selectively interpreted in terms of the current situation or the world as it is, when one thing that we should be doing is thinking idealistically. For schooling makes a major contribution to shaping the future, as well as providing for it.

I conclude that we should not avoid giving individual consideration to the main things that schools try to do on the grounds that all we need to do is that which is useful or relevant. On the contrary, we still have a pressing need to establish whether things like socialisation and vocational study are worth doing and are best done by means of schooling. I shall begin with the question of education.

2 EDUCATION AND CRITICAL THINKING

Before considering whether education is something of value and something that schools are or could be well-suited to provide, let us consider carefully what it is. Let us analyse the concept or consider what exactly is involved in the very notion of education— never mind what is actually going on in its name. [Since this is the first example of conceptual analysis in the book, the reader may care to recall what was said about it in the previous chapter; what actually happens at this point is that I attempt to explicate my conception of education for you to consider and assess in terms of clarity and coherence.]

There is a popular phrase to the effect that education is of the whole man. I am not sure what precisely this is supposed to mean, but if it suggests that being educated has something to do with some transformation of all aspects of the individual (his appearance, his health, his intelligence, his feelings), then it seems plainly false. It may possibly be argued that schooling, a much larger operation, should concern itself with the whole man, but that is a different point, which we shall consider later. What I am suggesting here is that education, far from being concerned with all dimensions of the personality, is essentially to do with the mind and is purely cognitive (to do with knowledge, understanding and perception). To put this claim to the test is a matter for introspection [as explained above in Chapter One]: what on reflection strikes one as intelligible?

Surely it does not strike one as intelligible to reckon whether a man is more or less well educated by reference to such things as his physique, his athletic prowess, his capacity for love, his moral stature, his emotional maturity, his imaginative powers or his creative capacity. The fact that somebody is morally repugnant to me does not in itself show him to be uneducated. The fact that somebody is emotionally immature is likewise not an indication that he is uneducated, and the fact that somebody has a great capacity for love, though no doubt admirable, is not to the point either.

What, then, do we look for in estimating whether a person is more or less educated? We judge him by his understanding and his capacity for discrimination. To educate a person is to develop such understanding and such a capacity, and schools, if they are seeking to educate, must contribute to such development. I deliberately say "understanding" rather than "knowledge" because the word "knowledge" can imply mere possession of a stock of information, and that does not seem appropriate. A walking *Guiness Book of Records* or a Mr Memory is not, as such, an educated man. Peters is correct when he says that we expect the educated man to have understanding of the reason why of things or a grasp of the underlying principles, and not simply know-how or a collection of pieces of information.[4] The fact that you happen to know that Franklin D. Roosevelt was re-elected President of the United States for a third term of office on November 5th 1940, and that November 5th is the anniversary of Guy Fawkes' attempt to blow up the Houses of Parliament in Britain and many other such facts and figures, does not reveal to us whether you are relatively well or poorly educated. Nor would the fact that you also know the election dates of all the other American Presidents suggest any the more that you are an educated man. But if it becomes apparent that, besides knowing the date of Roosevelt's third term, you also have some sensible things to say about how and why he won it, you are beginning to show the sort of signs that we look for in judging whether people are more or less educated. (Just to be on the safe side, let me stress the phrase "the sort of signs". I am *not* suggesting that knowing about Roosevelt is a necessary condition of being educated. I am using Roosevelt as an example to illustrate the sort of thing educated people, by definition, should have understanding of: explanations of political success rather than dates.)

That example brings me to another point on which Peters' early work on the concept of education was surely convincing. Education implies some breadth of understanding rather than narrow specialism, however profound or erudite that specialist knowledge might be. A brilliant historian or a front-rank scientist is not necessarily an educated man, and if a man's historical *nous* or understanding, or his scientific know-how was *all* that he had, we should not take him as the epitome of an educated man. Furthermore not only is deep knowledge, if confined to a very limited sphere, not sufficient to constitute education, but such exceptional specialist knowledge is not a necessary condition of being educated either. Being educated is not synonymous with being clever. One might be a well-educated person and not very brilliant in academic terms, and one might be extremely clever in some particular field such as science or history and yet not very well educated, since that term suggests a wide range of understanding. Breadth rather than brilliance, good sense rather than genius are characteristics of the educated mind.

In two important respects, then, I think that Peters' original work on the concept of education was correct. His further elaboration of the concept, including work where he joins forces with Paul Hirst and they introduce what Hirst originally termed *forms of knowledge*, seems to me less convincing.[5] Hirst argues that out of the myriad subjects that could be categorised by reference to their subject matter or content alone (e.g. photography, angling, finger-wagging, science, history) there are seven which are notable in that unlike other subjects they also each have their own unique logical structure and special way, appropriate to the unique subject matter and logical structure, of seeking to establish truth. These seven are listed as: religion, philosophy, literature and the fine arts, physical science, mathematics, morals and interpersonal understanding (i.e. "explanations of human behaviour in terms of intentions, wills, hopes, beliefs, etc.").[6] Hirst calls these "forms of knowledge" and argues that they are logically fundamental in that, for example, a purely religious proposition (e.g. "God exists") has to be examined in its own unique way, and so on through the rest of the forms, while propositions arising in other subjects will always turn out to be basically religious, scientific, etc. or else hybrids drawing on more than one of the forms. (He calls subjects which may draw on several forms *fields of knowledge*.) He and Peters go on to suggest that the breadth of knowledge or understanding required of the educated mind is provided by these forms, and that therefore what it means for a man to be fully educated is at least that he should have been initiated into the seven forms of knowledge.

What Hirst calls forms of knowledge (or, in later writings, modes of knowledge and experience) are defined by three criteria:

(*a*) They have their own distinctive concepts, as, for example, gravity, accelerations and hydrogen are characteristic of the sciences.

(*b*) They have their own logical structure. That is to say, largely because of the meanings of the distinctive concepts, there is a limit to what may meaningfully be said employing such concepts. (Ways of talking that may make sense in one form do not necessarily make sense in another.)

(*c*) They have their own distinctive manner of testing the truth of their claims.

Since many subjects have their own concepts and even logical structure, the most important criterion is the third. So what Hirst is saying, at rock bottom, is that, if we look at the domain of knowledge in general (the range of things we might claim to know), we will find that they can be classified in seven different groups by reference to the manner in which we would set about trying to establish their truth. Thus, "the truths of formal logic and mathematics," he points out, "involve concepts that pick out relations of a general abstract kind, where deducibility within an axiom system is the particular test for truth."[7] That kind of test for truth is to be distinguished from that found in the physical sciences. The latter "are concerned with truths that, in the last analysis, stand or fall by the tests of observation by the senses. Abstract though the theoretical concepts they employ may be, the sciences necessarily employ concepts for what is seen, heard, felt, touched or smelt; for it is with an understanding and knowledge of the sensible world that they are concerned."[8]

So far, so good. Mathematics and the physical sciences provide clear and good examples, for they are obviously to be distinguished not just by their different content, but by their reliance on quite different kinds of test for truth, just as Hirst says. There are, then, at least these two forms of knowledge.

The difficulty starts when we try to push this further; the remaining five of the seven forms that Hirst and Peters discern are by no means so obviously distinguishable. It is suggested that there is an interpersonal form which incorporates concepts like believing, intending and wanting, and which gives rise to claims about our own and other people's minds, such as, "I hope to become President", or "He did not intend to kill her." Now it is quite true that these kinds of claim "do not pick out, in any straightforward way, what is observable by the senses." You do not test the truth of the claim that he did not intend to kill her in quite the same way as you test a claim in the physical sciences. The trouble is that it is not entirely clear how we do or whether we can test such claims at all. Perhaps there is a unique way, as Hirst and Peters suggest. But there are other possibilities, such as that we should treat them as if they were scientific claims (perhaps assessing in behaviouristic terms), or that they are untestable or that, so far as the logic of testing goes, they resemble mathematical propositions and their truth or falsity is a matter of "deducibility within an axiom system"—the axiom system in question being the product of understanding concepts such as believing, intending and wanting.

The next two candidates for status as forms are morals and religion. Here again, although these are clearly distinct areas by virtue of their distinct concepts alone, it is far from clear that each one of them involves a distinct and unique way of assessing their truth. Indeed in these areas there have been persistent and persuasive attempts to argue, either that they are not the kinds of matter where a question of truth or falsity arises, or that they can be reduced to scientific or factual questions involving tests of the senses. In a subsequent chapter, I shall argue that truth here is once again a question of deducibility from certain axioms, those axioms being the product of the basic concepts in either case. Here I merely want to make the point that it is far from certain that there is a unique way of assessing moral or religious truth. The sixth suggested form of knowledge is philosophy itself, though yet again many would argue that philosophical truths are logically similar to mathematical truths. The final form, literature and the fine arts, raises a particular problem concerning what Hirst means by it.[9] Some interpret him to mean aesthetics, in which case it is subject to the same queries as I raised about morals and religion.

But it seems to me evident that he is not thinking of aesthetic propositions of the type "this painting is beautiful", but of the proposition that a work of art might itself be said to embody. Thus we are asked to consider not statements about a piece of sculpture, but the piece of sculpture as a statement. If this interpretation is correct, it is difficult to reject or accept the contention too readily, for a great deal of prior thought will be needed to make sense of the idea and to consider whether, if the artefact is seen as a statement, there is indeed some unique way of testing such statements for truth.

The above is intended as no more than a crude sketch of a very important thesis, and the barest outline of what is problematic about it. It cannot be dealt with in depth here, because the question of whether, say, there is a distinct form of aesthetic knowldge, is one and the same thing as the question of what the nature of aesthetic judgements may be, which could be a lifetime's study in itself. This perhaps explains why some have felt very dissatisfied with Hirst's original paper on this subject; it seemed to presume so much that is in fact hotly disputed, such as that moral judgements involve meaningful propositions that can be true or false (while others would argue, as Hirst is well aware, that they are subjective utterances or not propositions at all). But the important thing to remember here and now is that there is a distinction to be drawn between the outline and the details of this theory and that the broad outline certainly has something in it. Two things at any rate are surely correct:

(a) Mathematics and the physical sciences are distinct by the criteria Hirst points to. So there are at least two forms of knowledge, and the notion is not an absurd or abitrary one.

(b) The concepts that are peculiar to a subject have a lot to do with assessing sense and nonsense and truth and falsity in that subject. The reasonableness of a moral utterance, for example, is partly and importantly related to what is meant by goodness, ought, duty, etc.

A question mark, however, must remain over whether there are indeed seven such forms, as maintained by Hirst and Peters. It is a difficult matter to judge, given the complexity of the areas and in view of the fact that here their comments are too obscure and questionable to settle the issue. But, quite apart from reservations about the theory itself, I have reservations about the relationship between education and understanding of the seven forms. Hirst's and Peters' view is that education involves initiating people into these seven basic forms; the forms, as I said above, are regarded as constituting the required breadth of knowledge. Whilst agreeing that such a person would be educated (assuming that one or two other conditions, to be introduced below, were met), I do not see such initiation as necessary to being educated. Although an individual with such breadth of knowledge would have to be accounted educated, an educated person would not have to have the entire range of this particular set of forms. Though breadth of understanding is a necessary condition of education, it doesn't have to be precisely this range of items that constitutes the breadth. Education is like beauty in this respect; all beautiful people must have something in common, in order to earn the same epithet, but nonetheless their beauty may take many different forms. In the same way any educated person must, by definition, have a breadth of understanding, but different people may arrive at breadth in different ways: a scientist who knew no history, but knew something about literature and bee-keeping might reasonably count as being to some extent educated, whilst a theologian who was also something of a botanist and a philosopher, though having little specifically in common with the scientist, might also. (Implicit in everything I have so far said is the obvious truth that education is a matter of degree. People are not simply educated or not, they are to a greater or lesser extent educated.)

Does what I have said entail that any breadth of understanding, never mind what items it comprises, makes a man educated? Not quite, I think, for I now want to argue that there are certain elements (more specific than the formal necessity for breadth) that are necessary to being educated. Firstly, an educated man must have some awareness of our place in the totality—awareness of the cultural and historical tradition to which we belong and of rival traditions, and in addition awareness of man's place in relation to the wider story of the universe. I need hardly say that I am not here thinking of detailed information, but a general appreciation of the pattern of the evolution of the world. Secondly, an educated man is by definition one who appreciates and is alert to people as individuals and to the power of individuality. I emphatically do not mean by this that he needs to be a student of psychology or psychotherapy. I mean that the understanding of anyone whom I would recognise as educated would have to encompass awareness of the unique quality of every individual and the consequent need to balance any sociological generalisations or ideological fiats with appreciation of the fact that particular personalities are always involved. For all I know, people may for the most part be the victims of circumstance, but the plain truth remains that they need never be passive victims. There will also be awareness of the responsibility we have, as an inevitable counterpart of man's ability to manipulate as well as react to circumstance. A third and vital aspect of being educated will be the ability to distinguish logically distinct kinds of question. Whatever the strengths or weaknesses of Hirst's thesis in point of detail, it is undeniable that there are logically different kinds of question, and it is important to recognise them as such, even if we do not have a definitive account of their differences to give. There are empirical questions, there are aesthetic questions and there are moral questions (and there are others and also hybrid questions). Educated people should be able to recognise such distinctions, as well as basic logical distinctions such as those between explanation and justification or cause and correlation. Finally there is what I call the capacity for discrimination, by which I mean the ability to think in terms of precise and specific concepts rather than blurred and general ones. The possession of precise and particular concepts gives one *discriminatory power* by which phrase I refer to the control, manoeuvrability and penetrating power in thought that the ability to make fine discriminations provides. What I say here is simple and important. In discussion about matters as diverse as whom to vote for, the merits of Evelyn Waugh as a novelist or the acceptability of capital punishment, one's contribution will be the more significant and illuminating, one's thinking will be the better, in so far as one is in possession of more, clear and specific concepts. If you cannot get beyond broad and general concepts (communist/capitalist, comic/realistic) you cannot contribute much. We must remember that it is a question of both clarity and specificity. [See above, Chapter One.]

It is in respect of the last of my four proposed criteria of education that we have most obviously failed, to date. By and large, people do have some grasp of man's place in the world and their own culture's place in mankind's history, they have some appreciation of individual responsibility and some grasp of the distinction between an empirical claim and a moral judgement— at any rate in so far as they don't, it is not for want of trying on the part of teachers and parents. But, despite that, we have not really succeeded in developing people's capacity for discrimination, which is the key feature of good or critical thinking. Hence the plethora of slogans to be found even in matters where serious intellectual discussion is supposed to take place, the ubiquity of crude advertising, and the abundance of political and ideological formulae, rich in generality, banality and ambiguity. Hence a widespread inability of people to grasp complexity and to reject dogmatic and facile responses.

Since the educated man is a person with breadth of understanding, incorporating specifically a grasp of logical distinctions and discriminatory power, one might reasonably say that one clear goal of education is developing powers of *critical thought*.[10] For what I mean by critical thinking is thinking that is concerned about and embodies good reasoning and coherent steps, conceptual clarity and discrimination in planning, discussion, explanation and any other form of ratiocination. It is necessarily good thinking (in the sense that it is necessarily coherent thinking rather than confused or illogical, not in the sense that it is necessarily appropriate to all situations. And "necessarily" here refers to conceptual necessity, i.e. it follows from the meaning of the concept.) There are of course great difficulties in judging whether critical thinking is going on in practice—difficulties that arise largely out of deciding what are good reasons in particular cases and how to conceptualise situations—but there is no difficulty about what I mean. What it is important to do here is distinguish it from and explain its relationship to various other concepts such as intelligence, logic, lateral thinking and creativity.

Knowledge of formal logic is neither a necessary nor a sufficient condition of critical thinking. As was pointed out in the previous chapter study of logic involves the classification of valid and invalid forms of argument, the recognition, cataloguing and labelling of points of logic. Such study is not sufficient to improve critical thinking, because there is more to critical thinking than recognising *see earlier* an invalid syllogism or being able to classify a particular fallacy. It is not necessary, because it is possible to recognise a fallacy when it crops up, without being able to classify or label it. It may empirically prove a way of developing powers integral to critical thought, but a critical thinker is not the same thing as a student of logic.

Nor is he a *lateral thinker* or a *creative thinker* as normally understood. There are glaring problems in lateral thinking and creativity tests, examples of which might involve participants in thinking of suitable titles for stories, in filling in circles to make pictures, or in puzzling out an explanation of how a room in which Antony and Cleopatra were said to be present has a floor covered in broken glass and water. Problems such as who determines good or correct answers in response to open-ended questions, and how? Whether quantity of answers is being used as a qualitative measure, if so why? But the basic point is that skill at this sort of business, like skill at crossword puzzles or solving detective story plots, has no immediate bearing on everyday life, and is not the same thing as critical thinking. The unexpected is seldom the answer in everyday life, most situations are anyway not open-ended, and the critical thinker is characterised in terms of competence rather than ingenuity. [For further consideration of creativity tests, see below, Section 9.]

One thing that the accomplished critical thinker is, is *intelligent*. I must make it clear therefore that in talking of intelligence I am not referring to some supposed faculty or attribute comparable to a sense of humour, which people have and may bring in to play when they choose to. In calling somebody intelligent I am referring to what I take to be his capacity to do things in a certain way, namely in a thinking way that is both efficient and successful. Intelligent people do not have to be moral or aesthetically appreciative, nor do they necessarily exercise their intelligence (except when there is good reason to do so. If a little thought could save your life and you do not want to die, then it is a mark of unintelligence not to think). Of course intelligence, like so much else, is a matter of degree, and being overcome on occasion by passion may testify not so much to a lack of intelligence as to strength of passion. Intelligent people, then, are essentially the same as critical thinkers in my vocabulary. It should be noted that IQ tests have absolutely nothing to do with intelligence in this sense. They certainly don't test it, and, though they may serve as reliable prognosticators of some things, they are not of intelligence. It may also be pointed out that the fascinating question of whether, or to what extent, intelligence is innate, is not of very much educational or schooling interest, because one thing that is certain is that we can materially improve or impair the extent of practically everybody's intelligent behaviour to some extent. Beyond that nothing is certain anyway; the empirical evidence does not unequivocally either establish or disprove that either genetic factors or environment are of greater importance.

So the educated man might also be termed a critical thinker or an intelligent man. The last two terms are in my usage synonymous. But the phrase "educated man" is not actually synonymous with them since, besides being intelligent, the educated man must also have that sense of individual responsibility and of our place in the totality, neither of which are criteria of the concept of intelligence. Finally, I should draw attention to the fact that my conception of intelligence to some extent involves using the word in defiance of ordinary use. Frequently people use "intelligence" with connotations of mystery, strong mental powers and even genius, and with implications of some inner faculty. I ignore that usage because it seems to me vague and mysterious, misleading where it is comprehensible and at variance with other equally ordinary uses of the word. What this boils down to is my claiming that after giving much thought to the matter, the only entirely

clear sense of "intelligence" I can see is that given, which makes it
synonymous with "powers of critical thought".

That last comment re-introduces the question of philosophical
method, so we may reasonably pause here to remind ourselves of
the nature and status of the above analysis of the concepts of
education, critical thinking and intelligence. It would be true to
say that you have read no more than the author's attempt to
explain and clarify his own idea of education (which led him to
state what he understands by "critical thinking" and "intelligence").
The question of whether it is true, if that means the correct
conception, does not arise. It doesn't make sense. Nor does it
matter whether your idea is the same as mine. The first question is
whether this conception is internally coherent and clear. Do you
understand this notion of education (*not* do you understand why
someone should have it)? Is it comprehensible to you? One might
then ask a second question, namely do you, on reflection, share
this conception (or share parts of it)? The phrase "on reflection" is
important, because it is quite common for us to find that we do not
really appreciate what our view of something is until we are forced
to think about it. So it is quite possible that some people who
would not, off the cuff, have described an educated man in the way
that I have, might nonetheless agree after some thought that this is
more or less their view of the matter. If you do not share this
conception, nothing necessarily hangs on it; a more important
question would be where you stand in relation to this conception;
that is to say, granted that this is not what you would call education
(or an educated man), what do you think of it? That is the question
to which we must anyway now turn.

Now that we know what we are talking about, is this something
to value? Some might be tempted to rephrase the question and
ask "Is education of any use?" but that begs the prior question of
whether it is supposed to be of any use. Certainly a lot of people
seem to have thought so—particularly all those who over the last
twenty years or so have become increasingly keen on evaluating
the success and worth of educational programmes, and making
teachers more accountable to the tax-payer. Admittedly, the mere
demand for evaluation and accountability need not indicate a
concern that education should be seen in terms of crude economic
and social utility, but a casual glance over some of the evaluation
programmes (i.e. the ways in which evaluation has been carried
out), and some of the things for which people have demanded
teachers should be accountable, particularly in America, indicates
that as a matter of fact it usually does. [Issues relating to accountability will be examined in Chapter Three.] There is in fact, as we

shall see, a very real sense in which education is useful to society. But as a first strike, it is important to insist that it is simply wrong to try and judge education in this way. If "useful" is going to be interpreted in terms of things like increasing the labour force, then education isn't supposed to be useful any more than art is. Let it be roundly declared: you do not educate people in order to boost the Gross National Product or to make sure there are enough dentists for the coming decade. And therefore you do not judge the success of educational programmes by reference to the GNP or the number of dentists around. Education is something we provide because we believe it is valuable to be educated, just as it is valuable to be beautiful. However it is also the case that in some respects education is useful. Education being what it is, to open democratic societies with goals of truth and rational decision-making, educated people are obviously very useful and uneducated people are a considerable nuisance. (In closed totalitarian societies the situation is radically different: educated people are the nuisance and consequently, in closed societies, schools do not provide true education. This book is written in the context of Western democracy.)

But, granted its value, whether intrinsically, extrinsically or both, is there a case for entrusting education in the sense delineated to schools? I would say unequivocally "yes", but can here do little more than draw attention to the main considerations for and against. The obvious argument against is that schools may stifle and kill enthusiasm, and fail to capitalise on genuine interests that children may have. As a diagnosis of troubles to be found in our schools, the deschooling argument is illuminating. As against that, it has not been established and it is in fact preposterous to suggest that schools must necessarily do the job badly; enthusiasm can be generated in the school context and there is anyway no guarantee that in a society without schools people will become educated. Fundamentally, the argument in favour of a system of schooling to provide education is that education is regarded as very important, the acquisition of the requisite kind of understanding is not automatic, but usually depends on guidance and encouragement, and above all individuals often do not appreciate the value of it of their own accord soon enough. We may summarise the matter thus: if it was true that by and large people would educate themselves or find access to education in society without the institution of schooling, we should not need schools, at any rate for that purpose. But that time has surely not come, and in the meantime education is so valuable, both for its own sake to the individual and on wider grounds of utility to society, that we must encourage the schools to provide it, while conceding their shortcomings and continually trying to remove them.

3 SOCIALISATION AND INDOCTRINATION

Recently a number of people have become increasingly restive about the way in which schools become the dumping ground for each and every social problem. Increases in vandalism, shortage of trained technocrats, increases in sexual promiscuity, chauvinistic attitudes, lack of patriotism, decline in sales of books, decline in quality films—there are those who attribute the blame for all these alleged cracks in the plastering of civilisation to the failure of the school. And, as I say, there are those who object to the way in which the school is so often made (sometimes retrospectively) responsible. But this question of how one may set a limit to what the school should be concerned with is a very difficult one to answer. After considerable pondering on the matter, I've come to the conclusion that one cannot set limits *a priori* on the responsibilities of schooling. Although I feel intuitive sympathy with those who say that it is wrong to throw everything on to the schools, I cannot see a clear line of reasoning to suggest any principle or set of principles whereby we may set a limit to what schools should do. To be sure, issues like reverse discrimination, bussing as a means towards racial integration and sex-role stereotyping are not educational matters, but why should schools not, nonetheless, play a decisive part in respect of them? They are crucial matters in respect of how our society is going to get along, and schooling is, amongst other things, about precisely that. However, what we can do is point out two very important restraints on this business of pushing everything on to the schools.

Firstly, we can object reasonably enough to the schools being called upon to do anything that would hinder them while trying to do things it has already been agreed they should do. For example, although schools should do many things besides educate, they shouldn't be expected to do anything that is actually incompatible with or anti-educational. Secondly, we must not accept that the school should automatically respond to the needs and pressures of today, for as I have already said, what the future will be is partially determined by what the schools do now. Schools are by no means bound to reflect current practice and experience. What I suppose they are bound to do is reflect current demands (which is why one writes books like this in an attempt to influence the demands of thinking people). This does seem to me to imply that if, for example, the democratically elected government determines on a policy of bussing, school authorities should carry it out. (They may meanwhile continue to argue about it, the question of whether this policy is the right one being quite distinct from the question of whether, emanating from the duly elected government as it does, it should be carried out.) Beyond these two broad restraints, however, we cannot do other than look at each case on its merits.

Socialisation is certainly one function that schools currently perform or contribute to. By socialisation I mean familiarising the child (individual) with and initiating him into the customs, conventions and expectations of society and habituating him to a culture or way of life. Socialisation may involve such diverse aspects as cultivating presumptions about driving on one side of the road rather than another, about not picking your nose in public, about not being drunk in the course of a day's work, about sexual mores, about being considerate towards others, about waiting your turn to get on the bus or about the value of free speech. The customs, conventions and expectations of a society will obviously form a motley collection, and will seem of varying importance to the society itself. Some of them will pass in and out of fashion at various times. At any given time some of them will seem objectionable to some of us within the society, but that is a distinct question, as is the question of whether we, as outsiders, approve or disapprove of a particular culture into which others are being socialised. Bearing that in mind (i.e. that we are not necessarily hereby defending any particular attempts at socialisation), it seems very difficult to me to object to the notion of socialisation in itself. Social life depends upon a set of agreed conventions; indeed up to a point it is defined by them, since a collection of people is not a society and only becomes one in the light of some principles of organisation and conduct. And in any case a degree of socialisation will inevitably take place. It is quite inconceivable that a child should grow up in a particular culture with particular manners and values and not become familiar with them and to a greater or lesser extent influenced by them. Once that is recognised, it must be absurd to refuse to take steps to see that such influence is orchestrated.

There may conceivably be theoretical arguments for valuing a complete absence of influence, were it possible. But once it is conceded that people are going to be influenced by their surroundings, I can conceive of no convincing argument to show that it would be best if such influence were left to chance, or if children were to be subjected to a barrage of random and often contradictory demands. Besides, the very point and purpose of influencing children in respect of the norms of society is denied, if there is no uniformity. Socialisation, to be effective socialisation, must involve steering all children in the same sort of direction, namely in the direction of appreciating how things actually are in the society in question. There may come a point at which individuals revolt against some of the features of the society, and have moral objections to the way in which society as a whole would habituate their children to acceptance of those features. Issues like the war in Vietnam for Americans or Suez for Britain may bring about such conflicts, or, on a more limited scale, national and individual attitudes to things like capital punishment and abortion may not coincide. But the fact that there will be occasions when any one of us may want to fight the forces of socialisation is not incompatible with the point that, generally speaking, being a member of society involves acceptance of the idea of socialising the children of that society into its ways. The fact that we may honourably hold different views about the moral acceptability of American involvement in Vietnam does not mean that we must have similar crises of conscience over whether our children are brought up to familiarise themselves with and respect the traffic code, the laws and the manners of our land. The difference between Western democracies and totalitarian regimes such as those of Soviet Russia, Nazi Germany or South Africa, and the objection to the latter, if there is one, resides not in the fact that the latter call forth commitment to their code of living (with rather more success than democratic states), but in something about the way in which they do it or the content of their code or both. There can be no inherent objection to initiation into the requirements and expectations of a society as such—which is to say, socialisation.

But what we do need to do is to distinguish between socialisation and something else which is usually termed *indoctrination*.[11] Socialisation involves giving people information about the society in which they live, and habituating them to what is demanded or expected by that society in terms of behaviour and attitude. It will of course have repercussions in terms of belief, since most of us tend to form opinions about our way of life (such as that it is a good way of life or a miserable way of life). Nonetheless socialisation is not defined in terms of promoting beliefs. Getting people acclimatised to the fact that in this society we don't walk around the streets naked is one thing. Getting them to believe that it is immoral to do so (never mind what this or any other society thinks) is another. Only the former has a place in socialisation as I

conceive it. Indoctrination on the other hand is about implanting
beliefs. That much seems to be agreed by all who have considered
the concept, though there is a lot of disagreement on the questions
of what kind of belief and what methods of implanting them are
crucial to the notion.

There are those who maintain that only doctrinal beliefs can be
indoctrinated. A doctrinal belief is a belief that is part of some
ideological system (i.e. a set of interrelated beliefs having repercussions for how one lives one's life and based upon one or more
unprovable proposition(s)). A closely related view is that only
unprovable propositions themselves can be indoctrinated (i.e.
ones that we do not know how to set about proving or disproving
rather than ones that we simply haven't yet managed to prove or
disprove. [See Chapter Five.]) It must be borne in mind that since
we are talking about the meaning of the concept here, the claim is
not an empirical one about the practical impossibility of indoctrinating other kinds of belief, but a point of definition; the
claim is that the meaning of indoctrination is such that imparting
other kinds of belief wouldn't count as indoctrination. However, I
know of no convincing argument for accepting either of these
proposed limitations. The etymological point that "doctrines" and
"indoctrination" are obviously connected, which is sometimes
advanced as an argument for concluding that only doctrinal beliefs
can be indoctrinated, deserves about as much respect as the
parallel claim that one can only sing songs would do. (i.e. none: I
can perfectly well sing the telephone directory, if I want to.) More
to the point, I see nothing unintelligible, logically odd or peculiar
in the idea of indoctrinating people with simple falsehoods or even
truths. This is because indoctrination is surely to be defined in
terms of the way in which and the purpose with which you implant
belief, as can be seen by comparing telling a lie with indoctrination.
To tell a lie is to misinform, which you might do for any number of
reasons (for a joke, to gain something, to hurt somebody, to save
your skin, to protect someone else, etc.). But indoctrination,
though it may be engaged in for some such ulterior motive,
certainly doesn't have to be, for a sufficient motive is embedded in
its meaning, which is to implant a belief unshakeably in someone's
mind. So indoctrinating a lie is distinct from telling a lie, the
former by definition involving an intention of getting the lie
believed in once and for all, while the latter carries no such
implication. Similarly one might conceivably indoctrinate a truth,
that is to say put something across that happens to be true, with
the intention of getting it to stick.

But if we leave it at that there is an obvious drawback, for if indoctrination is to be defined simply as imparting beliefs with the intention that they will stick, then a great deal of routine teaching and upbringing is going to constitute indoctrination. In getting people to believe that four times four equals sixteen, that H_2SO_4 is the chemical formula for sulphuric acid, that naked light sockets are dangerous, that dogs that foam at the mouth are best avoided, we would be guilty of indoctrinating. There are two objections to accepting this conception without further qualification, and hence that conclusion. Firstly, it doesn't account for the fact that the word "indoctrination" has pejorative connotations for most of us. We think of it as a bad practice, but, if it includes teaching people the multiplication tables or to beware of dogs with rabies, it surely isn't in itself a bad practice. Secondly, if we nonetheless persist in using the word in this broad way to cover the sort of examples cited, we are missing an opportunity to label and hence pinpoint a distinction, which is certainly there to be made, between on the one hand teaching people that four times four equals sixteen and on the other hand teaching them that the theory of evolution is iniquitous and false. The difference is this: the former can be explained and taught in a rational manner. The latter cannot, for there are not adequate rational grounds for describing the theory of evolution as iniquitous and false. (Note my unusual choice of example: remember that the theory of evolution *may* be false in its entirety or in points of detail. The point here therefore is not that describing it as iniquitous and false is ridiculous, although many will understandably feel that it is, but that no such charge could be explained and supported in rational terms in the way that the multiplication example could be.) I would therefore add as another defining characteristic or criterion the use of non-rational techniques of imparting belief. What precise means are used is not important to the definition, provided that they are non-rational. Thus one might rely on charisma, threats, magical incantations, torture, blinding with words—anything, in short, other than the provision of reasoning that inclines one to the conclusion.

It was explained in Chapter One that there is no such thing as a correct conception of anything. So in putting forward the view that we should include the last mentioned criterion (use of non-rational means of imparting belief) I am doing no more than suggesting that its inclusion gives us a more useful, because more specific, conception of indoctrination than its absence would allow. My definition of indoctrination, therefore, is: the use of non-rational means with the intention of implanting belief(s) unshakeably. Now this seems to me inherently obnoxious; we do not want a world full of people with unyielding and inflexible commitment to ideas they have acquired for no good reason. Beliefs based on reasoning are far more flexible and susceptible to adaptation or modification than those acquired by non-rational means. If I believe something for particular reasons then changes in circumstances or argument may lead me readily to modify that belief; but if I hold the belief for no good reason in the first place, then no reasoning is likely to moderate it. More to the point, indoctrination in this sense is incompatible with education, because education is essentially about promoting understanding, the antithesis of non-rational belief. So if the schooling system or individual teachers within the system (or parents) seek to induce unyielding commitment to various beliefs, that is to be deplored. Being actually anti-educational or a hindrance to it, it cannot be accepted as another legitimate function of the school. And let us not pretend that indoctrination as defined does not take place: it happens in an institutionalised way in Soviet Russia and China, it happens in some Muslim states and in some religious schools in Britain and North America, and no doubt throughout the Western World there are individual teachers in ordinary schools who are guilty of attempting to indoctrinate students. But that is to be distinguished from socialisation which does not involve using non-rational techniques to impart beliefs such as "One ought to drive on the left hand side of the road" as if they were unquestionable truths, but habituates people to the fact that that is a demand of society. By all means let children know that they live in a democracy or a Marxist state or whatever, and let them be habituated to the demands and expectations of that state—that is socialisation. But don't bring them up to believe, as could only be done by non-rational means, that the fundamental tenets of their particular state are inviolable truths.

It may finally be asked why schools rather than individual families should take responsibility for socialisation. But the question betrays a lack of understanding of the nature of the case. Socialisation is, as we have said, the name given to the process of influence and habituation that comes to bear on people as they grow up within a community. There cannot be a question of anyone or any group or agency opting out of its contribution towards socialising, for it is defined in terms of all the agencies there are; one is socialised as a result of the impact of one's family, one's neighbourhood, one's peer group and, of course, one's schooling. The only question can be whether an agency like the school should take thought for the matter or let its contribution be haphazard. Common sense implacably and forthrightly replies that, since socialisation is going to take place and is a crucial aspect of society, it would be best for those who will inevitably play a major part in it, such as schools, to put a lot of thought into it.

4 CHILD-MINDING

If schools are institutions for bringing people up, which includes at least offering them the good of education and a well-planned contribution to the necessity of socialisation, what about their custodial role? Should they have what Reimer has called the task of baby-minding?[12] It is interesting that while some raise this question, others are asking questions about the traditional roles of parents, particularly of mothers. While some are seeking to absolve schools from responsibility for keeping an eye on the child's daily whereabouts, others are seeking to absolve parents from it too. Certainly, if mothers are going to enjoy more of the freedom from family concerns conventionally granted to fathers, and if the latter are going to remain much as they are, we will need institutions of some sort to exercise custodial care on a wider scale than heretofore. I shall not discuss the alleged rights and wrongs of demands for more freedom for women, partly because I don't believe that it is a matter of right and wrong and partly because it would take us too far out of the way. [I don't believe that it's a matter of right and wrong in the sense that I don't believe it is, so to speak, written in the heavens that women—or anybody else—should or shouldn't devote so much time to their children. My own ethical position is such that so long as anything, including a social convention, promotes happiness to a greater extent, taking the long-term overall view for all people affected, than any alternative arrangement would do, there is no moral objection to it. Thus the question of whether women should or should not have more state aid to allow them to be released from the practical necessity of looking after children is the largely empirical (though exceedingly difficult) one of whether we have reached a point at which, on balance, there will be more happiness to the community as a whole, if we give priority to such a strategy.]

But it seems likely that the arrangements of the past, whereby the mother is tied by young children and gains a degree of freedom when they go to school, will be regarded increasingly as unsatisfactory; more and more parents will want more freedom from the limitations imposed by looking after children, and will want more baby and child minding facilities provided by the state. In the absence of any obvious objection to such a tendency, that desire seems a good enough reason for providing such facilities.

The question must be whether schools, already concerned with education and socialisation, should have to take on this further responsibility. Since the provision of education and socialisation already require some degree of attendance, the real issue becomes whether schools should be expected to do things like ensure attendance, crack down on truancy and generally take active steps to superintend the child's behaviour and welfare throughout the day.

The point has been made that such a role for the school may make its other jobs harder to perform successfully, and an alternative, more open model of schooling has been put forward, whereby education is available on a voluntary basis and socialisation left to other social agencies. Between that and the traditional model of compulsory school attendance there are a number of alternatives such as free schools, where daily attendance is compulsory, but what the child does while there is largely a matter for him to determine, or the typical university model, where there is a reasonable amount of freedom and choice amongst a limited range of options. One might even envisage a schooling system run on the lines of business or industry where attendance is encouraged more by incentives, rewards and, perhaps, penalties, than by compulsion or choice. But the obvious difference between university students and adults in industry on the one hand, and young school-children on the other, is that the former are in a better position to make informed choices; the obvious difficulty of free schools and deschooling is the fear that many children will not be in a position to appreciate the potential value of what schools might try to offer. There are those who will point out that some ten-year-old children are as wise as some twenty-five or seventy-five-year-olds, and that stopping compulsory schooling at a particular age is quite arbitrary. But that line of argument is not very compelling. It is true that any cut off point for compulsory school attendance will be arbitrary, if that means that it might well have been fixed at some other, if not any other, point, just as any speed limit is arbitrary in that sense. Similarly there is no doubt that some adults are more stupid than some children, just as some drivers are more dangerous at 30 kph than others at 90 kph. But just as the existence of dangerous slow drivers and the arbitrariness of a chosen speed limit in no way amount to a case against having a speed limit, so such observations about some children don't materially affect the case for schooling. By and large, nine-year-old children do not freely choose to do a lot of the things that from the long term point of view of both themselves and society it would be sensible, useful and rewarding for them to do.

To this it has been replied that it is treating people like children *to* that makes them childlike. Treat them like adults and give them *sweeping* responsibility, and they will exercise that responsibility like adults. As a general principle the claim that people will act exactly as they are treated is overstated and implausible. It is anyway impossible to argue about in a coherent way, so sweeping is the claim. The specific claim that children would freely (and as a result more efficaciously) embrace all that is of importance in compulsory schooling is hardly less tricky to deal with, since it may involve so many different kinds of claim, ranging from views about what is important, through to assertions about what does happen and speculations about what would happen in different circumstances. But at least it can be faced. The question is, would the majority of children, if given freedom from any formal schooling requirements, (*a*) safely look after themselves, (*b*) refrain from anti-social activity here and now, (*c*) become socialised in a manner acceptable to society, and (*d*) come by the education which it has already been argued they ought to have?

The actual evidence relating to that four-part question is paltry and inconclusive. Experimental schools such as Summerhill in Britain are extremely atypical in intake and above all in their consciousness of being special, which they wouldn't be if they were the norm. So the tiny amount of evidence they supply is scarcely representative. In any case there is no clear evidence that even in such special cases the answer to the question would be affirmative on all four counts, particularly the fourth. The more extreme tactic of ridding society of schools altogether takes us into the realm of sheer speculation, where there isn't any relevant evidence one way or the other. I have already indicated that I doubt very much whether deschooling is a sensible solution, but an important point to grasp is that this is not a point of principle. I would not argue that deschooling must necessarily be wrong. Indeed rather the opposite; for I share with many of the deschoolers a certain conception of education, a desire that it should be valued for its own sake, and a dislike of indoctrination. Where I differ from them is in thinking that deschooling is a realistic option. In a better society we wouldn't need schools. In society as it is I fear that deschooling would not improve matters so much as remove one potential bastion against the worst features of our society.

But while there is no reason to accept the contention that things would be better without a system of schooling, there is every reason to take the criticisms of schooling made by those who would rid us of them seriously; we are always covertly teaching more than we may realise; in particular we covertly teach that what is learned in school is more valuable than what is learned from neighbours or television or by chance; our examination systems exert considerable pressure on what we teach, often with undesirable consequences; we are too inclined to proceed as if there is in all matters one straightforward objective reality, and to underplay the role of individual perception; we too often teach passive and uncritical acceptance. My argument would be (and this too is necessarily speculative) that in practical terms the best way to counteract these evils is through an improved schooling system (particularly through improved education). "Far from relaxing the grip of the schools we need in some respects to increase it to meet the very shortcomings noted by the radicals."[13]

To return to the immediate issue: it certainly isn't going to make the schools' other jobs any easier to perform if they are seen as penal institutions by students. But on the other hand the goods cannot be delivered if the students aren't there. The only satisfactory way out of this impasse is going to be the difficult one of establishing the idea that schools have something to offer, both in the national consciousness generally and in the minds of students in particular. My argument in this chapter as a whole leads inexorably to the conclusion that in both a positive and a negative way this is so, and that even a reluctant student may gain from school both advantages that he does not necessarily welcome or recognise as such (as the reluctant patient gains from going to the dentist), and advantages that sooner or later he sees as such (as the reluctant first-time concert goer may someday thank the person who dragged him there). My argument at this particular juncture is that we must work hard at getting this point across and making the experience as enjoyable as possible, rather than give up the point in despair or indulge in a bout of utopian daydreaming.

The conclusion is that, notwithstanding all the dangers and drawbacks, schools should continue to act to some extent as childminders. Children should be expected to be there.

5 VOCATIONAL COURSES

A favourite question in philosophy of education examination papers over the years has been "Is vocational education a contradiction in terms?" I think that it probably is. We have already seen that education by definition implies breadth of understanding acquired and valued for its own sake, whereas usually vocational courses are narrowly specific and undertaken for instrumental reasons. Training as a motor mechanic, as a secretary or as a printer might serve as good examples of vocational courses, and they do not in themselves constitute education.

Now one might reasonably argue with that, and point out that a vocational course could perfectly well serve as part of an educational curriculum or, again, that some so-called vocational courses are actually of such a sort as to be indistinguishable from education. For example a university degree course in medicine or law might arguably be regarded as both educational and vocational. But really there is no need for such disclaimers. Indeed it is probably strategically foolish for one who wishes to defend vocational courses to do so on either of these grounds, for both lines of defence implicitly admit that education should be the sole criterion for establishing what should be taught in schools and colleges. But it should *not* be the only criterion. If one thing is clear by now, it is that education is only one of the things that schools should be concerned with. Most vocational courses, if not all, are probably not strictly speaking educational, but that does not in itself mean that they have no place in schools, for schooling is about more than education. Admittedly there are dangers here; we should not want vocational courses to oust education, for instance, or to impose constraints on thinking where there should be liberation of the mind, or in any other way to get in the way of or interfere with education, since that is certainly a prime function of schooling. But surely it is eminently sensible that in bringing up our children, besides educating and socialising them, we should have an eye to their future employment; besides giving them education for its own sake, we should try to develop their talents and then match them to likely opportunities, for the sake of their livelihood and satisfaction and society's smooth functioning.

One of the most extraordinary things we seem to have done in recent decades is come to think of education as merely another profession, comparable to the legal and medical professions. This way of looking at things intensifies the idea that there is some kind of conflict between education and other matters, just as there would be between a medical training and a legal training. But there is no conflict between education and vocational courses. They are different aspects of upbringing. People should be educated and people should have the opportunity to pursue a vocation. (The word "vocation" seems to have lost overtones of work undertaken in response to some inner, quasi-divine, call, and I use it to refer to any trade or profession.)

But while we must defend the place of vocational courses in school, we must avoid letting a realistic concern for vocation run away with us. The danger to avoid is that of limiting people under the guise of helping them; for example, we must avoid devoting all our attention to training people to be gas fitters and fit for little else, in a world that has increasingly little use for gas fitters.

Without assuming that we will get a perfect solution it is evident that, particularly in the later years of schooling, we should give some thought to people's particular talents and interests, and seek to match them up against likely job availability. Surely it is highly desirable that schools should concern themselves far more than they do now with the broad question of what those who are going to leave school in two years' time are going to do. And little harm can come of thinking in terms of broad categories such as engineering, shopkeeping, nursing and insurance, or in seeking to build on specific proclivities. The dangers to be particularly avoided are, firstly, that already referred to of effectively dictating the future in the name of preparing for it (e.g. training people to be telephone engineers so that that is all that they are ready to be), secondly, providing too specific a training, thirdly, wasting time and resources on training that is readily available elsewhere, and finally wasting them on that which is essentially trivial. Teaching typing during school time really does seem unjustifiable, not because typing isn't useful to many people, but because teaching typing does not require the expensive back up of schooling, and there are other things that do. Similarly it is extremely difficult to see why cookery or home economics should warrant a place in the school curriculum any more than gardening or house painting. These are activities which can be readily practised without the benfit of schooling either now, in the child's home, or in the future. To train people for a trade and thereby to stamp them for a particular future occupation is a risky undertaking and is far better left to the years of apprenticeship or technical college. The secondary or high school should limit itself to concern with a range of broad vocational areas.

6 Primary and Physical Instruction

Two of the largest groups in the teaching fraternity, primary or junior school teachers and physical education instructors, are in the interesting position of being only marginally related to education. By and large primary school teachers do not educate so much as lay necessary foundations for education or contribute elements of education. This has sometimes worried them, but there is no obvious reason why it should, for it is to say no more than that, rather than contributing directly to the provision of some part of that breadth of understanding that constitutes education, they teach certain skills that in practice are necessary to the later development of such understanding (skills such as those of reading, writing and numeracy). That is a most worthwhile role. Besides overseeing a necessary first step towards education, they play a crucial role in schooling both by developing a favourable disposition in children and by taking the first steps in socialisation.

The case of the physical education instructor is slightly different because here we have a case of the leopard trying to change his spots (or somebody else trying to change his spots for him). Not so long ago PT, i.e. physical training as it was then called in Britain, was a common feature of the curriculum of most schools. The rationale for having PT lessons was straightforward enough and owed something to the Roman poet Juvenal's tag about the need for a sound mind and a healthy body.[14] The idea was to keep young bodies fit and healthy, possibly with the additional aim of teaching a few basic principles of physical health. But one of the unintended consequences of recent emphasis on education being a serious and valuable business, essentially bound up with understanding, has been to make devotees of many schooling activities that were seemingly unconcerned with understanding rush to emphasise a cognitive element in them. This is exactly what happened with PT. Firstly, the element of theoretical understanding was emphasised, courses gave more attention to the rationale for various types of physical exercise, and the enterprise was renamed "physical education". Subsequently, the intellectual aspect has been even more emphasised and yet new names have been coined such as "human movement studies", with the result that many courses are at least as concerned with theories about the nature, point and purpose of various physical activities as they are with physical activity itself. Some of the claims made to satisfy this latest phase are absurd, and many of them turn what started out as a programme of physical activity into something quite different, such as a study of the sociology of sport or aesthetics.

Though in principle it must be possible to devise perfectly good arguments for studying aesthetics or sociology of sport, or for doing ballet or improvisation, or for playing baseball or cricket, the main feature of the current situation is a remarkable dearth of clear argument for the value of what is going on.[15] Presumably this is because, for the most part, the situation leads competent practitioners of particular activities into the uncharted waters of trying to justify those activities as compulsory elements in a curriculum—something which they are not particularly competent to do. The result has been a plethora of curious claims, such as that movement is crucial for the development of the intellect, that some children might gain access to the forms of knowledge through kinetic experience, that sport is art, or that "the important role [for PE] might be in the education of the feelings and senses and in achieving a high degree of self knowledge".[16] I would not presume to say that such claims could not be interpreted in a way that makes them meaningful, though I would venture to suggest that, in so far as they make sense and have some truth, they will turn out to be pretty trivial. The main point that needs to be made here and now is that various types of physical activity (games, gymnastics, dance, swimming, etc.), that either are or might be part of the curriculum, are currently supported by a most confused and hazy body of argument, largely as a result of the feeling that they must prove themselves respectable by showing that they too are intimately concerned with the cognitive and hence education. Yet clearly there was something of value in what we started with, namely physical health and physical fitness. There is plenty of evidence that people work better and feel better when fit, that they live longer and are able to engage in more potentially enjoyable activities when they are healthy, and that a great deal of enjoyment is to be derived from various forms of physical activity. Surely that is quite sufficient justification for devoting school time, firstly to keeping children fit and healthy and, then, perhaps, to giving them some understanding of how to keep that way. Certainly this has little to do with education as such (one may be educated and sick or healthy and uneducated), but that doesn't stop it being a proper concern of schooling.

(To say that most forms of physical activity can legitimately claim curriculum time, without contorting their very nature to make themselves educational activities, and to say that, currently, most arguments seeking to justify physical activities in intellectual terms are pretty embarrassing, is not to say that such an argument could not be coherently presented or that it should not be attempted. This might be a suitable place to draw attention to the distinction between arguing that schools ought to do certain specific things, and arguing that there is value in studying certain specific things if people want to study them—a distinction between candidates for some kind of core curriculum and various curricular options. I am maintaining that children's physical fitness and health ought to be a concern of the schools, while it is far from clear that studying human movement necessarily should be. That is not to say that the study of human movement, whatever exactly it turns out to involve, would not be a suitable and worthwhile option to make available on a curriculum.)

7 Social Role Selection

Finally there is the matter of what may be generally termed social role selection. As a preliminary to considering this issue, let me introduce the observation that how things are and how things ought to be are two distinct questions, and that the fact that something is the case does not justify it being the case. The fact that big fat bullies successfully intimidate the weak and the meek does not mean that they ought to, have a right to or are justified in doing so. Conversely, the fact that there are no instances of societies that do not use animals for their own advantage (so that it is regarded as natural to make use of them) does not show that there ought not to be. It is evident to most of us that as a matter of fact schools do contribute to social role selection in various ways, and indeed that it would be difficult to stop them doing so. But so long as it is conceivable, however difficult in practice, that they might not, we have to face the entirely distinct question of whether it is desirable or acceptable that they should. [The error of interpreting questions of value as if they were questions of empirical fact is sometimes referred to as committing the *naturalistic fallacy*. That is actually a rather loose use of a phrase originally introduced by G. E. Moore to pick out the more specific habit of trying to define moral goodness in terms of some natural quality, as, for example, some people might claim that to call an action morally good means that it is an action that promotes pleasure. Moore himself went on to classify any attempt to define goodness, even in terms of non-natural qualities, as similarly fallacious. The distinction stressed above is perhaps best summarised in a phrase that derives from David Hume, although he didn't actually use it: "no ought from an is". See below Chapter Five.]

The problem is that schools make a contribution to social role selection almost without trying, certainly without the people concerned such as teachers necessarily thinking that it is or should be part of the school's function. There are, broadly speaking, three ways in which they make this contribution.

(*a*) They may, as we've just seen, equip people to do certain things rather than others. They may in other words take an active part in selecting people for some roles rather than others. But to pillory the school for this would be an absurd case of putting the cart before the horse (especially since we've just argued that this is one of the things that, with due caution, schools ought to do). The school helps the individual who wants to do one type of thing rather than another, to do so; although, as has been noted, there is a danger that schools may make individuals become some things rather than others, they do not have to do so. In this respect they are institutions that may offer a range of broad preliminary types of training. This seems both acceptable and compatible with other functions of schooling.

(b) A slightly different part in selection is played by schools from a rather earlier date, in that in most systems children are gradually sifted and sorted out by reference to aptitude for certain broad categories. Thus, as the years of schooling pass, it becomes clearer just who is going to make a quarter-back, a mathematician, an oarsman, an artist and so on. Even allowing yet again for the point that to some extent and in some cases the school will be creating mathematicians, etc., as much as revealing them, it is difficult to see any objection to this function. Neither we nor the individuals concerned know in advance who is going to have an aptitude for mathematics or whatever (indeed for those of a very environmentalist persuasion, the idea scarcely even makes sense). What then could be more sensible than to take children step by step into the world of mathematics (rowing, football, art etc.), and to find out as we go along whose interest and/or talent thrives and develops, and whose wanes and falls short?

(c) Schools classify people. They classify them in general as good and bad students. They classify them in broad categories as technological, artistic, sporting, good material for medical school. They classify them more specifically as having good grades, eight 'O' levels, 'A' level maths or whatever it may be.

One objection to this is that even the more specific kinds of judgement (e.g. "not very good at French") tend to be seen as general judgements on character and ability, though even the broadest kinds (e.g. "a poor student") ought not to be. To be poor in school is not the same thing as being poor—period. A bad student is not necessarily a bad citizen. This tendency of society to inrerpret judgements made in the context of schooling as of permanent global significance is a most unfortunate by-product of schooling. But still it cannot be used as a conclusive consideration against such classification, especially if there is some other good reason in favour of it, since it is essentially an objection to the use to which the classification may be put, rather than to the notion of classification itself. The matter of assessment itself will be looked at in more detail below [Chapter Six]. But here it has to be said that schools certainly should not organise themselves with a view to sorting and classifying, since that emphatically should not be one of their primary functions. They should organise themselves with a view to education, socialisation and the other things that have been mentioned as their proper functions. Now, if the outside world, if society at large, insists on making use of classifications that will inevitably crop up in the context of schooling, in a wider context, that is another question. There is not much that can be done to stand in the way of society saying that it wants competent doctors, and that it regards certain examination papers as a necessary condition of medical competence; if big business sees certain grades as indication of the type of man it wants, there is not a lot that schools can do about it. What schools can do, however, is refuse to allow employment qualifications to dominate the courses they lay on. They can refuse to allow what big business or medical schools want to be the yardstick of what they provide. What schools teach should be decided solely by reference to the functions (e.g. education, socialisation, etc.) of schooling, not by reference to the qualifications that other social agencies happen to look for.

There are then some respects in which schools should, or at any rate reasonably may, play a part in social role selection, but even so it seems clear that this is a minor and secondary function of schooling which must be subordinated to the primary functions of education, socialisation, broad vocational preparation and maintenance of physical health. The success or failure of schooling should be judged by reference to those four factors, and not by reference to considerations such as social mobility or the subsequent success of one time students.

8 Education of the Emotions

We have considered the nature of education and dealt with some of the other main functions of the school. One thing that has not so far been mentioned, although it is widely thought to be of great importance, is the affective side. With this in mind, many people might want to go back to the concept of education itself and ask "Is it really convincing to depict education in purely cognitive terms?" or to raise the more general question "Is there no place for the affective side of things in the school?" Before answering those questions, let us get a clear conception of what an emotion is.

Some people use the words "emotions" and "feelings" more or less interchangeably. There is no law against that. But note the consequences: firstly, if we regard emotions as just feelings in the sense of sensations, so that the emotion love is presumed to be a particular kind of feeling on a par with a sensation of thirst or pain, it automatically follows that there is not a great deal that we can do or say about emotions. For a start, if the emotion of love is just some sensation, then there is no way of judging whether what you call "love" in any way resembles what I call "love", and no way of checking an individual's claim that he is experiencing love. Secondly, to classify emotions as feelings is merely to deny oneself the opportunity of making distinctions that can be made; for, as we shall see, though an emotion such as love is no doubt a type of feeling, it is in important respects different from a feeling such as pain. Thirdly, if emotions are, like all feelings, reduced to mere sensation, then the only way to study them would be through behavioural patterns. Now behaviourism is a very sensible methodology for psychologists to adopt—that is to say it is sensible to proceed in terms of what is observable rather than what is not. But to offer behaviourist definitions is very crude and dangerous; certainly, jealous people may be defined as people who do x and y, but sometimes people do x and y for reasons other than those of jealousy, and sometimes people who do not do x and y are nonetheless jealous. (So at least it generally seems to most ordinary people. Of course in terms of a particular behavioural definition that cannot happen, for being jealous is, and is only, doing x and y.) If we want a full understanding of the emotions, if, that is to say, we want a proper understanding that nonetheless does justice to our everyday assumptions and statements about them, we need to improve on both behaviouristic and subjective (i.e. sensation) accounts of them.

In point of fact this is not too difficult, as we see if we contemplate a list of what appear at first blush to be emotions and a list of what appear to be feelings. Emotions are undoubtedly feelings, but they are feelings of a particular sort; they are, if you like, a subspecies of feeling, and while all emotions involve feelings, not all feelings are emotions. The question is, what is the difference between on the one hand feelings such as hunger, thirst, pain and pleasure and, on the other hand, emotions such as envy, jealousy, pride, guilt, shame and love? (Or, to ask a similar question, the answer to which will later prove revealing, "Why is it that something like fear seems hard to categorise as obviously either one or the other?") The answer in outline is that emotions are feelings directed at a particular object or objects and arising out of a particular way of looking at a situation (a particular form of cognitive appraisal, as it is sometimes phrased).[17]

Imagine that you wake up one morning with a particular feeling that you classify as hunger. You may feel hungry for something specific like a piece of ham, and you may be thinking of the fact that you haven't eaten for forty-eight hours. But neither condition need apply; you might not be hungry for anything in particular, and you might have no particular view of your situation. It makes perfectly good sense to wake up and just feel hungry.

The same thing cannot be said of something like jealousy. It makes very little sense to claim to wake up one morning, *à propos* of nothing, with a feeling of jealousy stabbing one's vitals. On the contrary, if you claim to be jealous, we would naturally expect you to be jealous of somebody or something, and to have this feeling because you see your situation in a particular way. For that is what being jealous means. When we say that Othello is jealous we are hardly referring to the kind of feeling he experiences at all (about which we know nothing anyway). What we are saying is: he is experiencing some kind of sensation directed at Desdemona, because he sees her as being unfaithful. Incidentally, it does not matter whether one's view of the situation is adequate or not: if I think my wife is being unfaithful, I may feel jealousy which is real enough, even if I am mistaken and therefore have no cause to feel jealous. (Or start at the beginning of the paragraph again and consider this: why, when you wake with this feeling stabbing your vitals, do you call it a feeling of jealousy? Is there a distinctive jealousy feeling that may be experienced in any context?)

Some of the words in either of the two lists above might refer to either an emotion or a feeling. That is why fear is hard to classify. Sometimes we just feel fear (i.e. just experience a sensation which is of a broadly distinctive kind and for which there is no obvious explanation, if there is one at all); sometimes we are afraid (i.e. interpret our situation in a particular way and thereby fear something specific). The important point is that there is a distinction to be drawn between mere feelings and feelings attached to objects in the light of a particular cognitive appraisal. The latter are what most people would seem to have in mind, however hazily, when they refer to emotions.

Feelings, though they might be trained, schooled or cultivated, cannot be educated. You can no doubt diminish or increase people's capacity to feel things like fear, hunger or pain; and you can school them not to express those feelings. But it's difficult to make much sense of the idea of educating them. By contrast one could educate the emotions, because there is that element of cognitive appraisal in emotional responses, and education is about understanding. Emotionally mature people or emotionally educated people (I use the phrases interchangeably) are those whose feelings are appropriate and allied to cognitive appraisals that are reasonable. People who feel jealous when and only when circumstances warrant it, for example, are emotionally mature (at any rate in that respect), while those who unreasonably see cause for jealousy in the quite innocent behaviour of others are emotionally immature. Those who mistake infatuation or lust for love, those, that is to say, who do not fully understand the circumstances in which it is appropriate to classify a feeling as a symptom of the emotion love, would thereby again betray emotional immaturity. To educate the emotions would be to give people greater understanding of the subtleties of human relations in life, such that they are enabled to classify their feelings in line with a discriminating and realistic appraisal of circumstances. It would therefore involve refining blunt stereotypical responses, opening up a wider range of discrimination and developing a more perceptive view of the world. The mind is involved both in experiencing one's own emotions and in judging the emotions of others, and the question of correctness or reasonableness may arise: it is not reasonable to assume that you love somebody because the sight of their naked body sets your pulse racing; it is incorrect to regard yourself as jealous, if your feeling is merely occasioned by resentment at not being put before someone else. In all these cases no one doubts that feelings are involved, but they are being wrongly classified as a result of inadequate perceptions and conceptions.

To say all this does not involve going back on the claim made above that education is essentially cognitive, and not a business that necessarily involves the affective side of man. Very much the reverse; it is only because emotions have a cognitive element that we can sensibly talk of educating them. We have to distinguish between the question of whether being educated necessarily involves reference to the emotions (which is a question about the concept of education), and whether one can educate the emotions (which is a question related to the concept of emotion). To the former question I still return a negative reply: a person whose emotions are uneducated (i.e. an emotionally immature person) may still be an educated person. Emotional maturity is not a mark of the educated man, and, if schools were solely concerned with education, they would not be under any obligation to consider the emotions. But schools are not only concerned with education, and one might quite consistently argue that schools should look to the affective side of our nature too, and that they should seek to educate the emotions.

That they should seems to me to be clear. Emotional immaturity is a dangerous and debilitating limitation for both the individual himself and society as a whole. Ignorance in this sphere is no less harmful than any other kind of ignorance, and possibly a great deal more harmful in that whereas one can steer clear of matters where one's ignorance of physics or literature would be exposed, it is practically impossible to steer clear of the emotional dimensions of life. (One might go further and say that emotional understanding should be regarded as an important element in the breadth of understanding one would require of the educated man. But in that case one would be modifying what was said above about the concept of education.) So, in answer to the questions raised above, I suggest that it remains convincing and adequate to depict education in purely cognitive terms, though one might plausibly require that the educated man have understanding in this sphere. On the other hand, there is nonetheless a strong case for educating the emotions. Schooling should take account of the affective side of human nature as well as the physical, the cognitive and the social, because schooling is about providing important lessons and superintending growth into the kind of adulthood we want; on either count we want rounded individuals. (Schooling, possibly, though not education, should be of the whole man.)[18] This is scarcely something we need or want to argue about; ideally we would like to bring up a generation of physically healthy, socially minded, vocationally prepared, emotionally mature, educated people.

9 THE CREATIVE DIMENSION

Finally, we must consider whether we should go one further and insist that schools also develop the individual's creative side. Before answering that question, however, there is a need to sort out a certain amount of verbal ambiguity surrounding "creative", and in one case some conceptual difficulty. The verbal ambiguity arises quite straightforwardly out of the fact that different people mean different things by the word "creative". It is variously used, for example, as a synonym for being extrovert, or for being inventive or productive or for expressing oneself. The simplest procedure to adopt will be to look briefly at some of the more prominent senses the word may have, commenting as and when it seems appropriate.

(*a*) If "creative" is used to mean "productive" (as Agatha Christie in writing one hundred or so detective stories may be said to have been creative) or "expressive" (as a three year old child splashing paint about at will may be said to be), it seems hardly worth detaining ourselves. Talk of developing creativity in these senses through the agency of the school just doesn't seem apposite. There may be a case for encouraging children to express themselves or to produce things in quantity, but these can hardly be goals of schooling. The role of creativity in such a sense is far more likely to be motivational or therapeutic (that is to say something that may have value as a means of adapting the child to the environment of the school). Much the same may be said of the view that creativity is involved in presenting some version (painted, written or whatever) of one's own image of the world, without further qualification. I am not suggesting that creativity in these senses is a bad thing, merely that they don't seem plausible objectives for schools to aim at, or with which they should be fundamentally concerned.

(*b*) A different kind of problem arises with a conception such as that of Jerome Bruner, and that is that it is difficult to grasp it or see how we could make practical use of it. For Bruner, creativity is displayed in the act which occasions a feeling of effective surprise.[19] This formula leads to a distinction being drawn between subjective and objective creativity, the former being involved where the surprise is occasioned to the agent, the latter when it is occasioned to others. The difficulty of grasping this conception is obvious. We have no idea what counts as or what constitutes a feeling of effective surprise. More than that, we have no way of knowing whether somebody is experiencing it subjectively, and it is not clear how many people or which people have to experience a feeling of effective surprise on viewing my painting for it to be legitimate to describe me as objectively creative. Some of these objections apply to any attempt to define creativity in terms of a process, without any reference to the qualities of an end product. If being creative is to be defined solely in terms of what the agent experiences, only the agent can actually be in a position to assess whether he is creative or not. This means that there is no public meaning in the concept (since the beginning of time there has been no way of knowing whether different people, in using the word creative, are talking about the same thing, even granted that they are trying to use the word in the same sort of way). It also means that we cannot sensibly have views about whether people who are dead and gone, and who left no commentary on their inner state of mind—people like Shakespeare and Mozart, for example—were creative or not. But it must surely be a grave shortcoming in a conception of creativity that makes it impossible to attribute it to the sort of people who most immediately spring to mind as examples of it! The shortcomings of Bruner's conception are even worse, because in this case even as agents we don't know what it is we are looking for. We can't begin to determine whether we are subjectively creative, because we haven't the first idea what this feeling of effective surprise is. (Is it the kind of feeling I get when I hear a bump in the night? When I see a beautiful sunset? When my girl friend says she loves me? When my wife says she's leaving me? When I manage to stop the table wobbling?) So creativity in this sense could not possibly be controlled, cultivated or measured with any assurance, even if we wanted to do these things. It is anyway far from clear that we should want to do those things, or in any other way be much concerned with it. Creativity in this sense, obscure as it is, doesn't seem that big a deal.

(*c*) Then there is creativity as measured by creativity tests [referred to above. See Chapter One]. Examples of such tests include those that ask participants or subjects to think of uses for a brick (an old shoe box, whatever) or to listen to various story synopses and suggest suitable titles for them, or to fill in empty circles in such a way as to make them drawings of something (e.g. a smiling face ☺).[20] One problem with many of these tests is a lack of clarity about the criteria that are to be used for assessing performance on them. In particular it is often unclear whether quantity of response (without reference to quality) is being used as a measure. If so, one badly needs to know why. What is the value of being able to think of a lot of silly or impossible uses for a brick? If, on the other hand, silly answers don't count, if, in other words, there is some qualitative difference other than quantity, we need to know, which we are never told, what it is. In the story title test we are told that the testers divide responses into clever and non-clever, but still we are not told how they do this. This means that despite the trappings of scientific detachment and objectivity surrounding these tests, it is still a matter of an individual adult's judgement of quality in reference to a particular exercise. What such tests therefore reveal is the tester's judgement of who is good at this particular (usually rather unusual) task. The testers not only make the judgements, but they also define the terms of reference. If the qualities that the tester is looking for could be clearly articulated, if the tester's judgement could be independently shown to be reliable, and if it could be shown that good performances (as now clarified) on these tests led to or indicated similarly good performances in respect of things that we cared about—such as good answers to problems arising in marital life or sensible answers to political problems—we might be on to something important. But that's a lot of "ifs". As things are, the tests seem of little or no importance. They do not appear to bear any relation to everyday problem-solving and they are not known to provide useful prognostications of anything. It is hard to dissent from Gribble's conclusion that "creativity testers confuse that which is merely unconventional with that which is imaginative",[21] or more generally that they unwarrantably try to place importance on things like the ability to think of lots of things to do with a brick by calling it "creative". Being creative in that sense has nothing to do with the creative imagination that Shakespeare displays or that one of my brothers displays more than the other. (The exception that proves the rule amongst empirical testing related to creativity is Liam Hudson's very cautious and sensible research that largely eschews grandiose terms and claims, and limits itself to saying that there is evidence that those who do well on a certain kind of test are more suited to arts than sciences.)[22]

(*d*) This brings me to what is probably the fundamental sense of creativity in dictionaries, if not in educational journals; creativity as applied to a few select figures through history such as Shakespeare, Mozart, Einstein, Marx, Plato and Brunel. "Creative" in this context is clearly a normative term (one that by definition implies evaluation as "beautiful" does, as opposed to one that contingently implies evaluation as "fascist" does) and one thinks immediately of originality and quality. A problem will arise in trying to judge who actually is creative in this sense, because of unavoidable arguments about quality, but that does not present us with a conceptual difficulty. It's a difficulty about making certain kinds of qualitative judgement. We know perfectly well what we mean by creativity in this sense, though we may argue about who deserves the label. But there *is* an interesting conceptual problem in this sense of creativity, and that is what counts as originality. On the one hand we want to avoid saying that anything that in any respect differs from other things, or has not been done before, counts as original, for that makes everything under the sun original —and "when everyone is somebody then no-one's anybody".[23] On the other hand, it seems incorrect to interpret originality too stringently, and to insist that only the entirely revolutionary is original; for surely something like Rachmaninov's variations on a theme by Paganini is original work. I believe that here we must re-introduce the idea of expressing one's own view of the world. Above I dismissed this as inadequate as an account of creativity. So indeed it is, in itself. But it might help to explain the notion of originality, which is one aspect of creativity in the sense we are now considering. For surely what distinguishes the work of people like Shakespeare and Mozart is that, while working within a quite familiar tradition and with quite familiar themes, they produce work that is both different from that of others and unmistakably carries a seal of authenticity; that is to say that it unmistakably represents their way of looking at the world, despite being expressed in terms of a quite familiar form. (Note that authenticity of this kind would be impossible for the very young unself-conscious child.) What I am suggesting in fact is that originality must be construed in terms of difference combined with authenticity, and that, where originality in that sense is combined with quality of output, we have creativity in the sense that we attribute to the great masters, be they thinkers, writers, painters, scientists or philosophers.

The value of creativity in this sense is self-evident. It is, as I said above, a normative term, which means that it is defined in a way that makes it necessarily valuable. But not all things that are valuable are worth doing or need or ought to be done in schools. (Sex is valuable; deep-sea diving is valuable, I dare say; mountaineering is valuable. It doesn't automatically follow that all or any of these ought to be on the school curriculum.) I must here confess that I hold an apparently minority view amongst educationalists that creativity, even in this esteemed sense of the word, is not merely something schools probably can't do much about, but is something they should anyway not be much concerned with. They could do a little bit about it, for they could lay down the foundations of knowledge and understanding in a given sphere, without which originality, divorced from quality, would be mere idiosyncrasy. But to do that, to provide such knowledge and understanding, which schools should be doing anyway, though it happens to serve as a foundation for creativity, is not to be concerned about creativity as such. I started this chapter with the contention that being educated is not to be confused with brilliance or cleverness, nor even particularly associated with such things. I would go further in conclusion and say that schools should not see themselves or set themselves up as hot-houses for rare genius, creative giants or intellectual colossi. By all means let there be places for nourishing such people—indeed, by all means let schools provide nourishment for such people where appropriate. But don't let schools focus on any such role for themselves. The whole point about schooling and education, which, remember, is but one function of schooling, is that they are for everybody. Schools should promote education, socialisation, health, vocational preparation and emotional maturity for all because these are the important lessons, the valuable instruction, they can readily provide.

3 Control and Authority in Schools

So far I have argued that schools should seek to perform a number of specific functions: to educate, to socialise, to offer vocational preparation, to develop emotional awareness and to ensure physical health. We now come face to face with a cluster of questions relating to authority, responsibility and control in schooling. Granted the above functions, who is to interpret them? Who is to be responsible for what decisions? Who should have the ultimate say on which matters? In this chapter I shall address myself particularly to the questions of whether there should be a common core curriculum, if so who should devise it, what responsibilities teachers and individual schools should have and to whom they should be accountable, how decision-making within the school should operate and, finally, the question of teacher neutrality within the classroom.

1 INTERESTS, NEEDS AND THE COMMON CORE CURRICULUM

The term "curriculum" refers to the content or what is taught in schools. Sometimes it is confined to what is overtly timetabled and taught. However its use may quite reasonably be extended to include reference both to things that are not actually timetabled and even to what the school is not consciously aware of teaching (what is sometimes called the hidden curriculum). Since there is indubitably a hidden curriculum, any proposed curriculum or planning must take account of that too. For the remainder of this book it may therefore be assumed that when I use the word "curriculum" I do so in its broadest sense, and I am referring to everything that is taught, whether consciously or otherwise and whether clearly advertised and timetabled or not. However, most of the detail, particularly in the next chapter, will relate to the timetabled curriculum. By a "common core curriculum" is meant a limited element of curriculum content that virtually all children would be expected to study. (The "virtually" is necessary to allow for very exceptional children such as those suffering from extreme brain-damage; in practice one means the vast majority of children.) In Britain it so happens that recent official thinking has favoured such a *core curriculum*, but can its imposition be justified in principle?

There are those who argue that no predetermined curriculum requirements, whether common to all children or not, can be justified, on the grounds that content, or what children study, should be entirely governed by their *individual interests or needs*, which may vary considerably. There is an ambiguity in the phrase "governed by their individual interests" which has to be cleared up immediately. One's interests might imply a reference to what is in one's interests (i.e. for one's good or benefit) or to what interests one. Though the two may sometimes coincide, they obviously do not necessarily do so (it may be in my interests to do the jogging that doesn't interest me, and it may interest me to get involved in a criminal act that turns out not to be in my interests). The suggestion that curriculum content should be determined by reference to what is in the interests of children seems quite unexceptionable, but it is also rather unhelpful, in just the same way that appeals for a useful or realistic curriculum are [see above Chapter Two], for it leaves open the hotly-debated question of what is in their interests, an answer to which would be necessary before one could actually teach in accordance with this adage. Arguments for the extreme view embodied in the other interpretation, however, (that what children study or do should be governed entirely by what interests them) are totally unconvincing. No doubt we should agree that what interests children is important. We would presumably rather interest them in what we have to offer than bore them with it, we may want to take some notice of what already interests them for a variety of reasons, and we may in particular wish to motivate them through their interests. (For example, a child's interest in railways might serve as a basis for studying changing patterns of communication.) But those are qualified claims, in no way adding up to the extreme view, and one could consistently concede all that and still maintain that there should be some predetermined curriculum content.

What there seems no reason to accept is the view of those who claim that education must be defined in terms of the child's interests, so that education as such is not taking place, by definition, when the child's interests are not the governing factor in the matter being explored. The clearest exposition of this view is probably that of P. S. Wilson.[1] First he makes it quite clear that he is not thinking merely of using children's interests as a motivating factor to get them to study something previously decided on by the teacher. He quotes John Dewey's objection to that (very common) approach: "I know of no more demoralising doctrine . . . than the assertion that *after* subject matter has been selected *then* the teacher should make it interesting",[2] and he endorses Montessori's claim that situations centred on adult values are not truly educational. He goes on to say that "even when a person who is being educated is a child and even therefore when his interests often seem 'childish' or silly or undesirable from the point of view of his adult teachers, nevertheless his education can only proceed through the pursuit of his interests."[3]

Nobody can stop somebody defining education in this way. But you cannot define things into existence. To define education in this way won't change the way things are or remove the need for justification for a policy of following only the child's interests. If this is what we take "education" to mean, then I for one am not that concerned about education; education in this sense will seem to many of us to be less important than other things such as schooling or instruction in various subjects. Interestingly, Wilson seems to come to more or less that conclusion himself. Well aware that to concentrate exclusively on the child's interests might limit one to exploring trivial or even harmful interests, and prevent one from pursuing various important lessons, he classifies the study of adult values and interests as schooling and says that of course, schooling too is important for children. In any case, though we cannot say that it is incorrect, we can say that this proposed definition of education is most idiosyncratic and unpersuasive. For most of us, as we have seen, being interested is neither a necessary nor a sufficient condition of being educated. A man may be educated and uninterested in what he has learned, and he may be interested in various things but not educated to any marked degree. So the claim that education is to be defined in terms of interest carries little or no weight. The rather different, empirical, claim that through the actual interests of the child all the ground that we want covered will be covered is dubious; but if it is correct, it comes to the same thing as saying that there should be a predetermined curriculum. For to know that the ground will be covered involves knowing what ground we're talking about. To be sure that it can be covered through an approach centred on interests, we should need to determine beforehand what it is we want to do.

Nor will the notion of a curriculum based on needs help, for either we presume that needs are predictable, in which case we have a predictable curriculum, or we presume that needs are to be identified with expressed interests, in which case see above, or we are faced with the problem of determining what people need. There is a tendency to talk as if what needs people have is a question of straightforward empirical fact, comparable to the question of how tall they are, what colour they are or even what interests them. But that is not so. To say that somebody needs something is to say that they lack something that is necessary for an objective. I need penicillin, if I lack it, if I am ill, and if I want to get well. This is to say that judgements about need always involve reference to objectives. Sometimes these are fairly uncontentious. We say without hesitation that people need water, because we assume that they want to survive. If, however, somebody is trying to commit suicide, he does not need water. To say that a curriculum should be based on needs does not make things any easier therefore. We will disagree beyond a certain minimal level relating to things like food and shelter, about what they do need, because we will disagree about what we ultimately want for children. If on the other hand we say "yes, up to a point that may be true, but we can agree on certain needs that children have", that is another way of saying that we agree that children lack certain things that they ought to have. But to say that involves a predetermined curriculum. If we agree that they need to read and write, then we are in effect saying that reading and writing should be part of the curriculum. If we are not saying that, then we obviously do not agree that they need to read and write. It is clear then that, for needs to guide us in respect of curriculum planning, we have to settle what needs children do have. But settling that is a way of settling what they ought to study.

There is one final way of attempting to extricate oneself from this dilemma, but it also fails. If you say "well, let the curriculum be based on what each individual says he needs", you are back with the problem facing the view that it should be based on expressed interest. It is not an incoherent or impossible suggestion. It just looks totally unconvincing. By and large we see no reason to leave children to do whatever and only what they think they need to do. Such a policy seems calculated to lead to anti-social and anti-individual interests sooner or later.

But it is the obverse of this point that there is no convincing argument to be raised against having a predetermined curriculum that is critical. Schools are set up to serve a number of purposes. They can hardly be expected to serve them if they don't have some kind of curriculum. Just as if you want to be a deep-sea diver or to master Chinese philosophy, there are some things that have to be done, so if we want to socialise and educate our children, rather than train them to be ballet dancers or prepare them for life as monks, there are some things that we have to do (or, to be more cautious, there are some things we have to ensure happen). We have to do, at least, whatever is necessary to help people become socialised and educated. In order to socialise, we have to convey understanding of the attitudes, behaviour and beliefs that are fundamental to our society, because that is what is involved in being socialised. In ensuring that we talk of them, exhibit them, express and encourage them, we have the beginnings of a curriculum. (Remember that the term is being used to cover both what are sometimes called open and hidden curricula.) Given what education is, we have to ensure initiation into a breadth of understanding and such things as reading and writing which are in practice necessary prerequisites. In short, it follows from the desire to provide education and socialisation to all that there is some minimum content that should be presented and made available to all. Of course, if you don't want to socialise or educate, or if you have quite different conceptions of them, the case may be different. But if we are talking about the same things when we refer to education and socialisation, and if we want schools to provide them, then we have a core curriculum on our hands already.

(Perhaps we may add reference to the view that another good reason for some kind of core curriculum is that it makes for greater efficiency in the overall administration of schooling. In particular, if there is some degree of uniformity, it is easier for the system to cope with changes in staff and with children who change neighbourhoods. The point is valid enough and adds weight to a case already established, though I would not myself think it strong enough to justify a core curriculum on its own.)

We have established that there should be a common core curriculum of some sort. It should contain the ingredients vital to education, socialisation, emotional maturity, etc. It should be noted, however, that firstly to demand a common content is not to demand common packaging. We can quite consistently say that all children should be taught to read, taught maths and taught good manners, and leave great flexibility in the question of where and how particular children or groups of children should be taught these things. [On methodological issues, see below Chapter Six.] Secondly, a common core curriculum is not necessarily compulsory. The practical question of whether it is more effective to make children attend classes by various means, or to leave them free to choose to attend is quite distinct from the argument dealt with here. The argument here does not lead automatically to the conclusion that there must be compulsory formal classes in, say, aspects of socialisation. It does not rule out the possibility of a so-called free school. But free schools too have their curriculum, i.e. a content that they intend to convey as well as a content they unconsciously convey; they merely hold the view that a free environment makes it easier to get that content across. By and large I believe that that approach is impractical and implausible, but that is a separate issue.[4] All I wish to assert here is that schools, in having some clarity of purpose, must have some minimal content to get across to all children.

That is the principle of the thing. The question now to be raised is who should determine the content of the core curriculum in broad outline. The candidates most often put forward are the teaching profession and the state. The argument generally put forward for leaving it to the profession is that this is their business. Unfortunately that is not quite accurate. By and large, teaching is their business. Certainly, many educationalists, such as myself, believe that teachers should ideally have a much wider perpective, and hopefully many of them do take a wider view of and interest in education and schooling. But being a teacher does not in itself make you well-qualified to talk on the nature of education or the proper limits of the curriculum. The practical experience of being a teacher doen't even guarantee mastery of all relevant empirical data, let alone assure skill at the conceptual level or competence in rational thought. Furthermore these are issues that are not simply factual. They relate to ideals, and there are good logical grounds for denying that some are known to have a surer grasp on the truth in the realm of ideals than others. What we should do in schools partly depends on what sort of a society, ideally, we would like, and there is no obvious reason why the teaching profession should be thought particularly well-qualified to pronounce judgement on that. All in all, there doesn't seem any compelling reason why teachers should be presumed competent, as a matter of course, to lay down the law about curriculum content.

[We shall examine moral value in some depth below, see Chapter Five, but here it is sufficient to point out that how one determines whether something is good, whether morally or more generally, is by no means certain to anyone who has given the matter serious thought. You and I may happen to agree on the superior value of a certain body of literature to most pop songs, but, if we do not, it is not clear how we could rationally settle our differences, establishing that one or other of us is correct. It is altogether easier to offer rational defence of value judgements within one area (e.g. one can give reasons for valuing one book more than another, or one song more than another), for particular purposes (e.g. books are better at character-study than most songs), or given some agreed premises (e.g. we are considering what is better at giving pleasure). But the real difficulty comes when we try to determine rival claims about intrinsic value (e.g. poetry is superior to sport). I would argue myself that there is no mechanism for resolving that kind of disagreement, unless there is a shared premise to be found, and that remarks of the form "this is intrinsically valuable or valuable in itself" have to be construed as having emotive rather than descriptive meaning, and that they serve primarily as conversation stoppers. They are ways of saying "I value it and that's that". Since decisions about curriculum content, if you push them far enough, inevitably end up in this area of judgements about inherent value, they cannot be a matter for a group of experts to settle on their own. No doubt some people are better-equipped than others in respect of the empirical facts of the matter, foreseeing likely consequences, and even in terms of having given some thought to their values (though these people won't necessarily be teachers). But at the end of the day, if you say, "Yes, but I just don't value the sort of country and the sort of citizen your curriculum would produce", we have a difference that we do not know how to resolve. Certainly, being a teacher doesn't give one any particular qualifications for dealing with it.]

Most of what has been said about teachers applies to parents too. One difference that might be cited in their favour is the claim that they have a direct interest in what happens to their children. But although that is a popular assumption, it is not clear that they actually do have any more of a direct interest than the state. Such a claim is partly evaluative and as such very difficult to know how to determine. Of course parents have a direct interest in their children in various purely descriptive ways. (They have legal interests, they are personally concerned about them, they brought them up, they gave birth to them, etc.) The question which is far from resolved is whether amassing a number of those kind of points amounts to a case for saying that parents have a direct interest in the further sense of having some special rights in the matter. Furthermore, granted the state did not give birth to the children and so forth, it did nonetheless contribute in various ways to their growth and welfare and these children are the citizens of tomorrow. Perhaps the state, too, has some rights in this matter.

Besides, counting against the far from established possibility that parents do have some special claim when it comes to dictating school policy, just because they are parents, is the point that almost certainly the majority of parents know even less about children and have thought even less searchingly about schooling and education, than teachers.

The state comes next, and the first problem here is who or what counts as the state. If it is left as an obscure abstraction, then it cannot be left to do the job. If it is taken to mean the government, it is not immediately clear that we should welcome it making decisions of this sort. Certainly, the argument that the content of the curriculum is a political matter and that it should therefore be left to the politicians is fallacious, since the sense in which it is political bears little resemblance to the sense in which politicians are political. It is ultimately a political matter, as we've seen, in that, pushed to the limit, the arguments for one curriculum rather than another involve a view of the good life for the body politic or for citizens. But that doesn't make it political in the sense of a matter to be determined by those who practise the art of the possible, the business of governing or however else you like to define politics. If the state is identified with the government, then there is a real problem about seeing the state as a repository of wisdom. Indeed in some states I could see no reason whatsoever to desire or think it appropriate to leave educational matters to the state. What on earth would there be to recommend the idea of leaving educational planning to a Stalin, an Amin or an Ayatollah Khomeini?

Contemplating that question gives us the clue we need. There surely is no argument for leaving broad curriculum planning to the state *per se*. What there is, is an argument for leaving it in the hands of a democratically governed state, and that argument is identical to the argument for having a democratic state in the first place. Nobody believes that the argument for democracy is that democratic government is always wise, or even necessarily best in terms of propagating and serving agreed values, or in accommodating or synthesising differences of value. The most plausible argument for democracy takes the line that it is a relatively fair and tolerant method of organising government, and preferable in practical terms to alternatives, especially because it protects us all from domination by other minority extremes. The only people who necessarily lose out in democracy are those who regard the imposition of their viewpoint on others as being of supreme importance. (Democracy may take many forms, although there are also quite misleading uses of the word to refer to entirely distinct concepts. East Germany, for example, is not democratic in the sense we are concerned with. For present purposes I am assuming that any system of government involving elected representatives, whom the people can in due season vote out of office should they want to, is democratic. To pursue the important subsidiary set of questions about the strengths and weaknesses of rival democratic systems would be to go beyond our present purposes.) Just as democratically determined social policies are by no means always the most sensible or effective, so decisions about schooling made by a democratically elected government are not necessarily going to be exemplary, but nonetheless by and large it seems better to proceed by giving it, rather than any subisidiary grouping, the right to determine and the responsibility for determining broad curriculum policy. Better for our common policy to be imposed by a body that represents a variety of interests and is answerable to us, than for it to be imposed by a more selective and less answerable body. Certainly a number of groups fitting the latter description would be very likely to come up with more clear cut, more positive, and sometimes to some of us, in some respects, more acceptable policy. But any such group would nonetheless be dictating policy with no obvious qualifications or right to do so.

Naturally, because we have not gone into an examination of different forms of democracy, the conclusion that the state should be responsible for the broad parameters of the curriculum leaves open detailed questions of what that actually amounts to in practice. In the United States what it means will depend upon the prior question of the way in which a balance is struck between federal and state legislature ("state" here being used in the way appropriate to America and not as it has been used above). In Britain or Australia to say that it is the business of the government does not necessarily mean that policy has to be thrashed out and voted on in the Houses of Parliament. Government can, and presumably will, continue to operate through a number of means such as select committees and public commissions. All that I wish to establish is that it is in the final analysis for the government to lay down broad curriculum requirements. The buck stops there. What is being argued, in sum, is that since decisions about what in outline should be studied in schools involve a crucial element relating to people's view of the ideal and good society, and since it seems that the merits of rival ideals are not finally to be determined by any expertise, we must respect varying viewpoints, provided they do not involve conceptual confusion, empirical error or logical fallacy. Democratic machinery is designed precisely to reflect and institutionalise such respect, while ensuring some practical policy. The fundamental point is that what our children study should be a community decision, taken as decisions about capital punishment or taxation are taken (i.e. taken by the people through their elected representatives) rather than a decision taken by any one group, be they teachers, trade unionists, parents, industrialists, Catholics or whatever.

In a democracy one does at least get a chance to air one's views, which brings me to what some may see as an anomaly between all this talk of nobody being wiser than anyone else when it comes to determining curriculum content, and the fact that I am here writing a book involving arguments for various particular recommendations as if I for one were certainly wiser. There are two points to be made. Firstly, there is a substantial contribution to be made by philosophers to the business of drawing up a curriculum, because as well as weighing various alleged empirical facts, to do it well one has to have a pretty clear idea of the nature of the enterprise. Certainly, philosophy, though it provides a necessary piece of expertise, is not sufficient to guarantee access to truth. It is just a contribution, but it is a very important one that is generally overlooked. The second point requires us to distinguish between rules and umpires or referees. Umpires and referees interpret and administer rules, sometimes wrongly in our view, but, though they do not necessarily have the right to make the rules, they are the final arbiters of the matter while the game is in progress. In soccer, for instance, there is a clear rule relating to a player being off-side. Actually judging whether somebody is off-side however is sometimes a difficult matter. But if the referee says that you are off-side, then, remonstrate as you may and whatever the facts of the matter, you are. It is the fact that he decides that you are off-side, conjoined with the rules of the game, that makes you so. Using this analogy, I have been arguing that it is a matter for government to referee the game. And that is entirely proper, for it is very much the function of books like this (i.e. books by educational philosophers) to seek to determine what the rules of the game should be and who should to the refereeing. That is to say, questions such as what schooling should be all about, what constitutes real education and who should determine curriculum content are questions in the domain of the philosophy of schooling. If the argument then suggests that government should be given responsibility for seeing that our schools do indeed provide a curriculum suited to the aims of educating, socialising, etc., that is entirely consistent with our continuing to guide their actions with our arguments, in so far as we can.

2 RESPONSIBILITY, MONITORING AND ACCOUNTABILITY

In the previous section we have been concerned only with responsibility for broad curriculum requirements. There is an important distinction to be made between determining the sort of areas or ground that ought to be covered by a curriculum (its broad framework), and determining what schools should do in order to meet those broad requirements (its detailed implentation). To say that the state should be responsible for the outline or the framework of the curriculum does not entail that it has to be responsible for the details within it. It does not mean that we have committed ourselves to something on the continental model, where, one is led to believe, the relevant Minister of State can say what is going on at 10 am all over France. In the first place I have only been arguing about the broad curriculum framework, and not about points of detail. In the second place I have been arguing in terms of overall aims of schooling and not in terms of yearly stages or limited objectives for given age-groups. And finally, no reference has been made to methodology, which might vary considerably from place to place. All that has been said is that since what goes on in school affects the state and is not finally assessable in terms of any known expertise, the state should superintend the general framework. This will almost inevitably lead to the appearance of some kind of bureaucracy, but that constitutes a practical problem requiring careful watching rather than an objection to the principle of state control. It is after all a failure of our system when the civil service dictates policy regardless of the efforts of elected representatives, and not a feature of it. But, accepting that the government should superintend the broad requirements, who should fill in the *detailed curriculum demands*?

This brings us to the role of the individual school. (We will consider the organisation of school government and the question of who should have what powers within the school in a moment.) Questions of how to implement the general framework, and at what stages of children's school lives, must be individual school decisions, for such decisions depend upon knowledge of particular children, particular teachers and local circumstance. It is one thing to insist that it should be a national decision that children study English literature rather than Japanese culture, and quite another to say that it must always be studied in such and such a way, with respect to this rather than that, at a particular age, and without any reference to all kinds of individual difference. There are innumerable ways in which one might adequately conform to the general framework, if it contains only the broad prescriptions that we

University of Cumbria

Learning, Information and
Student Services
Tel 01524 590871

Borrowed Items 08/11/2010 19:36
XXX3483

Item Title	Due Date
Learning to teach geography in th	08/11/2010
* philosophy of schooling	15/11/2010
* Blackwell guide to the philosopl	15/11/2010
* Readings for reflective teaching	15/11/2010
* Learning to teach in the second	15/11/2010
* Educational objectives and natic	06/12/2010
* Contemporary debates in educa	06/12/2010
Geog 1 geography for key stage	13/12/2010

* Indicates items borrowed today
Thankyou for using this unit
E.LISSlancaster@cumbria.ac.uk
Website www.cumbria.ac.uk/liss

envisage it would. Even the uniformity currently imposed by national systems of examination must be unwelcome. The argument for demanding that all children be taught to read, write and understand literature to the best of their ability, is not an argument for saying that all children should have read George Orwell's *1984* by the age of fifteen. On the contrary, there is very little to be said for such a specific demand at national level. One teacher might be able to get far more out of Jack London's *White Fang*. One school might have copies of Charles Dickens' *Little Dorritt* and no money to spend. Some children may have read *1984*. Those kinds of consideration are important. Those considerations are also essentially empirical and best determined by the people on the spot. That is why it cannot be for parent associations or government to decide this kind of detailed question. Detailed curriculum implementation is a school matter.

However to say that individual schools should decide upon the details of implementation is not to say that they should be accountable to no-one. We need here to distinguish between the questions of someone's *authority*, *responsibility* and ultimate *accountability*. It is the responsibility of the policeman on the beat (the patrolman in his car) to act as he sees fit in specific situations, but this does not mean that he is accountable to no-one. To be accountable to someone means that that someone has the ultimate right to assess you and reject or accept you. A good model is provided by the ancient Athenian custom of demanding that political figures, at the end of their term of office, render their accounts to the people. While in office they were responsible and they took decisions, but afterwards they had to account for their acts and decisions, and they might find themselves summarily rejected as a consequence. It might therefore be perfectly reasonable for the state on the one hand to give individual schools freedom to determine what they should do (within the parameters of the broad framework), but nonetheless turn on some of those schools and condemn them and their ways, should the results seem in some way unacceptable to the community as a whole. (Something very like that effectively happened recently in Britain in the case of the William Tyndale School, which was finally closed down.)[5]

But, before asking to whom schools should be accountable, we have to clarify the issue of what they may be accountable for, and that brings in another important distinction between on the one hand the general conduct and behaviour of teachers, and on the other hand their success or achievements as teachers in the more limited sense of people with specific lessons to teach or matters to impart. Although schooling involves many elements, some of which, like education, are not at all easily measurable or assessable, one thing that it surely is reasonable to demand of teachers is a degree of success in one of the jobs that they are there to perform, namely teaching some part of the overt curriculum. So how is success or lack of it to be monitored in this department, and to whom should teachers be accountable for it?

One way of trying to monitor teaching success is by reference to examination results, which has the advantage that it doesn't require much further organisation, since national networks of examinations already exist. Another way, which is similar in type, but much more specific in detail and which therefore would require considerable organisation, is to specify various goals and objectives and test whether, after teaching, children attain them. A notable example of this latter approach is afforded by the Michigan State Accountability system to which Hugh Sockett has recently drawn attention.[6] In Michigan the teacher is seen as contracting himself to the taxpayers to perform a particular service and detailed checks and tests are made on his progress; in addition Michigan operates an incentive scheme which closely resembles the system of payments by results employed in Victorian England. Sockett carefully itemises six objections to the Michigan model. I think all six are valid, but we can more simply dismiss both that particular system and other approaches of the same type, including use of examination results, on two decisive counts. Firstly, measuring children's achievements is not a fair way of testing teachers' skills for all sorts of obvious reasons, and that is what all such methods of monitoring are doing. Secondly, if monitoring of this sort is to take place then we reduce the criteria of success to quantifiable or measurable elements, and that, besides having a limiting effect on the scope of what is taught and examined, totally distorts the nature of the complex business of schooling, most particularly its educational dimension. To put it simply, the things you can most readily ascertain whether a student has acquired during a year are not the sort of things that any intelligent teacher who had given some thought to schooling would want to be judged by—and he would be quite right.

Also to be resisted is any form of monitoring that unconsciously operates with aims and objectives that differ from those of the school. (I am not suggesting that the school should operate with whatever aim it chooses and that the rest of the community must judge it on its own chosen terms. We are not at this moment discussing who should determine the aims or what they should be. I am arguing that once the aims are determined the success of teachers should be monitored in those terms and not, as so often happens (particularly if the monitoring is done by parents or local government bureaucrats) in terms that presuppose different ideals and different conceptions of schooling and education.)

There is surely a strong case for saying that, provided there is broad agreement on the sort of things the school should be trying to do and the ground it should be trying to cover, and provided that there is some form of accountability, individual schools should be given considerable freedom to devise their own ways of proceeding, and that monitoring of progress should be as flexible and informal as possible. Flexible, in order to allow for a hundred variations in local circumstances and, indeed, national requirements; informal, in order to avoid the hideous distortion and straightjacketing that is the inevitable consequence of trying to measure such subtle, impressionable and unobservable concepts as education as if they were chunks of cheese. Given that, it would be hard to beat, in principle, the British system of Inspectors, whereby monitoring is placed directly in the hands of a small number of experienced ex-teachers who visit schools (at necessarily rather lengthy intervals) and take a close look at what is going on. This, to put it crudely, puts the emphasis on the intuitive judgements of an experienced few, rather than the Procrustean bed of tests and measurements. It is but one more indication of the contemporary infatuation with the superficial trappings of science that many people take it for granted that the latter must be more reliable and objective, whereas, in point of fact, the former is capable of giving us a much truer and more sensitive appraisal of the state of affairs.

To whom should schools be finally accountable for their overall success or lack of it? Not presumably to that same small body who should have the job of monitoring their success or lack of it. We do not want an Inspectorate that is both judge and jury; besides, on what conceivable grounds should this small and unrepresentative group be the body that may decide the fate of individual schools and teachers? It is the task of Inspectors to report whether, in their experienced view, the job is being well or badly carried out. It is not at all the same thing to decide what the job should be, or what should happen when evidence amounts to suggest that it is not being done. But does any identifiable group have that right? Is there any good reason why schools should be accountable only to local government, or to parents, or to teachers themselves or to any other specific group?

Surely it is at this point (rather than in connection with drawing up a core curriculum or with judging the competence of teachers) that the fact that various different groups of people may have an interest or a stake in what is going on becomes important. Parents, who according to my argument have no particular right to demand the curiculum of their choice or to judge their daughter's teacher unfit to teach biology, surely must at the end of the day be accounted to in some respect, to some extent, for what happens to their children. But equally headmasters and local government may reasonably expect teachers to be accountable to them for their daily performance as teachers. If it comes to that, teachers might reasonably claim that they should ultimately be accountable for their performance to a body of their peers and colleagues. If we bear in mind (a) that we are currently concerned with success and failure in terms of teaching, which must involve some reference to specialist expertise and experience, (b) that we are nonetheless dealing with a matter where there is bound to be divergence of opinion as to what constitutes success, partly as a result of different priorities, and (c) that there are a number of interested parties, we see that there is a strong case for concluding that schools should be accountable to a governing body, specifically constituted to take account of the points made. Thus each school might have a School Board or a Governing Body consisting of something like the head teacher, two parents, two local government representatives, two teachers from the school in question, two teachers from another local school, and two local citizens not coming in to any of the previous categories. The details are obviously not to be settled here, but some such composition would ensure a representative, yet informed, body. The purpose of designating some body to whom one is accountable is to guarantee that there is a safety net, a check against abuse or excess. What is at issue in this context is neither what constitutes success nor the question of who should be authorised to decide that, but who should have the final authority to determine whether individual teachers or schools have or have not seriously failed in the performance of their duties. My suggestion has been that that delicate kind of a question (thankfully rare) is best entrusted to a representative body of citizens with varying kinds of interest in schooling.

So far we have been thinking in terms of the teachers' or schools' performance in terms of teaching an agreed curriculum only. That is to be sharply distinguished from the question of to whom, if anybody, teachers should be accountable for their broader life style, for the claim that I teach mathematics badly is of a quite different order to the claim that I have a mistress or have had two drunken driving charges laid against me. The latter kind of claim is not in itself of any particular concern to those whose interest in the education and schooling of children gave them some reason to be concerned about my teaching performance. Of course there are those who think that teachers should be accountable to them (or to something like the Governing Body) for their private life too. But provided we leave aside illegal behaviour or behaviour that may clearly affect teaching performance, why should teachers be subjected to any more rigorous a code of private life than anybody else? If, for example, it is not illegal to be homosexual, then whose business is it that he is homosexual? Some would argue that the mere fact of being homosexual, should it become known to the children he teaches, sets a bad example or is an unfortunate influence. But so in somebody else's view might the fact that another teacher is a Methodist, or likes rock'n'roll music or votes Republican or is a Marxist constitute a bad example. The point is that we, as fellow-citizens of varying opinions, don't have any right to interfere with other people's lives simply as a result of those opinions. If the law of the land says that people may be Methodists, atheists, Marxists, rock'n'roll freaks or homosexuals, then teachers may be too.

What, however, one may argue is that it is sometimes very difficult to judge whether an individual teacher's life-style, or some aspect of it, is deleteriously affecting his performance in the role of teacher. Clearly the above paragraph was not designed to, and would not, lead to the conclusion that it does not matter if a teacher initiates a child into homosexual practices. That is entirely different from being homosexual in one's private life. The practical problem arises from the fact that between those two extremes it may be very difficult to judge whether the teacher's behaviour is such as to warrant public objection or not. In matters of this sort the case for teachers being accountable to some professional body made up of their peers, on the model of the medical profession, seems to me overwhelming. For what we are saying is that teachers, like doctors, and for essentially similar reasons to do with public confidence, must have a code of conduct, and that there must be some body to which they are accountable for conducting themselves according to the code, in order to ensure that it has force. But when we bear in mind that what is really being determined (in both the medical and teaching example) is not what conduct is in itself morally accept- able, but what conduct is professionally acceptable, it is clear that it must be a decision for the profession to make. For what is pro- fessionally acceptable has to be decided by reference to such things as what is possible and what is probable in the professional situation, and to an estimate of the consequences to the standing of the profession of certain kinds of conduct. Only teachers are placed to be able to answer those kinds of questions in the context of schooling.

3 THE DECISION-MAKING PROCESS

The above proposals leave the individual school with considerable autonomy. True, there is a common core curriculum to be implemented, there is some monitoring of achievement, and the school and the teachers within it are accountable to a governing body and a professional body. But that leaves a great deal of freedom for the school to decide things for itself. The question must now be raised, therefore, of the way in which *the decision-making process* within the school should be organised. Should the head teacher exercise a regal or presidential control, as leader and ultimately superior officer to his staff, should he be *primus inter pares*, or should he occupy a role divorced from leadership and authority such as that of executive manager? Should the staff function as a democratic unit (with or without the head teacher) and act as the real centre of power, should it function something like a second chamber that can restrain but seldom initiates (a House of Lords or a House of Representatives), or should it follow a traditional hierarchical pattern whereby orders from on high emanate downwards? Should individual teachers be given freedom to make their own decisions? Should the children, for whose benefit the whole structure is primarily designed, have more of a say, either as individuals or as part of a democratic whole formed with the staff?

The possibilities are many, but we can keep some control over the otherwise unmanageable realm of options to be considered, by recalling what sort of things the decisions we are now concerned with will relate to. Given what has already been said, the question is now limited to who should determine (and how they should do it) the particular organisation of the core curriculum appropriate to a given school, and various other aspects of the curriculum, such as what further subjects to teach, whether to make them optional, what sporting facilities to provide, what social functions to encourage, what books to use and whether there should be a school uniform. According to the argument so far these are certainly matters for individual schools to decide. But how should they come to their decisions? Who should be involved in the decision-making process? (It is perhaps worth drawing attention to the fact that I slip in here matters like the wearing of a school uniform and a decision as to whether the non-core curriculum should be compulsory, for these are not insignificant matters. But it is right that they should be here, for a decision about the merits or demerits of school uniform is not on a par with questions about the general curriculum framework. It involves considerations about the consequences of a particular policy, but not fundamental political questions about what kind of a society we want and what schooling is for. By definition the same is true of non-core curriculum subjects, since whatever is thought to be crucial as a contribution towards our ideals will be part of the core curriculum. Issues like school uniform, optional subjects, and whether to play basketball or football will be assessed in different ways by different people, and different schools will be differently placed in respect of providing them.)

I have already pointed out that this book is written in the context of liberal-democratic societies. I value democracy, presume my readers do, and presume that we are considering schooling for such a society. But it is fallacious, though not uncommon, to argue that, if we are democrats, we must favour democracy in schools. It is in principle quite coherent to approve of democratic organisation in one context and not in another, provided that one's argument for democracy in the one case is not simply that in all matters every human being should have an equal say with all others. In that case of course one is committed to democracy in schools, in nurseries, in hospitals and everywhere else. But most of us do not defend democracy on such simplistic terms. Almost certainly we approve of it as being in practice the most morally acceptable and tolerant form of political organisation at national level. We do not automatically assume that within the family newborn babies should have a say in how the housekeeping money should be spent. And we do not necessarily automatically believe that in all conceivable circumstances democratic procedures would be best. (We might accept some limitations in time of war; we might even go further and argue that if a group of saints existed and had the desire and authority to rule over us, we might prefer them to do so.) So our endorsement of democracy in the state does not commit us to anything in particular in respect of schools. We have to examine that idea on its own terms.

When we do that, it is at once apparent that a strong democratic thesis is most implausible. By a "strong democratic thesis" I mean the view that decision-making should be the prerogative of all members of a school—pupils, academic and non-academic staff. Such a view has been put forward before now, and from time to time an attempt is made to put it into practice, but the practical experiments always turn out to have certain qualifications when one looks closely, and the theoretical pronouncements are without exception muddled and weak. To that it may be added that since there is no clear and convincing theory justifying the position, it would be difficult to judge the success or failure of the attempts at practical implementation. For how can you judge whether a democratic school is successful, if you are not clear what its justification is supposed to be? Successful at what?

The principle that all beings count equally and have interests deserving of equal respect, which is cardinal to democratic theory, seems to me quite acceptable, and would indeed be the cornerstone of anything that I would recognise as a truly moral position. But to say that my interests count for no more than those of my grandmother or your two-year-old son, is not to say that my opinion is no more worth having on any issue, so we cannot move directly from this premise to the conclusion that everyone should have an equally weighted vote on every issue. Sometimes knowing something about an issue may be as significant as being affected by it in some way. Now the main reason for saying that adults nonetheless should have an equally weighted vote in the political context is the point already made above, that political decisions involve reference to matters where nobody knows the answers and one person's preferences therefore have as much weight as those of another. But that point clearly does not apply in matters where a distinction can be drawn between knowledge and ignorance, and understanding and confusion. Medical doctors, to take the obvious analogy, despite the fact that they undoubtedly make some mistakes, ought to be listened to when it comes to matters of public health, in a way that you and I ought not to be. And it is not unreasonable to give them powers in this respect. So why should we give weight (preponderant weight, given their greater numbers) to students in matters to do with schooling? Because their interests are at stake? So are patients' interests in the medical example, and in neither case is it proposed that interests should be ignored. But they must be the best judge of their interests? That is simply not true, and indeed the fact that they are not is one of the best reasons for arguing against this view. The sort of decisions we are here talking about can be taken with more or less good sense — and the sort of good sense needed is that acquired through experience and study of educational matters. Children's opinions may certainly be worth taking note of, but whether it is or is not wise to make children study French, though in the final analysis it may not have a definitive answer in the abstract, is a question they are not likely to be well-qualified to pronounce on. They do not know what they may gain from it (or what they may lose by it), they have little experience of the world to judge it against, and they have not thought long and hard about schooling.

All that may be conceded, but, it might be said, it misses the point. The point is rather that by treating children as responsible adults you hasten their development as such. There is obviously some truth in this, but that doesn't make it a particularly strong point. Given the opportunity to partake in decision-making some people may sooner become more responsible, in the sense of willing to give serious attention to their decision-making; but you cannot hasten the development of people's knowledge and understanding by pretending that they know and have experience of what they do not know and do not have experience of. By all means let us treat children as adults to a greater extent than we do, but don't let's pretend that they are adults when they cannot be. This raises a second point: why do we so readily accept that it is bad to be a child for a while? Certain educationalists have made great play with the claim that childhood is a concept we create, as if in so doing we create a monster. But, in the first place, childhood is not entirely an idea we wish upon people. And, in the second place, it is not something that is necessarily and obviously good or bad, so why not leave children to be children? (Let no one bring in reference to what is natural here, for who can say what it is natural for a twelve-year-old child to be like? The matter gets even more difficult the more we emphasise environment with suggestions such as that we create the concept of childhood. If environment is the crucial factor, then what is natural is what the environment throws up. If environment is not the crucial factor, then how is it that children are childlike?)

Another argument has it that correct or rational decisions are not expected or required. Granted a wise old head teacher might be more rational than a group of schoolchildren, but the point is that each individual should be free to have his say. This, as stated, is coherent, but can anyone seriously believe it? Can anyone, that is to say, seriously believe that freedom is more important than anything else? Certainly nobody acts as if they believe that, whatever they may say, as can be appreciated by reflecting that, if a staff democratically decided to kill or maim someone, no advocate of freedom would stand about and accept the decision, however ruefully. He would say that here freedom must be curbed. But as soon as one concedes that something (never mind what) may be more important, it is no good saying that all that matters is freedom. More to the point in this case, we have already argued that schools should perform certain specific functions; there are certain specific things we want them to do because we value those things. We hope ideally that children will enjoy them and see the value of them, but we maintain their value nonetheless. It would be quite inconsistent for us to retain that view and try to embrace the view that it is not important whether or not children do these things. In saying that schools should socialise and educate, and in elaborating what socialisation and education involve, we are saying that there are things that ought to be done. And in doing that we are committing at any rate ourselves to a position that cannot consistently regard freedom as being of supreme importance. (What might be said is that as far as the issues we are now talking about go, it really doesn't much matter what the decision is. But even if this was true, it would be a somewhat double-edged argument for democratic decision-making: everyone may have a say on this sort of matter because the outcome is unimportant.)

The empirical claim that as a matter of fact people get more out of democratic organisation is difficult to assess. More of what? Obviously, if it is the case that they get more of something we want to get across, that provides a good reason for such organisation. But it is not sufficiently clear what advantages are supposed to accrue to the individual from the mere fact of participation in a democratic organisation, nor is there sufficient evidence to show that any particular advantages do accrue better by these means than any other, to make it possible to take this line of argument very seriously at this stage. Equally, the rather different view that the intuitive wisdom of children is a match for the experienced understanding of adults is beyond the scope of reasoned assessment.

All the above argument relates to the point of principle. I have been concerned to show that there is no good reason to accept the inherent value of a democratic school (in the strong sense). If instead one looked at different issues on their merits, one might conceivably come to different decisions about different ones. How to teach subjects, it might be said, really is and must remain a matter for teachers to determine, likewise whether and what other things to teach besides the core curriculum. But questions about uniforms, it might be argued, or social rules of the institution, could be decided by democratic vote of staff and students, because here there is no clear relevant superiority of knowledge or expertise possessed by staff. (But even that view has a weakness, because, as we shall shortly see, the fact that an issue does not lend itself to resolution through any particular superiority of knowledge or expertise is not the same thing as it being arbitrary or a matter that anyone may equally well determine). It should be said that the conclusion that children do not obviously have a right to determine or to play a part in determining school decisions does not imply anything about the relationship, treatment or attitude of staff to students. The fact that a physicist should be listened to in preference to a poet when it comes to discussing the risks involved in nuclear power reactors does not mean that he is entitled to pontificate, sneer at or despise the poet.

Much more difficult to come to a conclusion about is the issue of staff organisation—whether in particular we should veer more towards a democratic staff or an autocratic head.[7] Something of what was said about children (concerning their lack of knowledge, for instance) might be thought to apply equally to some adults, and some disenchanted readers might exclaim with frustration, "Well, if you're prepared to say that you know more than any of the children you teach, why not go the whole hog and say that you know more than most of your colleagues. Set you and your kind up as dictators, while you're about it!" Well, it is of course the case that some people are more rational, more experienced, more knowledgeable, indeed better educated than others. But generally, amongst adults, particularly belonging to one profession such as teaching, it will be much more debatable as to who those people may be. But it is a mistaken strategy to approach the question of decision-making and -taking by asking who is best suited to do it, because one tends to think not in abstract terms of arguments for autocracy, democracy or whatever, but in personal terms of heads I have known and colleagues I have worked with. The crucial question, and one that in logic should determine who should be looked to with respect, is what criteria or what qualifications are necessary for good decision-making. There have been several references already in this book to unprovable or open issues; but though there are such issues that admit of no known answers, there is still room for better or worse understanding of these issues. There is room for expertise in relation to them, if not for an expert solution.

Consider the various elements involved in making a decision about a matter such as whether children should have to attend lessons other than those related to the core curriculum, or whether to offer geography rather than carpentry as an option, if only one can be provided. In either case ideally one would need to know the answers to various empirical questions (What is involved in teaching geography? How might it be done?) to have a clear conception of the nature of one's task (What is education?) and to be able to reason competently. A well-informed discussion about whether geography is deserving of limited curriculum time would presuppose:

(a) appreciation of what geography does or might involve,
(b) awareness of various possible approaches to the teaching of geography,
(c) understanding of the different claims that might be made for different methodological approaches and of the distinct objectives that might be arrived at or served by different conceptions of geography teaching,
(d) familiarity with what is actually available and possible within the school in question,
(e) knowledge of the character and idiosyncrasies of the staff,
(f) information about children in general (e.g. how to motivate them, what interests tend to be at particular ages)
(g) familiarity with a wide range of suggested schooling aims, and
(h) knowledge concerning means or methods of attaining those ends.

But there is still one thing missing, for determining policy involves more than having information pertinent to decision-making. It involves actually making the decisions. An individual in possession of all the above knowledge is not thereby equipped to make a sound judgement on the matter, for nothing has been said about skill or lack of it in respect of sifting, weighing and using the information. In practice, often there is no obvious distinction to be drawn between people's information and their ability to marshal it. By and large, perhaps, people who know a lot about football make intelligent use of the facts they have acquired. But it does not have to be so. A man may know a lot about football and be a very bad captain, coach or commentator. At any rate one can make this distinction in theory. And one should do so, for as far as logic goes it is a distinction that cannot be broken down between, on the one hand, knowing what does happen if such and such is done, and, on the other, deciding what ought to be done. All the information in the world cannot logically, in itself, determine what ought to be done. Competence in the sphere of policy-making, therefore, cannot be defined exclusively in terms of information.

What is missing from the above check list is (i) what I have elsewhere termed philosophic competence.[8] Philosophic competence is to be characterised in terms of such formal requirements as consistency, coherence, concern for good reason and impartiality. But its three most important strands are discriminatory power, the ability to avoid conceptual muddle and the ability to recognise different kinds of question for what they are. This competence does not guarantee arriving at the correct answer, even in conjunction with all the available information, but it does ensure that one will know how to set about disentangling various

strands interwoven in specific problems, how to approach resolution of those strands, and what kind of reasoning is appropriate
to answering any particular question. To have such competence is
to be in a position to unravel complex issues and to treat them
adequately, appropriately and reasonably.

To illustrate this, let us take the example of a topic referred to
above. Should children be free to decide for themselves whether
or not to attend non-core curriculum classes? What would be
necessary for a thorough and competent examination of this issue?
Firstly, claims that are distinct in kind must not be confused. The
evaluative claim that children ought to be free from the interference of adults is to be distinguished from the empirical claim
that children learn better where they freely choose to engage in an
activity. Secondly, each distinct kind of claim needs to be pursued
in the distinct manner appropriate to it, and with proper understanding. If it is claimed that freedom leads to wise choices, we
need to know both what is meant by the claim and what the
evidence for it is. Does it mean that, given freedom, people choose
what we (the speakers) think is wise? Or that whatever is freely
chosen is for that reason (i.e. by that criterion) wise? What do we
think is wise? Is consensus a criterion of wisdom? Is there evidence
for any of these contentions? How, if at all, could one validate the
claim that whatever is freely chosen is for that reason wise?
Thirdly, there must be conceptual clarity. In order to cope with the
question at issue one needs to have a clear idea of what constitutes
free choice, wisdom and better learning. Fourthly, there must be
concern for and commitment to the rational mode. Nobody who is
drawn towards the charms of being first and foremost persuasive,
self-interested, ideologically sound, partial or prejudiced is going
to be reliable when it comes to offering a rational response to the
question.

Possession of the above nine elements does not guarantee that
one will come up with a right answer to problems, but they are
necessary conditions of a well-informed answer nonetheless. [I call
the ninth element philosophic competence with good reason, but I
would not want it to be thought that academic courses in philosophy are either necessary or sufficient for acquiring it. An
academic philosopher might not display such qualities, and there
are certainly other ways of developing them. But one would expect
philosophy to contribute to their development.] We now come to
the question of who has these qualities. In theory I suppose that
educationalists do, but in practice very few seem to have. Certainly
head teachers as a breed do not, nor teachers as a race. One quite
sensible line to take here would be to say that though head

teachers, as things are, do not have all these qualities and are indeed often chosen for quite other qualities (such as management abilities), they ought to have them, and that competence in educational theory ought to be a *sine qua non* of being a head teacher or school principal, whether courses designed to promote it be provided for them on appointment or it be demanded from them as a condition of appointment. Certainly there is a case for saying that head teachers need this theoretical grasp more than teachers do, for you can teach successfully within unquestioned parameters without reference to the sort of points mentioned, whereas you cannot take organisational decisions competently without them. So, if headmasters are to make such decisions, they ought to have such qualities.

But a very reasonable alternative is to argue that, ideally, all teachers should have a wider interest in education, and that since the range of skills and information involved in a school overall is really rather great and cannot be possessed by every teacher, all teachers ought at least to be grounded in the qualities in question here. Then, on the assumption that they are (but not very convincingly otherwise), it could well be argued that the school staff should be organised democratically. Of course in practice, just as in a political democracy, different individuals will still have different strengths and weaknesses, but the overall assumption will be that all have some appreciation of the nine points on the check list, filled out by experience and a particular interest in the decisions taken.

To some people the above issue (Should schools be democratically organised?) is of burning importance. I cannot see it that way. At the theoretical level, it seems to me to make little difference who calls the shots, provided that they are called in a competent manner. I do not recognise an obvious or weighty point of principle. In practice, therefore, I would see no reason to complain at variations between schools, some autocratically led by wise and inspired heads, others given over to democracy. All that does matter, both in theory and practice, is that decision-making should be carried out by those with the requisite qualities, which must include philosophic competence.

4 Authority, Neutrality and Impartiality

Teachers are set in authority over children, and this chapter has raised certain questions relating to the limits of that authority. It is now time to consider the question of *authority* and expertise in connection with the task of the individual teacher. It is possible to draw a distinction between being in authority, being an authority, being authoritative and having authority. Being in authority may be a matter of being officially granted a position of authority or legally empowered with one (hence known as *de iure* authority, from the Latin meaning "by law"), or on the other hand it may be a matter of taking such a position without any particular entitlement or official status (known as *de facto* authority, from the Latin meaning "by the facts of the case"). The policeman at a road accident has *de iure* authority, but a calm strong-minded citizen may exercise *de facto* authority. "Having authority" is ambiguous; it may mean that one has it *de iure*, as the general has authority or, typically, the head teacher, or *de facto*, as when a member of a group asserts his leadership and finds it accepted. One may in particular acquire *de facto* authority as a result of being an authority, which is to say being an accredited expert in a field. Thus Sir Kenneth Clark is an authority on art and this gives him authority (*de facto*) although he has no official authority (*de iure*). Being authoritative is also ambiguous; it may mean simply acting or speaking in manner that betokens one's authority (either *de iure* or *de facto*, and whether acquired through being an authority or howsoever). But there is also a common pejorative use of the term that makes it more or less synonymous with authoritarian and implies a hectoring or bullying manner, backed by no cause or grounds for it.

Clearly teachers of particular subjects, whether in school or anywhere else, ought to be authorities in their field. If they set themselves up as purveyors of, say, mathematical understanding, then (no matter what methodology they espouse) they should be authorities in that subject, and from that alone they will gain some *de facto* authority from any sensible audience. Teachers are generally set in authority in a much wider way, but here again, the assumption is that, compared with their students, they have more knowledge or expertise in relation to wider aspects of life. But it is at about this point that the matter begins to get more problematic, for there are surely some matters on which teachers do not necessarily have any relevant expertise, and should not therefore be regarded as authorities or arbiters of truth or correctness.

There are some subjects, such as most obviously social, political and moral issues where what is in dispute are not only facts, which a teacher might be expected to be or to get himself apprised of, but also judgements of value of a type that there is no readily agreed way of settling—the sort of open or unprovable proposition we have already referred to. When discussing issues such as the merits of one political party, the morality of pre-marital sex, the case for or against nuclear power reactors, the case for or against economic sanctions against nations with whom we are in' dispute, or the acceptability of capital punishment, there is always a bedrock of unprovable and contentious evaluation which will affect one's view, whatever the facts of the matter. For example, whether you put happiness before freedom, whether you believe in God, and whether you approve of competition. (For the sake of simplicity I am ignoring the point that some so-called empirical points may turn out to be far from proven, if not unprovable in fact, as opposed to principle. Claims such as "This policy will make people happier", "The way to make these fellows listen is to hit 'em hard first" or "Illegitimate children feel a permanent stigma as a result of their illegitimacy".) It has been pointed out already that an unprovable proposition (and here we are back with logically unprovable rather than unprovable in practice) is not the same as an unproven one. Let us look a little more closely at this distinction. It is unproven that cigarettes cause cancer, but it is not unprovable in principle. We know the sort of evidence that would settle it, and if it cropped up we would accept it (or, if you prefer, when it is sufficiently-well attested we will accept it). But if I say that everything that happens in the world is caused by a gremlin called Simon (whom, incidentally, no one can see, hear, touch, smell or taste) there's really no way of proving or disproving what I say. By putting in the qualification that he (he? she? it?) is beyond the reach of any of the senses, I also put him beyond any obvious means of being verified or his existence being checked. For existence is something we usually verify by reference to one or more of the senses. Now it may, in the final analysis, be unfair to assert that propositions such as "All social change is the product of economic forces", "God exists" or "Freedom is good" are of that order. There are other options to be considered: they might be regarded as utterances that have only emotive meaning and therefore are not unprovable so much as not in the market to be proved or disproved; or they may turn out to be provable or disprovable as time goes by and new evidence, that unmistakably shows itself to be relevant, presents itself. But it is quite reasonable, indeed it is correct and extremely important, to stress, that at this point in time they appear to be logically unprovable, and as such form a distinct category of proposition. To insist that individual freedom should come before social equality (or vice versa), or that there is a God (or the contrary), or that building nuclear power stations is the best energy policy (or that it isn't), just is not like insisting that two times two equals four, that Queen

Victoria died in 1901 or that Hitler engineered the Second World War deliberately. Some try to ignore the distinction, arguing that they are all the same inasmuch as nothing is known for certain, and most agreed conclusions depend on shared premises and concepts. But that just misses the point, which is that, rightly or wrongly, we do agree that two times two equal four and that Queen Victoria died in 1901, because we agree on the sort of evidence that is appropriate to determining such matters; and even when we don't necessarily share an agreed view, as on the question of whether Hitler caused the war deliberately, we still know and agree on the sort of evidence that would be appropriate to settling it. The teacher therefore takes no unfair advantage if he draws on his greater expertise to correct his students on such matters. They may subsequently prove him wrong, because they may come to know and play by the same rules of evidence. In the meantime, to insist that Hitler caused the war deliberately without providing any evidence amounts to bad teaching, but to insist that he did and proceed to put up a good case for it is entirely acceptable, even though an element of judgement is involved.

But what should the teacher do when dealing with essentially contentious subject matter, that is to say matter not that people happen to disagree about, but matter that people must inescapably disagree about because there are no agreed procedures for determining it? Should they, as some maintain, remain *neutral*? If "neutral" means what I take it to mean, then I am not convinced that they should. "Neutral" means "uncommitted, favouring neither side to a dispute", whether the dispute be physical or verbal. To take the obvious example, a country is neutral in war that does not commit itself to either side and does nothing to favour one at the expense of the other. It is essentially a matter to be judged by what people do. Neutrality does not commit one to having no private views. One may be neutral, i.e. behave in such a way as to favour neither side, while being hopeful of victory for one side rather than the other. If you are going to remain neutral in discussion or action, you must not do or say anything to the advantage of either side, even if you think it morally warranted, expeditious, necessary for your own safety and so forth. So, strictly speaking, a neutral teacher would be one who said and did nothing to advance either side of a discussion.

One thing to be said against this is that it effectively gags the teacher and makes him redundant in the classroom (in relation to matters where neutrality is called for). For if he is to remain really neutral, he should not even point out obvious flaws in one side's argument, for to do so clearly weakens that side's credibility. (To try and balance this by finding some way to weaken the other side's credibility, quite apart from being rather bizarre, would not preserve neutrality. Neutrality involves leaving well alone, not interfering in equally measured doses). A possible way of avoiding this conclusion would be to distinguish between *procedural* and *substantive neutrality*, arguing that the teacher must remain uncommited to any substantive view on the subject, but that he need not be neutral when it comes to keeping an eye on the manner of discussion. That is a reasonable distinction in theory, and one that it is possible to maintain up to a point in practice. But in the end, as I say, to interfere with the presentation of the case of one party is to upset the credibility of its message, as every lawyer knows. So we are left with a choice between a suspension of procedural neutrality, which sooner or later means an end to substantive neutrality too, or a commitment to neutrality in both spheres which effectively gags the teacher.

It would be far better to ignore demands for neutrality and replace them with the recommendation that teachers should be *impartial* in such matters. Impartiality differs from neutrality in that one may openly espouse a view and yet remain impartial, for impartiality implies only that one follows where the argument leads. An impartial person will change his view, iff [= if and only if] the argument leads that way. But he will assess discussion in terms of good reason rather than in terms of his prejudices, popularity, or convenience. Thus the teacher may have his views, may freely confess to them even, but in terms of the discussion it is not his job to push them. It may be said that in practice he will inevitably end up lending weight to his own beliefs. He holds a particular view, which he thinks is well-founded; he is therefore bound to regard as relatively good, arguments and evidence that suit his case and to see the flaws in arguments and evidence that don't. There will certainly be some truth in this in practice, though there is no reason in principle why it should be so. Nonetheless it is better to aim for impartiality than neutrality. The value of the former cannot coherently be denied by those who value good reasoning, since it is defined in terms of good reasoning, while the latter is of dubious value in the teaching situation, where one of the premises of the whole question is that the teacher has something to contribute.

Perhaps we should raise the question of whether it makes sense to talk of justified partiality, as some maintain. Only, I think, if that means that there may be reasons beyond the immediate discussion for displaying partiality within it. Conceivably it might be wise to show partiality to a lunatic's argument, while he holds a knife to somebody's throat. But the notion that partiality within a normal discussion, and for no such extrinsic reason, may be justified, must be incoherent (unless one holds the strange view that discussion should proceed by its aesthetic or emotional appeal rather than in accordance with reason), for "partiality" means "favouring for no rational reason". As a matter of fact those who claim to favour justified partiality usually turn out to be confused, and mean rather that they favour what they see as a justified rejection of neutrality on occasion.

To summarise both this section and the preceding ones, the state, working through its democratically elected representatives, should be responsible for the general framework of a core curriculum. The detailed implementation of that core and other schooling decisions should be a matter for individual schools to determine, although schools should be accountable for such decisions to Boards of Governors representing all interested parties. The professional conduct of teachers is a matter in respect of which they should be accountable to their own professional body. The monitoring of teaching should be externally administered, but in a relatively informal way in order to preserve in particular the sensitive nature of education. There is no principled need for the decision-making process within the school to involve all the children or even all the staff. But equally a reasonable case can be made for welcoming decisions being taken by a democratically organised staff, provided that teachers are appropriately prepared for that responsibility. That is the main point: people who are going to be entrusted with such decision-making ought to be competent educational theorists, with more emphasis on philosophic competence than has usually been acknowledged or granted.

Within the school there seems no reason why the teacher should be expected to be neutral either in manner or in what he says (though there may be a limit to the terms on which particular schools will wish to employ him). Should he happen to be homosexual, for instance, or an atheist, or a Muslim, or a Marxist or an anti-evolutionist, then, provided he is not abusing his teaching role (by soliciting pupils, indoctrinating Marxism or whatever), there is no ground for expecting him to remain neutral with respect to these preferences. What he should do is be impartial when discussing them, and exercise due sense about when and whether to draw attention to them in the first place.

4   Curriculum Content

We have established that there should be a core curriculum and that its broad framework is a matter for the state to decide. But that does not prevent us considering the matter here and offering some reasoned considerations about the content both of the core and of the wider curriculum. The state has the final authority and responsibility, but it is to be hoped that it will exercise that responsibility in the light of careful reasoning. Firstly, it is necessary to consider two frequently encountered but usually unexplained remarks about school subjects in general: that the school curriculum is too *academic* and that *subject divisions* are *arbitrary*.

Is the curriculum too academic? What does the charge mean? The man in the street probably thinks of the academic in terms of mental as opposed to physical activity: the more you sit on your backside and reflect the more academic you are; the more you get out and do something, the less so. The dictionary definition of "academic" is a stringent one. It says that it means "purely theoretical, unpractical". If "theoretical" is taken to mean "speculative and not yet established by experience or experiment" (again I follow a standard dictionary) as a particular view of the origin of the world may be said to be theoretical, then few, if any, typical school subjects are purely theoretical. If it is taken more loosely to mean "concerned with the underlying principles or the rationale or the background to some practice or practices", as one may be more interested in the theoretical than in the practical aspects of baseball, so that one wants to reflect on it rather than play it, then much school study is relatively theoretical and hence academic (and it is far from being obvious that that is in any way a bad thing).

The division of subjects into practical and unpractical does not help much, being altogether too crude and equivocal. Stamp-collecting is not very practical, but it is not usually regarded as an example of something academic. Engineering, on the other hand, which evidently is a very practical subject, is generally classified as an academic one too. Nuclear physics would seem to be at one and the same time purely theoretical, highly academic and very practical. At the other extreme wiggling one's ears seems an unpractical sort of activity, but scarcely warrants the label academic. "Practical" is a term that functions in much the same way as "useful", and the question of whether something is a practical kind of study depends very much on what your objectives and interests are, whom we are talking about, and how direct and short-term a pay-off we are looking for. That many school subjects are unpractical from some points of view must be admitted, but that merely begs the question of the point of view. In any case, as we have just seen, the division into practical and unpractical is not the same as the division into academic and non-academic.

It is clear then that whether schools are too academic cannot be answered in the abstract, for one's judgement presupposes a whole philosophy of schooling such as we are here trying to elaborate. Most subjects can be treated more or less academically (in any of the senses discerned). If you perform a play you treat it, perhaps, less academically than if you discuss it in the context of dramatic subtlety. If you agonise over the classification of flowers in your garden, you are in a sense being more academic than if you just plant some bulbs. But as to whether and when more academic becomes too academic, that must depend upon your wider understanding of what schooling is all about. To pinpoint the matter with two extremes: for my money a school curriculum consisting entirely of the study of astrophysics and another consisting entirely of playing ice-hockey would be equally unacceptable, the former being too academic and the latter not being academic enough. But to say that is to reveal something of my view of schooling (namely that it is about more than merely mastering either ice-hockey or astrophysics), rather than to make a point about the degree of academic study required in the abstract. To object that either individual subjects or the whole curriculum are too academic is in itself empty, for, to understand why you say that, we need to know what you expect from schools and what you regret about what is going on; but, once you tell us that, you don't need to mention the word "academic".

If the curriculum is not self-evidently too academic and unpractical, are subject divisions nonetheless meaningless, and is all knowledge one, as some maintain? Here it is even more unclear what is being said. All knowledge might be said to be one in the sense of interrelated or connected in some way or other, but that wouldn't show that traditional divisions were meaningless or pointless. On the other hand, if the claim that all knowledge is one is taken to imply that all subject divisions *are* meaningless and pointless, it obviously isn't true. Is it, then, not so much that divisions are meaningless but that they are arbitrary?

The dictionary offers "of uncontrolled power, impulsive, capricious, or decided on inadequate grounds" as an account of "arbitrary". Sometimes the implication of the ideas of those who say that school subject divisions are arbitrary seems to be, even more strongly, that they are quite random, without rhyme or reason, and might equally well have been any-other-old-how. And certainly there is, even in this strong view, a half-truth lurking. The subject classifications that we have are not forced on us in the way that having such limbs as we have, or eye-colour, or indeed in the way that the physical world is, are. Instead of studying biology or living organisms, we might have chosen to institutionalise the study of four-footed life; and rather than recognising stamp-collecting as a conventional pursuit, we might have devised in its place a pursuit centring on the collection or tabulation of colours. The merits of a particular subject classification largely depend on how useful it is for our various purposes. To replace the study of living organisms with the very limited study of four-footed animals would be absurd. To try and enlarge the scope by studying living and inanimate matter together casts the net too wide and confuses the issue by lumping very disparate things together. But subjects do nonetheless wax and wane at least as far as their public recognition goes, in response to fluctuating usefulness. The rise of sociology did not herald a new area of inquiry. The interests of sociologists had long been the interests of other people such as historians and novelists. But a time came when it seemed useful for some to concentrate exclusively on social questions in as scientific a manner as possible. At the present time there are those who want to extract from the content of the social sciences and other subjects material that centres on interpersonal relations and focus on that. Thus a new subject may be born, which may draw on the methods of other subjects but may also conceivably evolve its own. In this sense then, subjects are of course man-made.

But two important qualifications must be recognised. First, there is a limit to what man can make. Not any classification is conceivable. Although to some extent we shape reality (i.e. impose a shape on what we find in the world), the process is reciprocal, and reality sets limits on our classification schemes.

There can and there always could have been a subject of sociology. As things are there cannot be a subject of four-winged horses, and there never could be a subject of married bachelors. Although it is true that man effectively decides what classifications to make and to concentrate on, he makes his choice from the many possible and not out of thin air; he is subject to the various restraints imposed by physical reality and logic. The second qualification is that there are certain fundamental distinctions that cannot be ignored once they are recognised, because they are logical distinctions. So far we have thought of subject classifications largely in terms of subject matter, but some subjects are also to be defined in terms of the fact that they ask, not simply questions about different subject matter, but different kinds of question, and it is difficult to see those different kinds of question as being arbitrary in the sense suggested. Biology, physics and chemistry are clearly different subjects, but they do not involve logically distinct kinds of question. Contrast that with the distinction between a scientific question (such as might be asked in any of those three subjects and a good many others) and an aesthetic question. These are not just different questions, or questions about different things, they are different kinds of question, in that the way one would set about answering them (or indeed understanding them) is quite different. In the end, scientific questions are resolved by appeal to one or more of the five senses, but that is not true of aesthetic questions. And that distinction is not arbitrary. It is not open to us to decide to treat aesthetic questions as if they were empirical questions, for in so doing we stop them being the aesthetic questions they were. (It is possible for us to just ignore the aesthetic dimension, but, if we want to recognise the question "Isn't the sunset beautiful?", we have to recognise that answering it is not simply a matter of empirical inquiry). Again, the distinction between the sciences and philosophy is not arbitrary in the sense of random, capricious or based on inadequate grounds. It is based upon the very good grounds (it is indeed forced on us on the grounds) that, whether we choose to take note of the point or not, science and philosophy are asking different kinds of question.

These remarks take us back to the work of Paul Hirst and others who have scrutinised the domain of propositional knowledge, in an attempt to locate the basic logical divisions that there may be and that may have some kind of fundamental importance. In Chapter Two I suggested that the detail of Hirst's argument is sometimes obscure and arguable, but there can be no doubt that his approach is well founded. It just is the case, so far as we can understand at this point in time, that there are a limited number of logically distinct kinds of question (or proposition), each of which may be asked about many things across a broad range of subject-matter and events. [Hirst talks about propositions. I prefer to talk about questions, but I don't think this point makes any difference. If "Two times two eqals four" is distinct from "Pearls dissolve in acid", then "Does two times two equal four?" is distinct from "Do pearls dissolve in acid?" My preference is based on the assumption that people more readily think of asking different kinds of question than of uttering different kinds of proposition.] Thus there are few, if any, events in life about which one might not ask moral questions, aesthetic questions, scientific questions and philosophical questions. And these are all distinct kinds of question, rather than questions about distinct things (though they may be that too).

[A full explication of this would require a complete excursus into moral philosophy, philosophy of art, philosophy of science and the nature of philosophy itself, for we are making claims here about the nature of morality, aesthetics and so on, which are the business of philosophy. I will say a little more in the next chapter about morality and religion, but I should make it clear that I exclude religion here, because I do not see so-called religious questions as being real questions at all. That is obviously contentious and, besides those who would deny it, there are those who would say that, if it is true, it is equally true of morality and/or aesthetics. What it boils down to is this: one may attempt to argue that moral claims, aesthetic claims and religious claims are reducible to empirical claims or emotive ejaculations. If moral or aesthetic claims can be successfully so reduced, the claim I am making here is defeated, but at the cost of denying a distinctively moral or aesthetic dimension to life. I maintain that religious discourse is reducible, but that aesthetic and moral discourse are not.]

Not only are moral questions (i.e. evaluative questions about what ought to happen, if justice is to be served, rather than what does or will happen), aesthetic questions (i.e. evaluative questions about the beautify of things), scientific questions (i.e. empirical questions about how things are, and why they are as they are) and philosophical questions (i.e. questions about the meaning and coherence of ideas and discourse) distinguishable questions that might be asked in relation to many different things (e.g. nuclear bombs, marriage, opera-houses, the White House), but, I would argue, all conceivable questions will turn out to be either instances of one of these four types or hybrid questions that may be broken down into elements, each of which will be an instance of one of these, or they will be questions that have only emotive meaning.

One might raise a host of sociological questions, but these will not be a distinctive kind of question. They will be, for the most part, empirical questions about a particular subject-matter. (They may not be answerable in the straightforward way that empirical questions in the natural sciences in principle are, but they are still straightforward empirical questions.) There are geographical questions, in the sense of questions asked in the context of studying geography or about geographical subject-matter, but they too will turn out to be empirical questions, or moral questions, or aesthetic questions or philosophical questions or some hybrid. There are historical questions, but these again are empirical. There are interpersonal questions (questions about things like motivation, beliefs and feelings), but these will break down into either empirical or philosophical questions.

These four subjects, then, have a unique status in being fundamental divisions arising out of logical type rather than subject matter. In no recognisable sense is there anything arbitrary about these divisions; and these subjects or disciplines, besides being logically fundamental, are of fundamental importance. Far from being impractical, they are of urgent practical value, for without a grasp of these distinctions you cannot think logically, and without thinking logically you have little chance of controlling your own world, while you become a considerable nuisance to others, particularly in an open society. If these subjects are academic, it is in the unpejorative sense of being intellectual pursuits, depending on a clear mind rather than a strong physique.

But these fundamental disciplines do not exhaust the important divisions in our knowledge that are not merely arbitrary. Various other subjects, while not embodying a unique kind of question and while not having the widespread application of the four, nonetheless are quite discrete and autonomous units, differentiated by a particular logical structure that is based upon certain key concepts. Thus physics is a discrete subject in a way that stamp-collecting, photography or education are not. The basic concepts of physics determine a particular kind of inquiry, while the other three examples are identifiable only by their subject matter; beyond that they draw on, and are an amalgam of, various other, discrete, subjects. The study of education, for instance, draws on philosophy, psychology, sociology and history; each of these four is a discrete subject, and one of them is, in addition, a fundamental discipline. (In distinguishing between four fundamental disciplines, an unspecified number of discrete subjects and various broader subjects, I have been pursuing the argument for its own sake. I have suggested that the four disciplines, being fundamental, should in some shape or form find their way into the curriculum, but as yet I have said nothing about the importance or otherwise of any other subject, discrete or broad, in curriculum terms.)

It is difficult to see what those who claim to deny that any distinctions can be drawn between subjects, or that there are any natural divisions in the seamless robe of knowledge, can possibly mean or hope to gain. The fact of the matter is that something such as what we choose to call "biology" is a discrete subject that one may pursue in isolation, without understanding or awareness of other subjects, and that is readily distinguishable from other areas of study. What is the purpose of asserting loudly that it is a random or capricious classification, or one made without adequate grounds? On the face of it, it is a good deal more capricious and inadequate to pretend that it is not readily distinguishable.

What is needed to make sense of the complaint about subject divisions is some reason for objecting to our making use of the distinctions tht undoubtedly exist. Here I can only think of one possibility. It may be that what the reproach is really getting at is that, if we teach in terms of distinct subjects, we may fail to convey to pupils a lot of the interplay and cross-reference that actually obtains between subjects. Biological man is not the whole man, it might be said, so to teach "biology" rather than "man" is to miss a great deal and to distort reality by partial emphasis. Equally, problems in everyday living tend to be diffuse and complex, so that you very seldom face a purely biological problem or a purely anything else problem. You face complex problems that draw on many subjects and disciplines, and consequently it is foolish to teach biology rather than to focus on actual complex problems.

Both points obviously contain some truth. But it does not follow that it would be sensible to teach by means of topics and problems rather than subjects. For that approach too has its limitations. If we teach "problems" we run the risk of giving children only the ability to solve the particular kinds of problem they have previously encountered, rather than the ability to recognise and classify elements in one problem that are common to others and hence familiar. One thing we particularly need to be clear about is whether the suggestion is that it is not important to have subject understanding (e.g. biological understanding), or whether it is a purely methodological claim to the effect that the best way to acquire biological understanding is through looking at complex problems that have a biological element, rather than studying biology. Now as a matter of fact I have made no methodological claims at all so far, so the latter claim is not yet at issue. I have been considering what knowledge is like, and I have argued that there are four fundamental disciplines and a number of other discrete subjects, failure to recognise which involves one in error. It certainly follows that adequate human understanding necessitates that one recognise such distinctions, but it does not automatically follow that such distinct subjects should be taught as distinct subjects. One might quite reasonably centre one's teaching on various complex projects for example, out of which recognition of distinct kinds of questions might arise. Or one might indeed teach discrete subjects and indicate their bearing on complex issues.

The question of whether we should adopt a subject-centred or a topic-centred approach, and of whether we should have an *integrated curriculum* in the specific sense of integrating subjects, became a burning one in the late 1960s in Britain. I, for one, am glad that the fire seems to have gone out of it, for this is surely a relatively profitless thing to argue about. The important thing is not whether you do it this way or that, but that, if you decide to teach subjects, you should make sure that students come to see the application of the subjects to complex problems, and if you decide to teach through problems, you should make sure that, by the end, students have extracted the common features from various problems that go to make a discrete subject.

2 THE CONTENT OF THE CORE CURRICULUM

Since in essence the justification of the core curriculum is that schools are set up for particular purposes, we can fairly quickly establish the vital elements—those things that are demanded by reference to the purposes of education, socialising, ensuring health, and preparation for life and leisure. At a basic level, reading, writing and numeracy are obviously vital skills, both for our way of life and as a means to education. These must not be left to chance.

Education, we have said, involves:

(a) Historical awareness, which entails that the curriculum should include the study of history in some manner, shape or form that bestows or leads to a general understanding of the path from past to present.

(b) Awareness of individuality. This kind of understanding is gained quite simply through experience of widely differing individuals and their unpredictable, idiosyncratic personalities; at one remove, it is gained through hearing about people. In practice, one excellent way of studying and gaining acquaintance with what may reasonably be termed human nature is through the vicarious experience provided by literature. Consequently some kind of study of literature (and, as a means thereto, English language) will be required.

(c) Awareness of logical distinctions of various sorts. Here it is not immediately clear what is implied for the curriculum. One might try to teach distinctions, such as that between justification and explanation, directly in lessons devoted to that purpose, or one might plan to cover such points as and when occasion and opportunity arise in other subjects. Equally, one might tackle the distinctions to be drawn between different kinds of subject head-on, or suggest that logically distinct subjects should all be studied, so that their differences become apparent. I am inclined to suggest, although I do not believe that there is any hard and fast answer here, that the best policy is to combine a general concern for logical discrimination in all matters with lessons specifically devoted to the study of informal logic, perhaps by means of one of the many excellent books concerned with clear thinking, such as Antony Flew's *Thinking about Thinking* (but see the bibliography and compare books by, for example, Emmett, Thouless, Scriven, d'Angelo).

(d) Capacity for discrimination, where again curriculum implications are not obviously limited to one policy. On the face of it, the obvious source for developing such a capacity is literature in the widest sense, though all studies should contribute to it by insisting on clarity and specificity. [I shall elaborate on this below.]

The questions of how, at what level, for how long and at what age any of these things should be studied are not here being discussed. Rather, the principle is being established that all children should be taught to read, write and calculate, to read literature and history with ease of understanding and to have a basic grasp of philosphy by the time they leave school.

The non-academic subjects, by which name, for the purposes of this section, I will continue to denote those popularly classified as non-academic, such as woodwork, typing, PT and games, may have as much place in the school as the academic subjects. But not as some allegedly more realistic alternative. The only sense in which woodwork is more realistic than history is that it is more physical. "Ah, but you can do it at home." You can do history at home. "Oh, but you will need to do woodwork at home." If you want to put your own shelves up, yes. But then, if you want to understand the Common Market, if you want to know something about Anglo-French relations, you will need to study history. Why should the former possibility be thought more likely or more important? On the face of it, it is far less important and only seems more likely because we make it so, by failing to bring up people in such a way that they naturally look at the Common Market in a historical perspective. We raise a nation of people to worry about the price of butter, and then assume that people are like that. Woodwork is not inherently more practical, it is not more realistic, and it is not more useful. It is more physical and less intellectually demanding, and we have presented it as a more normal thing for someone to engage in on a Sunday afternoon than historical reflection. Nor should things like woodwork be seen as an alternative pursuit. One of the most thought-provoking phenomena in schooling is that of grouped subjects. It is fascinating to wonder what process of reasoning leads people to arrive at some sets of alternatives. German or French is a straightforward enough sort of choice. You can't do everything, and, if you are going to study one language, it may reasonably be set against another one on the timetable. But how does it come about that children are sometimes expected to choose between home economics, woodwork and Latin? Assuming that there are reasons for doing any one of them, they are not likely to be the same in each case and how is one supposed to weigh up incommeasurables? Woodwork is not something that can sensibly be proposed as an alternative to history, since it bears no relation to it.

The non-academic subjects, therefore, are not to be defended as more realistic or in any other way as alternative fare. They, or rather some of them, have their own importance. Schools, as has been repeatedly stressed, do not only educate. They have the more general task of preparing the future. The phrasing there is important. We do not simply prepare for the future, because, as I've just indicated in the Common Market example, what we do now to some extent affects what the future will be; today's schooling helps mould the future, and that is why I say that schools make their contribution to preparing the future. That being the case, they must concern themselves with more than the largely cognitive business of education, important as that is even for practical purposes. Very properly they should be concerned for the individual's current and future physical welfare, leisure and emotional life and with skills useful for everyday living. There is no question of principle as to whether schools should be concerned with non-academic things, but a question of how much need there is to spend how much time on what non-academic matters at institutional level. It is a question of competing priorities rather than principle. The objection to an extensive course in cookery is not that things like that don't belong in the schools, but that it isn't necessay or warranted to spend limited time on it.

Critics of schooling such as Reimer and Illich clearly have a point when they say that, as things are, too much and too many different things are going on in schools, and that some activities might be better off if they were not institutionalised and not made compulsory objects of study. There are very real dangers in institutionalisation. It may divorce study from everyday needs and thereby induce alienation, it may kill enthusiasm and it may create an undeserved respect for authority in general and in particular the authority of institutions themselves. But these dangers are, on balance, offset by the other side of the coin; schooling does serve some everyday needs and it creates aspects of our future needs, which is a most important thing to do. It does not have to alienate, and it may create enthusiasm and interest. There is such a thing as deserved respect for authority, and, as I have already argued, there are further reasons for concluding that various functions of schooling should be institutionalised. As to the point about there being too many things going on, it is true that the school today is more like the supermarket than the specialist local shop, but in this too there are advantages as well as disadvantages. Specialist shops may tend to provide better service. But supermarkets may be cheaper, more efficient, more convenient, and more able to present the customer with a wider choice of things he might otherwise have missed. Arguing by analogy is of dubious value (since it begs the question of whether the two things really are analogous) and must not be used to do more than suggest, but it seems to me that the deschoolers have not adequately explained how they will ensure effective education, socialisation, etc. in the absence of schools; they have not, so to speak, explained fully how the local corner shop is going to cope when we close down all the supermarkets. I see no merit in institutionalisation for its own sake, but it is a matter of practical expediency, given that we want to realise certain aims, to rely on schools. The idea of disbanding schools altogether or reducing them to a more specialised role (comparable to adult education institutes) is not remotely practical, and, in particular, is likely to exacerbate some of the very dangers those who advocate this policy most fear.

What, however, we can say is that enough is enough, and we must resist enlarging the range of offerings made by schools yet further. There is a tendency, particularly amongst newspaper editors, to assume that any national problem from lack of moral fibre to lack of cereal fibre is best laid at the door of the school. The schools are blamed and the schools are expected to solve the problem. This tendency is certainly unwise. It is asking too much and often it is asking the wrong sort of agency. Moral upbringing perhaps is something that schools may do something about, but even then why should they alone be made responsible rather than parents? Why should schools be given a job like ensuring a market supply of various kinds of expertise at all? That really is a different kind of role, and one that does get in the way of some other tasks the school is seeking to perform, such as educating. If industry wants technicians of one sort or another, then let industry attract and train them. Why too should schools be given sole responsibility for the health and recreation of the young, as effectively they often seem to be? They have a part to play here, but so too should other agencies. So, although it is no doubt useful in some respect to be able to play golf, to drive a car or to play squash, to type, to repair television sets and to lay a brick wall, there is no case for automatically throwing such things into the school curriculum. It so happens that traditionally, in Britain at any rate, most of these particular examples have been provided by agencies other than the school, and there is no good reason for trying to alter that state of affairs. Slightly different are activities that are more private in nature such as cooking, handicraft, knitting or carpentry. Although I don't want to suggest that it is outrageous for schools to offer courses in such things, surely it should be a matter of secondary importance whether they do or not, for these are activities easily picked up through personal contacts at home or through friends and they can be well catered for by voluntary evening classes.

What we want to aim at is an uncluttered list of matters of potential social and individual importance, which it seems profitable to have taught by professionals in a group setting to people not necessarily initially interested. Anything that answers that description has a claim on school time, as a rule of thumb; anything that doesn't, doesn't. We have to say "potential" because we cannot predict the future with accuracy, even as we help forge it. But we certainly don't want to waste limited time on things we have little reason to suppose that many people will get much out of and society has little concern for. Laying on lessons in butterfly collecting, for instance, seems uncalled for, worthwhile though the pursuit itself no doubt may be. I say "taught by professionals" because schools are places where masters of a craft are called on to teach that craft, be it physics or physical training. Pursuits that do not require any initiation or instruction by the expert have no more place in school than teachers who have no expertise. Reference to "groups" is not made because group-teaching is in itself desirable. Indeed in many pursuits we might well wish for a one-to-one teaching relationship. But circumstances demand that we teach in groups (there are not enough teachers to go round otherwise, and I mean competent rather than officially certificated teachers) and we are wasting valuable time and resources trying to teach things that cannot be well taught to groups. Beyond a certain basic level, therefore, something like music should probably be a matter for personal tuition. (Though there is no reason why the state shouldn't pay for it; it just doesn't fit well into schooling. It is rather a curious anomaly in our system that schools very often still do provide music lessons, but the fact that students generally have to pay for them as an extra gives the lie to the policy. They are not really part of what the school has to offer.) I add the criterion of being "not necessarily initially interested" because a vital aspect of schools is precisely that they open up avenue and vistas that the child may subsequently be thankful for, but which he did not ask for. There is nothing wrong with the idea of people freely choosing, but schools are partly designed to make up for individual lack of foresight.

Including — Music

The above is an important paragraph, if rightly understood. I am not eulogising group-teaching of things that don't interest people. I am solely observing that schools are precisely a device for offsetting the sad fact that we do not as yet live in a world where individuals spontaneously want and are able to learn all that is desirable or they could be expected to. It is quite true that there is in schooling the risk that we dampen people's enthusiasm, that by providing schools we make society generally less inclined to be educative and to take responsibility for socialisation, health, etc., but on balance the risk is worth taking. Society will not change, just because we remove schools.

What we have to consider now is what in particular the various other aspects of schooling we have delineated (besides education) demand in terms of the curriculum.

Socialisation will cover things ranging from kerb drill to constitutional knowledge. It will involve imparting information, engendering habits and expectations. There may be a practical danger of indoctrination here, inasmuch as to get people to familiarise themselves with something like the Declaration of Independence, if mishandled, may slip into engendering unquestioning commitment to it. But logically there is a clear distinction between indoctrinating and providing information and understanding. It is the latter that is demanded by socialisation. Giving children knowledge about their society, geting them to observe habits and manners such as shaking hands on various occasions or to expect a black tie in a ballroom. Stimulating awareness of such things is to be sharply distinguished from preaching the unquestionable sanctity of such things. I should also make it clear that arguing for the need for socialisation does not necessitate arguing for classes in it. Most socialisation will come through the hidden curriculum (the unadvertised network of examples, expectations and assumptions) and benefits from, indeed trades on, the institutional setting; even much of the information about society will come through other curriculum subjects and other agencies. All that could be required of the overt curriculum is a little time given over to social studies, meaning straightforward imparting of information about the nature of society.

The physical side of things, it might be thought, does not need stressing, particularly in America. But it certainly needs sorting out. Firstly, it is no use trying to make it a part of or a rival of education. An educated man might study the world of sport, but in itself theoretical study of aspects of sport is neither sufficient nor necessary to being educated. Sport and physical activity generally should be practical rather than studied in schools. It is clear that individuals and society as a whole benefit if people are healthy and can turn to sport as one way of enjoying themselves. It is no less clear that the institutional setting of the school gives great scope for engendering physical health, knowledge about maintaining health and sporting opportunities. My argument then is that schools should continue to put the degree of emphasis on physical activity that some American and some English Public (i.e. private) schools do, but with a more straightforward rationale that makes no appeal to school spirit, the purifying quality of games, or the idea that a healthy body is an aspect of the educated man. Children should simply be taught how to, and given the opportunity to, keep fit, remain healthy and play games, particularly team games, since they are something schools are well equipped to promote. Note that in a real sense, time devoted to physical activity is curriculum time; ideally we want to break down the age-old assumption of children that sports day is a half-day off school. (But of course the idea is that they should come to see everything in the light that they once saw sports day rather than vice versa.)

Vocational preparation and emotional development make little and straightforward enough demands on curriculum time. In fact the latter makes no specific new demands at all, for it follows from what has been said about the nature of emotions and emotional maturity that the school will make its contribution in this area through the actual experiences it provides for children and through subjects such as literature and history. Given that it has been argued that schools should resist the temptation to fit people for specific jobs, all that is required in respect of vocational preparation is a much more serious attempt to help individuals think about what kind of skills and interests they really have, and to provide them with information about the sort of jobs they might consider. Not a great deal of time is needed for this, but a complete change in attitude probably is. Perhaps one lesson a week for the last two years of schooling is all that is needed in terms of time, but what is crucial is that, like physical activity, this should be seen and treated as a proper part of the curriculum. A great deal more curriculum time is necessarily going to be spent on education than anything else, but these other candidates for curriculum time are no less *bona fide* elements in schooling.

Preparation for leisure is a phrase that recently became briefly fashionable and schools were immediately given responsibility for this too. It is of course important that people should enjoy their lives over and above the time they spend earning a living (which seems to be more or less the implication of this unattractive notion of preparation for leisure). But hopefully we don't need to provide special classes in leisure. If we can get schooling right, then everything we do should be a contribution to enabling people to enjoy their leisure (and their work, so long as we have to make such a sadly violent distinction). Sport and other physical activities may obviously make a contribution. So may education (here therefore is another respect in which education turn out to have practical utility), for having the kind of understanding that is involved in being educated opens up a vast number of possible sources of interest. However, one mistake to be avoided is that of equating acceptable taste with educated taste. There are plenty of leisure pursuits which do not depend upon one being well-educated, but which are none the worse for that. Enjoyment of films, love of music (active or passive), love of nature and an interest in steam engines do not necessarily have much to do with being educated (though education might enhance them), yet they may have a claim on school time. It is a matter of practical experience that typically a home in Northampton, England, or Northampton, Massachusetts, does not open up for a child the potential pleasures of classical music, for example, and if schools do nothing, no other agency will. I have no intention of smuggling in an argument based on views of cultural superiority at this juncture. I am not saying that classical music is superior and worthwhile music and that therefore children ought to be introduced to it. I am saying that there are many proven sources of leisure interest that initially take some getting into, of which classical music may be one example, and that some attempt should be made by schools to help people get in to some of them, so that at worst they can judge for themselves and at best get something out of them. As far as this objective goes, what actually should be selected will have to be fairly arbitrary in the sense of based on no consistent rationale. All one can say is that some curriculum time should be given over to introducing children or students to activities that are difficult to come to grips with initially, but which have a track-record of proving rewarding to many who do get to grips with them; exactly what activities to concentrate on can presumably be left to individual schools to decide, on the basis of available expertise and resources.

In general, in building up the curriculum, we do not want to academicise the non-academic nor popularise the academic (academic here meaning theoretical and intellectual); we want to recognise that there is more to schooling than the academic, vitally important though that is, because there is more to schooling than education. I shall postpone summarising what seem to me to be the important elements in any school curriculum until I have dealt in more detail with certain particular suggestions. Firstly, I shall consider the very unfashionable subject of Classics in conjunction with the widely studied subject of modern languages, in order to illustrate and to put substantive flesh on the general points made above about usefulness and relevance. I shall then look in more detail at the nature and claims of English, history and philosophy, which have already been shown to be of crucial importance to education. Finally the claims of the sciences will be noted.

3 CLASSICS AND MODERN LANGUAGES

Traditionally a classical education was the education of the English gentleman. For a long time, therefore, knowledge of the classics was seen both as the necessary condition of education and as an indication of one's privileged position. It is scarcely surprising that in changed times the idea of retaining Classics in any significant way in the curriculum should be anathema to some and derided as class-based delusion or antiquarianism. But we must not make the elementary mistake of confusing incidental and accidental features with necessary characteristics of something. We must not foolishly imagine that merely to show that mistaken claims have been made about Classics shows that there are no important true claims to be

made, or more specifically that to show that it has been defended
for bad reasons establishes that there are no good reasons to study
it. Explanation and justification are quire distinct activities; when
we have finally explained the emergence of Stalin's regime with
the particular form, strengths and weaknesses it had, there still
remains the quite separate queston of whether his emergence was
for good or ill. By offering a social-cum-psychological explanation
of delinquent behaviour you do not bypass the need to evaluate
such behaviour. In the same way, in this case, no amount of
explanation of why people have valued Classics and no amount of
data revealing that it has not held its place for very good reasons,
would have any bearing on the question of whether there are any
good reasons for studying it. It certainly is the case that it has very
often been championed for poor and irrelevant reasons, but that
does not mean that there are not (and have not always been)
better reasons than were ever articulated. Whether there are good
reasons for studying Classics or not must depend solely on what is
involved in such study and the relationship of whatever is involved
to the goals of schooling.

I will make it clear here that I do not believe that a classical
education is the best or the only path to education, although I do
think that it would provide the basis of a very good one. I am
concentrating on it and drawing attention to it deliberately in
order to illustrate how unexpected a form educational relevance
may take. (Those who still cannot grasp the distinction between
explanation and justification will say that I dwell on it because I
studied Classics. They may be right; but what I say might be true
notwithstanding that.) It was explained above that relevance and
usefulness depend upon a relationship to chosen objectives. Thus
Classics is clearly more relevant than science or football to understanding eighteenth century literature. What I want to demon-
strate here is how wide of the mark is the man in the street's
assumption that a relevant schooling would naturally eschew
things like Classics in favour of things like modern languages.
("Nobody talks Latin any more, do they?")

In discussing curriculum content of any sort it is crucial to get a
precise and clear idea of what the various speakers actually
presume to be involved in studying geography, mathematics or
whatever they are talking about. Much discussion in practice is
vitiated by misunderstanding arising out of a failure to see that
different people have quite different conceptions of whatever is
being discussed. What I mean by the study of Classics would
involve the study of the two languages, Latin and Greek, some
part of the history of the Graeco-Roman world and the study of

the literature (poetry, drama, philosophy, history) of the two. Not everybody who has studied Classics has studied all these elements, but all would be necessary to the study I envisage. To be more specific, let us assume that the history studies will include an outline from 1,000 BC (roughly the date of the Homeric poems, the *Iliad* and the *Odyssey*) to AD 54 (the death of the Roman Emperor Claudius), with a deeper study of perhaps fifth century Athens (the age of Pericles and the building of the Parthenon) and Augustan Rome. The literature and philosophy studied would include works by Homer, Sophocles, Thucydides, Plato, Catullus, Virgil and Tacitus. Studying Classics in this way is obviously not something to be done in a one year course. Under consideration, then, is the idea of something like a three year period of study of the culture, history and literature of the period chosen, almost certainly preceded by another two years' study of the languages. Consequently, any defence of this is going to need to argue for it as a complete or a substantial part of the complete educational curriculum.

I am not trying to argue for the superiority of this over other similar packages. There are practical advantages in studying the classical world rather than many other periods of history, in that from the students' point of view it is more graspable. Relative paucity of material and evidence, combined with a smaller world stage, make it easier to select and integrate and to detect interrelationships without a sense of distortion. It is also more obviously related to our own culture than most other periods of history. But much of what I say could equally well be prefaced of other periods of history such as, say, eighteenth century France. What I am arguing is that though studying Classics (in this sense) is not directly relevant to being a football manager or useful in running a Woolworth's store, it is decidedly relevant to the objective of gaining a good education, an education, furthermore, which in turn is itself entirely relevant to the needs of today.

Consider what one would gain from such study. Firstly, disciplined understanding of language. Here I refer not to mastering a foreign vocabulary, which is neither here nor there, but to learning how language functions to express ideas and to make points. I refer not to learning grammar as such, but to beginning to appreciate the logical structure that grammar advertises. To give an example: you learn the difference between causal connection, correlation and concessive relations. Of course there is no logical necessity whatsoever to study specifically foreign languages, still less these particular foreign and dead language, to gain such understanding. Furthermore it is important to recognise that certain modern methods of teaching Latin and Greek cannot be justified in this way, because they don't proceed through a study of the structure of the language [see below]. The point being made is purely and simply that studying Latin and Greek can be one very good way (and as it happens a proven way) of gaining this understanding, an understanding which, as I argue below [see Section 4], is crucial to sound thinking. Secondly, and probably most obviously, we gain access to a rich store of art and ideas. Here again there is nothing inherently superior about all these ideas and all this art, but there are certain distinct advantages to be gained from studying them. If not superior, they are nonetheless amongst the best. They form the basis of much of our own art and thinking. Because of the small scale of the material available and the consequent thorough working over it has received through centuries, it is far easier in practical terms to consider such questions as the interplay between social conditions and the fermentation of ideas or between art and politics. Particularly in the context of school (as opposed perhaps to university) the classical world has the immense advantage of determinate limits and manageability. With the birth of historiography and authors who are keen to talk explicitly about how they see their task, we have also the perfect setting for introducing not just history, but the nature and problems of studying history. The whole, taken together, provides an excellent ground for cultivating discriminatory power, particularly given the quality of the work of authors such as Sophocles, Plato and Tacitus. The distance from our own times encourages detachment and impartiality in our study, and allows us to concentrate on developing and refining concepts of democracy, friendship, leadership, race, religion, art, politics, etc., without the distorting influence of our sense of how things happen to be now.

Now this certainly goes a long way towards providing an education as we have defined it. But is it relevant to today? Well, of course it is. The question in fact betrays complete misunderstanding of both the nature of education and relevance. It is an education relevant to today because education, being what it is, is not temporally bound in a way that the state of film-making, conceptions of drama or biological views are. The educated mind does not dwell on the level of the particular, the concrete here and now, but on the abstract and general level of principle. It is seen not in what facts a person can recite, but in what kind of understanding and discriminatory power he has. What dates is our grasp of the empirical world. Greek medicine and Greek science were, in a fairly uncontentious sense, less advanced than contemporary science and medicine (despite important apparent exceptions such as the atomic theory of Democritus). But, though fashions change, it would be absurd to talk of Sophocles, Thucydides or Plato being out of date in the way that the medical writings of Hippocrates might be. Naturally one would not deny that anybody is to some extent limited or affected by his times; it is a feature of their times that Sophocles dramatises for the most part in terms of mythology, that Thucydides hardly considers economic factors and that Plato contemplates censoring Homer rather than television. But such points are incidental. The ideas they wrestle with, the problems they discern, the concepts they grapple with—these don't date. If you want to think about revolution, civil disobedience or power politics you have as good a text (not better necessarily, but as good) in Book Three of Thucydides' *History*, Sophocles' *Antigone* and Plato's *Gorgias*, respectively, as anywhere else.

If, therefore, the reader accepts what has been said about education and the consequent importance of language, literature, history and philosophy in schooling, it is impossible to see how he could deny that such a classical education would be an excellent one and entirely relevant to the needs of today, so far as education goes. Note, however, as hinted above, that if you change the nature of studying Classics you may lose your argument. Recent changes in the manner of teaching Latin in both England and America have led to an increase in the number of students involved. But the basis of the new approach is to get people to read fluently in the original language more quickly. In so far as this approach leads to the ability to read something like Catullus' poems, it gains a part of the desired objective (access to part of classical culture); but, because of the nature of the direct method employed, one thing it loses is the kind of understanding and appreciation of the way in which language works, which more traditional approaches conveyed. Certainly the case for learning Latin, by this method and in isolation from a wider and deeper study of the culture and history, is by no means as strong as the case for a thorough classical education.

Consider now the claims of modern languages, which to a considerable extent are also moving over to teaching techniques designed to facilitate use of language for purposes of reading and more particularly, speaking. A case could be made for the study of modern languages in a manner akin to the study of Classics I have outlined, and the only likely difference would lie in the greater manageability of the classical period, arising out of the relative lack of source material and the apparent self-sufficiency of the period. But that is seldom, if ever, the kind of course offered in the name of Modern Languages at school level, or the kind of justification put forward for them. Instead, one of the most widely studied of all subjects is based on one of the most inadequate arguments ever mounted. For it is popularly supposed that a language like French or German is just what schools should teach, because it is useful and relevant. But useful for what? Relevant to what? In a country such as Canada, where a sizeable part of the community is French-speaking, it does have some utility. But the number of times anybody in Britain needs to speak a foreign language is minimal. Very few of the thousands of children who spend three or four years studying French in England ever have occasion to speak or read it. Of those who do, most will be those who take an occasional holiday in France, where they will not speak it well enough to gain much from it and where they could get by without it. A few will need it for business purposes, but we do not know in advance who they will be, and anyway such people usually need private lessons or years of experience to attain the proficiency required. If the object of teaching French were to promote widespread fluency that led to a real coming together and understanding between the two nations, then it would arguably be well worth doing; but that is not the stated objective and it certainly isn't the result. (Indeed the British are notorious for relying on foreigners to speak English). Besides being of no use whatsoever to most people, learning a foreign language in the kind of way here being considered, has got little or nothing to do with education. If through learning a language one comes to a greater understanding of language in general, and in other ways sharpens one's perceptions and conceptions, as may certainly happen, and is a by-product, if not an objective, of what are now very often regarded as traditional methods of teaching, then it is indeed an important contribution to education. But if the emphasis falls rather on the student acquiring an alternative vocabulary as rapidly as possible, as it often does today, then no contribution is made to education. And if we are thinking of the wider sphere of schooling and potentially useful skills, it can only be said that time spent in metalwork would be considerably better spent.

As I said at the outset, this section has been designed to illustrate a general point about relevance. Any reader who thinks that I have claimed that we ought to teach Latin rather than French has not read it carefully enough. I have said that a thorough classical education of the type outlined would be one way of providing a good education, and as such it would be relevant to schooling and useful to society (because education has a use). Whereas a subject that happens to be widely taught, namely French, turns out on closer inspection, if taught in the way it often is, to be of very limited use and not relevant to education at all.

4 ENGLISH AND HISTORY

It has already been argued that the study of English should be central to the curriculum. Here I want to explain what form such study should take and why it should do so. Basically it must involve close study of literature in terms of understanding content, and practice at what used to be called composition exercises. By "understanding content" I mean appreciating the answer to such questions as "Why did Miss Havisham delight in seeing Estella taunt Pip?" in Dickens' *Great Expectations*. By "composition exercises" I mean essays predominantly concerned with the rational mode of expression (rather than, say, the evocative or the poetic). I am perhaps deliberately using rather old fashion terms here, to draw attention to the unfashionable view I am putting forward. Certainly I am not necessarily advocating this at the expense of concern for creativity, aesthetic appreciation, stylistic sensitivity, self-expression and self-awareness, which are the more usual objectives enunciated by contemporary theorists, but I am advocating a shift of emphasis away from the affective and the stylistic. The argument for such a shift of emphasis hinges upon the point made above that education is essentially about good thinking. We have seen that that is not necessarily developed by such things as lateral thinking exercises or courses in logic. One of the crucial elements involved, I pointed out, is discriminatory power. A person whose vocabulary is small and predominantly consists of general and broad terms probably thinks in those terms, and will certainly only be able to communicate in those terms.

Now one may very easily classify literature precisely by its discriminatory power. What after all is it, but a body of publicly expressed ruminations that is good when it is well done? And in broad terms it is well done when it is subtle, yet clear, and accurately reflects the subtlety and complexity of the world. There will be arguments about when it is well done, but that is a separate point, just as estimating whether somebody is strong is to be distinguished from determining what constitutes strength. Besides, the observation that we disagree on matters of value can be overdone. Yes, we do argue about the merits of Joseph Heller compared with Kurt Vonnegut, or E. M. Forster compared with

Graham Greene, but at the end of the day that does not stop us recognising that there is a large class of *bona fide* literature which would include all four of these authors. It seems to me that Heller's *Good as Gold* is in various ways rather a poor book, but it is manifestly literature in a way that *Superman* is not. And part of what one is saying in making that claim is that here is an author who looks at the world with some degree of discriminatory power, and, in his own style, seeks to convey that to us. It deserves to be taken seriously and is worth reading for those who enjoy its style and subject matter, because it captures something of the complexity of the subject matter. (It is concerned with human relationships, ambition and motivation.) It is important that I should not rest my general point on some idiosyncratic view of literary criticism. So I need to observe that I am not trying to lay down the law about how people ought to assess books in each and every circumstance. There are, admittedly, certain curious creeds that are ruled out by what I am saying, such as the view that there is no distinction to be drawn between manner and content. But the only sense in which a view like that could be true would not affect my point. It is obviously theoretically possible to distinguish the two. If it were not, the claim that they are in fact indistinguishable would be meaningless. Furthermore in practice it is possible to distinguish them too. If it were not, two novels could not be said to have the same subject matter. What is obviously true is that how you express ideas affects the precise nature of those ideas. But that is a rather different and, in this context, unimportant point. What you can certainly do is read any author with particular concern for *what* he is saying, whether that is partially dependent on and demands attention to how he says it, as will often be the case, or not. So I do not say that novelists should only be judged in this way, or that this is a necesary and sufficient condition of literature. What I say is that it is arguable that it is a feature of everything that is put forward as an example of good literature, and that it is almost invariably absent from junk. Given, anyway, that whether we call it literature or not, we are thinking of books classified by this criterion, to be able to read them is, with certain obvious qualifications, a sure sign of having that discriminatory power.

Let us rapidly get the obvious qualifications out of the way.

(*a*) The claim depends partly on what is meant by "being able to read". Somebody might be able to utter the sounds of the words written on the page without any understanding. Naturally I mean "able to read" in the usual sense of being able to understand the meaning of what is written.

(*b*) This facility is not a necessary condition of having the discriminatory power. One might be unable to read because one is badly dyslexic or because one has never learnt how to, but still be able to understand what is being said, if it is read to one.

(*c*) Having the ability is not a guarantee that one will exercise it. One might be able to, but not enjoy reading books or one might not be interested in thinking about any of the things written about.

The fact remains that to be able to read D. H. Lawrence's *Sons and Lovers* with understanding is to have a fairly sharp and subtle appreciation of the matters treated in that book, because even if you dislike Lawrence as much as I do (which is why, to keep that cynic quiet, I chose the example) you can scarcely deny that he looks at the aspects of human nature and behaviour that he chooses to dwell on with a degree of subtlety and insight—in a phrase, with discriminatory power. The inability (as opposed to disinclination, etc.) to read it, if English is your language, probably (though assuredly not certainly) means an inability to think in those terms. In other words it is unlikely, though possible, that, while not understanding Lawrence, you can perceive the same things and make the same observations about the matters treated of in *Sons and Lovers* in different ways. But in any case it follows from the first point that to encourage and enable people to read such a novel is to increase their discriminatory power.

It has already been conceded, it is indeed an obvious point, that you don't have to do it this way. But apart from the fact that the realm of literature contains some of the most powerful and illuminating reflections on such a wide number of aspects of life, it has the immense pedagogic advantage of being initially teachable and allowing of progress to be monitored, while subsequently becoming a tool of self-help, not to mention the fact that few who have become fluent and easy readers have not derived great enjoyment from the fact.

I suggest then that in practice nothing could be more vital to the objective of education than getting people to read literature with understanding and enjoyment. We need to introduce children to literature slightly beyond their own experience in terms of matter and expression, so as to enlarge their conceptual repertoire and develop their reading fluency. We have to make them literate in the sense of giving them access to the entire realm of literature, giving them not so much understanding of the art of writing fiction, but rather understanding of the fiction, the story, itself. To some extent the mere increase in vocabulary is a contribution to an increase in discriminatory power, for to have a word that one understands, is generally to have a new conception. But I am thinking also of concepts that are revealed and explored without the appropriate word necessarily being used. *Othello* would introduce the concept of jealousy whether the word was used or not. The main point is this: we need to give children more specific and precise concepts. The realm of literature is the source *par excellence* for non-technical concepts. By studying literature with a view to content, one may continually question and refine one's own perceptions and conceptions. I should add that although I happen to be thinking primarily in terms of fiction, I see no reason why the argument should not apply equally to literature in the wider sense, including such things as essays and popular history.

The argument for the value of what I am calling composition exercises is even more essentially pedagogic. I am proposing that far more attention than generally is, should be paid to helping children to write essays, judged in the main by reference to the quality of reasoning rather than content, conclusion or style, in so far as such distinctions can in practice be drawn. It is quality of argument rather than plausibility of conclusion we should be concerned with. The two do not always go together. A child might, through ignorance of various factors, write an essay about comprehensive schooling that came to a less sensible conclusion than some adult's essay on the theme, but was nonetheless better argued. There are two main reasons for advocating emphasis on such composition exercises. First, practice improves ability, as the experience of anyone who has had to do a fair amount of writing of any sort shows, and, in line with the general argument, increased fluency in writing represents increased fluency in thought in various important respects. Secondly, thinking expressed on paper can be carefully studied and scrutinised. That is the main reason for preferring the written to the oral in schooling, and for having reservations about too rapid a move to technological hardware. Tape-recorders, televisions and audio-visual equipment of various kinds can in principle present materials as well and for some purposes better than books, and they can be used in different ways to replace the child's need to write. But we do not yet have anything approaching a repertoire of worthwhile material available in this form, let alone anything to match the content of the world's libraries, and we cannot control this medium nearly as well. In practice what the child says (on tape, audio-visual, or whatever) cannot be isolated, examined, pondered and experimented with in the way that the same thing written on paper can be.

But if we are to put more emphasis on composition we need to know what features to concentrate on. We must not confuse rhetorical style with effective argument. There are devices which are stylistically attractive and emotively effective, such as use of vivid metaphor, analogy, the "I need not mention such and such" technique, or *ad hominem* argument, but these are not our prime concern. Given the object of the exercise overall, attention must be focussed on clarity, and coherence of presentation; but what does this mean in practice for such old favourites as handwriting, spelling, punctuation, grammar and syntax?

Should neatness of handwriting be regarded as important? Is the day of copper-plate exercises to return? Appearances, perhaps, betoken attitudes and there may be something to be said for a general emphasis on clarity, precision and neatness in all things, including a visually neat presentation of a neat argument. But there is no evidence that I know of to suggest any logically necessary connection between tidy thought and tidy handwriting, and it is therefore difficult to see a particular case for making too much of this, provided that, to facilitate communication, it is legible. Spelling likewise would seem to be of relatively little importance so far as our objectives go. It is, in respect of writing, what accent is in respect of the spoken word. One can legislate that a particular way of speaking shall be regarded as the norm (the Queen's English, as we say) or a particular form of spelling as correct. But there is no proper accent or correct spelling inherent in the nature of things, and attempts to standardise serve only (the important) claims of communication. There comes a point at which your broad accent can't be understood and your idiosyn-cratic spelling can't be recognised for what it is supposed to represent. Then you are in trouble. Naturally, spelling has to be taught in the first place, otherwise you are not teaching people to read or write at all. But excessive concern over repeated spelling mistakes in words that are instantly recognisable (and that do not apparently hinder the individual from recognising the word in its standard spelling), timeless concern of teachers though it has been, is really time rather wasted.[1] The important elements are punctuation and grammar, including syntax. Punctuation is admittedly not a necessary feature of good writing; that much is shown by the example of legal writing, which eschews punctuation altogether, relying entirely on precision of expression to make itself clear. But that example is the exception that proves the rule. For, in the normal course of events, our language is not sufficiently exact to avoid all ambiguity and equivocation of its own accord. Punctuation is needed and serves to improve and aid precision of expression (or, to put the boot on the other foot, to make the task of reading that much easier for those who are finding concentration difficult). Punctuation rules may go in and out of fashion, and at any given time some are less important than others. (I remember being taught never to use exclamation marks, or shriek marks as they were derisively called; and I noticed on a recent stay in Canada that English-speaking Canadians are very much more sparing with commas and semi-colons than the British. The state of the world does not seem much affected by either habit, however.)

On the other hand, punctuation can be not simply a very important aid to clear expression but an absolutely crucial aspect of meaning itself. The difference in punctuation between "the man, who" and "the man who", for instance, represents a difference between two distinct points. If you are not aware of the convention then you are going to find it difficult to appreciate the distinction between the idea of the man, who happened to be a good thinker, also being a good reader, and the idea of the man who is a good thinker being a good reader, when you encounter the written claim that the man who is a good thinker is a good reader. I am not suggesting that without punctuation such a distinction is impossible. But I am suggesting that to teach in such a way as to show concern for punctuation is to teach concern for being aware of, and publicly making, various important distinctions. If no attention is paid to punctuation, then much of the time we cannot tell whether what has been written is coherent argument presented by somebody with something like a legal grip on language, or mere garbage. Punctuation, therefore, is of vital importance in the interests of communication.

Grammar and syntax are more or less in the same position as logic. [See above Chapter One.] You may not need to study grammar in a formal way, but you certainly need to be able to write grammatically, for that means in accordance with the rules that govern our language, and hence distinguish communicable sense from nonsense. Again, it would not be difficult to fasten on a few rules of grammar that don't seem to do very much, and which are frequently broken by everybody. But to cite cases such as the fact that many people say "who" when they should say "whom", isn't going to make much of a dent in the point that, if you want to entertain and express intelligent thoughts, you have to have a good grip on grammar. It is logically impossible to articulate a coherent statement about anything that will mean anything to other people in defiance of the rules of grammar.

The argument is, then, that while attention to appearances in respect of spelling and handwriting may be of some importance, the crucial thing to acquire is understanding of the important points of punctuation and grammar, for to understand these is to have understanding of means for expressing oneself articulately, coherently and precisely. By emphasising and cultivating such understanding we enhance our powers of communication and resist veering towards a clumsy, superficial view of the world in its non-technical aspects—a tendency that will be enhanced by putting self-expression before precise expression, and creativity and imagination before coherence. Children should be taught to express themselves clearly and coherently and helped to acquire discriminatory power, this being best done through literature and composition.

Such study will also make an important contribution to developing the awareness of individuality referred to above, and more generally it will introduce material, food for thought or information about the world we live in and the way we live in it. Finally, what is needed to complement the literary contribution (or if you prefer, what may be seen as an aspect of it, but one to be stressed) is a historical content to provide a sense of our place in a wider world and time-span, also referred to above. General history, as one would expect history to be at school level, is one of the surest ways of widening our horizons and sympathies in respect of the broad questions of life. It may provide us with an incredibly rich and diverse array of different kinds of life-style, faith, personalities, values, beliefs and ideals. It may promote an awareness of how these differences may affect events, both consciously and unconsciously. It helps us to lose our fear and suspicion of the strange and foreign; it may help us to understand ourselves and the present. It is the great eye opener; the great complacency shaker.

Lest I seem to some to be making rather exaggerated claims, let me conclude this section by repeating a point I have made elsewhere: we should be thinking of the above claims not in the context of specialists and scholars, but in the context of a contrast between those who are introduced to literature and history adequately in their schooling and those who are not. It is not to the pont therefore to say, with obvious truth, that a number of eminent historians have not been noted for their wide sympathies. The point is that you cannot expect people in general to be other than insular, provincial and set in their ways, if you never introduce them to anything but the here and now and the way *we* do things.

5 PHILOSOPHY

What is the case for introducing philosophy into the school curriculum? Although, under one name or another, some teaching of philosophy has often and still does go on in schools, there is a strong tradition, dating back to Plato and fostered a great deal by philosophers themselves, that philosophy is dangerous for the young.[2] Plato thought that a well-prepared mind might be ready for it at about the age of thirty. His main fear was that the young would only half understand its nature and point, and would use its techniques purely for cynical and destructive purposes. There is something in this. The power of philosophy to destroy and demoralise should not be forgotten, just because recent trends in philosophy in our part of the world have apparently buried all interest in anything to do with the real world. Many people do get only a half-grasp of philosophy, and proceed to abuse it and irritate us, by reciting, litany fashion, "it depends what you mean by . . ." on each and every occasion that somebody says something interesting. But despite the fact that that is always a true remark, nine times out of ten, for one reason or another, it is quite inappropriate to make it. The truth of the claim that some people are more intelligent than others is dependent on what is meant by "intelligent", and that is worth pursuing, because few, if any of us, have clear conceptions of intelligence, let alone shared or objectively assessable conceptions. But though the truth of the claim that some children are better at mathematics than others likewise depends on what is meant by "better at mathematics", standing on the demand to know that would generally merely impede progress unnecessarily. Remember the biscuit. [See above Chapter One.] And then again, horrific damage can be done by people half-grasping illuminating points, not to mention by their wholly-embracing unilluminating points. Much of the argument for various radical approaches to schooling and much of what calls itself radical sociology is based on philosophical insights insufficiently understood (or perhaps consciously, but outrageously overstated).

For example, Postman and Weingartner base their *Teaching as a Subversive Activity* on a crude and confused (alternatively on an irresponsibly oversimplified and popularised) understanding of Bishop Berkeley's contention that to be is to be perceived (*esse est percipi*), filtered down through Marshall McLuhan.[3] Apparently fired more by the intuitive recognition that you can *make* the medium the message, if you put all your energy into how you say rather than into what you say, than by any serious thesis about the nature of reality, Postman and Weingartner nonetheless insist that there is no reality out there, and that everything is as you see it. There are some very interesting questions that could be pursued here. Questions such as how we know that we exist or that there is a world outside our minds, what the criteria of reality are or how far we should trust our senses. But these questions are not taken up by Postman and Weingartner and, at the level at which they are operating, it is just plain silly to pretend that everything is entirely as you see it. Sometimes when it rains it really pours. (There is of course the entirely different and quite reasonable claim that how the individual perceives a situation modifies it. But that wouldn't be worth writing a book about.)

On a similar theme there are some important, if rather familiar, truths behind the view of radical sociologists that orthodox and traditional sociology has not seen or has ignored the fact that its conceptions and methodological framework contribute to shaping the reality it claims to reveal or uncover, and that how the observer conceptualises a situation has a significant bearing on the situation. But by the time this observation has led to it being denied that there is anything in the world except social constructs, the cure is worse than the cold. Some things just do happen, indeed are happening now, quite independently of how researchers, we or anybody else approach, contemplate or classify them. It just isn't true, for example, that differences between people are entirely the product of our ways of looking at them or that delinquent behaviour would cease to exist if society ceased to think in terms of delinquency.[4]

So, there are certainly dangers attendant on a half-understanding of philosophy. Equally disastrous is a complete inability to recognise the philosophical dimension, such as is sadly evidenced by rather a lot of empirical research in education. Many empirical researchers just do not seem to understand that the value of their work is dependent on a clear conceptual base, and that a stated verbal definition in perfectly familiar words does not necessarily amount to a clear conception. And that is to say nothing of the obvious need for a cool, logical head to sort out just what is being established by one's research and what is not, just what does follow from this or that, and what doesn't, and just how reliable the type of inquiry one is conducting could hope to be in respect of what. Ability to answer these questions is quite distinct from ability to carry out the empirical research in question. [See below Chapter Six.]

One further point to be noted is that most subjects, simply by concentrating on their own field of inquiry, naturally tend to make those who study them see everything in those terms. Historians may tend to take a historical view of political issues; scientists may tend to be hard nosed seekers after empirical data in all sorts of situations. One way to offset this tendency is to make sure that individuals have a breadth of knowledge, as we have already argued they should, so that they are never simply historians, scientists or whatever. But philosophy has a distinctive pedagogic value in relation to this problem, being what is sometimes called a *second-order discipline*. That is to say that while other subjects or disciplines use their own concepts and theories to interpret some aspect of the world, philosophy seeks to interpret and assess any concepts and theories, and thus comes to scrutinise the logical base of all other subjects. This means that while the physicist or social scientist quite properly takes his methodology for granted and gets on with the job in hand, the philosopher questions the methodology. (There is nothing to stop the man who is a physicist also questioning his methodology, but in doing so he ceases to do physics and begins to philosophise.) Philosophers, therefore, though no doubt as prone to dwelling on their own interests as anyone else, cannot in the nature of things be limited to a one dimensional view of the world in the way that specialists in other disciplines can be. (Again let it hastily be added that people who call themselves or are paid to be philosophers might nonetheless have a one dimensional view of life. But insofar as they are competent philosophers, they cannot have.)

So, despite the attendant dangers, something philosophical must be introduced to the core curriculum at secondary school level to save us all from perdition. For in the end the only thing that can cure both the problem of an inability to recognise the philosophical dimension and the problem of an inadequate grasp of it, is a more adequate grasp of it. What we have to do is get people into the habit of substituting thought for rhetoric, of articulating coherent ideas and arguments rather than mouthing words as talismen and ritual grunts in a permanent game of appearances, and above all of critically questioning their assumptions. Not only would this make them more powerful critical thinkers; it would also make them less likely to be the dupe of advertising, politics, professionals and other assorted groups who have a vested interest in putting conviction before truth. It is a question to some extent of ordinary people calling the Emperor's bluff. But to do that they need a voice. We have to get people beyond the stage of reacting to books like this by saying "I agree" or "I disagree", "God, what a lunatic" or "That's right, you tell them", and on to the stage of asking insistently whether the argument is clear, complete, consistent and coherent. If so, then we must accept the conclusion for the time being, whether we like it or not. If not, then it is up to us to point out where the argument is going wrong and to try and correct it.

One of the main problems may be to get ourselves to recognise a need for philosophy, rather than to persuade ourselves of its value in principle. Presumably we all agree that we don't want illogical arguments and hazy conceptions, but we don't think that we have them, and we don't recognise that that is what makes what our neighbour says absurd. (We put it down instead to his background or stupidity, or we blame the media—all of which are different and less immediately important kinds of response.) It takes a long time to learn that we do need to sharpen our conceptions and our logic, and the only path to recognising our shortcomings in this respect is itself that of studying philosophy. To some extent the path would be easier, if from the beginning we succeeded in cultivating a better control of language, as I have argued schools should seek to do. (As we have seen, verbal and conceptual points are distinct, but they are closely related.) [See above Chapter One.] If we do that, then it should be possible to successfully introduce lessons and courses specifically concerned with conceptual and logical clarity. Such things can be done in the context of other classes, and to some extent usually are. But demanding logical precision in a particular context is not quite the same as highlighting points of logic in an argument for its own sake. To engage properly in conceptual analysis would hold up progress in the subject being studied and to do the job too briefly would tend to reinforce the misunderstanding that conceptual analysis is equivalent to a firmly stated definition. There is, however, as I have repeatedly urged, a distinction between stating clearly "What I mean by democracy is one man one vote", in order to advance a discussion in a history lesson about whether Periclean Athens was or was not democratic, and attempting to analyse the concept of democracy, which would involve one in a more painstaking task that would have nothing specifically to do with Athens. Besides that, there is a danger that, if logic and conceptual clarity are introduced in various specific contexts, the strange pattern will continue whereby people have more precise ideas about, say, Periclean Athens than their own time and place. The lesson that needs to be learned is not simply the one we teach reasonably well at the moment, namely that good historians or good physicists need to know what they are talking about, and to have a concern for evidence, etc. The lesson that needs to be learned is that exactly the same applies to intelligent and educated people all the time.

Evolving suitable schemes for introducing various children to philosophy is a further question—one, incidentally, that is receiving considerable attention, particularly in America, at the moment.[5] But one thing that the whole argument of this book shows clearly is that few things could be more useful and educationally relevant than introducing philosophy in some way to the school curriculum.

6 The Natural and Social Sciences

So far, to adopt the perhaps rather outmoded terms of arts versus sciences, this is a very arts-orientated curriculum. Is there a case for involving the sciences in the core curriculum? There is an obvious and straightforward argument for introducing people to the natural sciences, based on two points. Firstly, to have a basic grasp of scientific aspects of our universe is to add another dimension to the breadth of knowledge necessary to educated men. It is not that this particular knowledge is necessary, but it is a species of knowledge which may quite properly contribute to the breadth that is necessary. Secondly, it is surely part of the business of schooling to give people a basic grasp of how their world works. From time to time somebody may be heard to remark that he studied science at school, but that it has not been of any subsequent use to him. One wonders slightly what such a person can mean. Does he mean that he does not use the scientific knowledge and understanding he acquired at school consciously and deliberately on a wide scale and a daily basis? Does he perhaps also imply that he doesn't use his scientific knowledge as a means of earning money or in relation to some consuming hobby or interest? If that is the sort of thing he means, as would seem quite likely, then the objection seems of very little force, for, as has been argued, no part of education and only a small part of schooling should be expected to be justified in those terms. At another level it can scarcely be true that the science studied at school has had no subsequent use or relevance. Our realisation, when the lights fuse, that we need to replace one burnt out piece of wire with another and that it is not a sign that God is angry, trivial as the example may be, is nonetheless an instance of our scientific understanding coming into use. The point being that at the sort of school level we are talking about ('O' level, tenth grade, let us say), estimates of the usefulness of science should take note, not of specific experiments learnt at school and repeated at home, but of the provision of a general appreciation of scientific phenomena and their part in our daily lives. The idea that schools should seek to make nuclear physicists or research chemists of us all would indeed seem quite unwarranted, but the idea that we should have some grasp of the basic way in which animal, mineral and vegetable life function and the nature of commodities like gas and electricity seems self-evidently desirable.

It seems plain, then, that a basic scientific understanding should be provided by schools. Scientific understanding is furthermore a likely and reasonable element in the breadth of understanding characteristic of the educated man, though not a necessary feature.

The social sciences, by contrast, seem to have little claim to being part of the core curriculum (which is not to say that they should not feature in the optional range of curriculum subjects). Two distinctions need to be made here. Firstly, I am talking of subjects like psychology and sociology and not social study or social studies. By the latter, which, it has already been argued, probably should have a place in the core curriculum, I mean little more than the imbibing and digesting of facts and figures about society, whereas the former are more critical activities, concerned with collecting data (recording facts) and considering methods of doing so. To inform people that there are in Britain *x* thousand Ugandan Asians, who hold such-and-such a set of beliefs, is one thing (and constitutes, in effect, a lesson in social studies); to carry out surveys of immigrant attitudes is another (and constitutes an instance of sociological inquiry). Secondly, we have to distinguish between what is necessarily involved in sociology (or any other social science) as a matter of definition, and what as a matter of fact sociologists invariably or often tend to do, even if it strictly speaking goes beyond sociology. Strictly speaking, sociology is the scientific study of the behaviour of groups of human beings and/or the organisation and growth of human societies. The inclusion of the word "scientific" is probably unfortunate (though it is far too late to drop it now), since it implies, as cannot be the case given phenomena such as human intentionality, that the study of human society can be strictly comparable to the study of physical matter. But at any rate it is clear that sociology is an empirical subject, concerned to find out what it can about human groups and societies by reference ultimately to the test of one or more of the five senses. However, many contemporary sociologists in fact range far beyond the limits of sociological inquiry. In particular, many of them are at least as interested in philosophical questions about the concepts with which they operate and the coherence and logic of their methodology. This seems to me an example of something that, while not being sociological, almost invariably characterises sociology nowadays, and in principle it is surely all to the good. If we are going to rely on the findings of sociologists with which we are fed, we must hope that they will have given careful consideration to the most effective and reliable way of ascertaining those findings.

The trouble is, of course, that very often the philosophical or other non-sociological aspects of the work are not handled very competently by people with no particular understanding of or training in them. And here we come to something that perhaps needs to be guarded against amongst run-of-the-mill social science graduates—although I stress, it is not inevitable and has nothing to do with sociology as such—namely a tendency towards an inability to recognise the distinct nature of various aspects of their work, and a consequent narrowness of vision that sees what is in fact an attempt to study an aspect of life empirically, as a comprehensive account of life itself. To some extent this is just a result of a failure to take other kinds of question seriously, which failure might in turn have any number of causes ranging from ignorance to lack of interest. Thus one may frequently encounter sociologists who simply do not recognise a moral dimension or an aesthetic dimension to problems or situations they confront. But it may also be nurtured more insidiously by the growth of the quite incoherent notion that there is something called a sociological truth, and a sociological perspective which is comparable to, but logically distinct from, a moral perspective, an empirical perspective or whatever. But this there cannot be. The only sense in which there can be a sociological perspective is that a person may concentrate only on sociological content. To look at football sociologically, therefore, means to look only at empirical questions relating to the behaviour of human groups in the context of football. It does not involve looking at football in a special kind of way, and is not therefore logically comparable to looking at football aesthetically. Similarly there cannot be a sociological truth in the same way in which there may be scientific truths or aesthetic truths. There can be truths involving the subject matter of social science (truths about football crowd behaviour, for example) or truths discerned by sociologists (whether as a result of empirical inquiry or not). What there is not is a logically unique kind of truth, as there may be in the domains of morality and aesthetics. Truths unearthed by sociologists are just a species of empirical truth. They are not, therefore, logically inaccessible to the outsider who is not a sociologist, in the way that the truths of physics or aesthetics may conceivably be. It is not possible for the complete outsider to understand propositions within the domain of physics or aesthetics. In order to understand, one has to acquire some grasp of the concepts and the logic of the areas in question. That is not true of propositions uttered in the domain of sociology. They may conceivably be couched in unfamiliar language, but what is actually being said (the proposition as opposed to the sentence), being a straightforward empirical claim about the behaviour of human groups, carries no logical problems for any normal English language user. (Outsiders may be ignorant of work done in sociology, and they may therefore not be in a position to challenge the sociologist who makes a particular claim, but that is a rather different point.)

An example that I encountered recently may help to illustrate the point and indicate how misleading a failure to appreciate it may be. Two sociologists were arguing about whether or not human nature is a social construct, whether, that is to say, there is any innate tendency to be of a certain sort in humans or whether they are effectively what circumstances make them. (Note incidentally that both disputants were sociologists, which helps to underline the point that what is being criticised here is not sociology, but a possible weakness induced by the study of sociology.) Now the question, surely one of the more interesting questions we might contemplate, is obviously a complex one. In the end it could only be resolved to our satisfaction by an empirical inquiry. But that inquiry could never begin in any serious way, until we had a clear conception of what constitutes human nature and even then the empirical research into the matter would be exceedingly complicated, if possible at all, in view of the difficulty of empirically locating something like human nature, or aspects of it, and the difficulty of controlling variables. In fact, it is fairly obvious after a moment's reflection that this matter cannot possibly be satisfactorily settled. The most we can hope for is a more or less well-thought-out hypothesis, supported by such strictly limited empirical inquiry as we can devise.

One of the disputants, seeking to argue that human nature is essentially a social construct, suddenly reverted to a more limited claim and asserted that sociology had at any rate established that human aggression was a social construct. The other countered by suggesting that, even with this more limited claim, "established" was too strong. "Surely", he said, "the best we can say is that many sociologists believe this, and have some evidence to support them. But we know equally well that some sociologists and a great many psychologists, as it happens, don't believe it, and they have some evidence to cite too." To this the first replied, and this is the part of immediate interest, that it wasn't a psychological question, so the views of psychologists didn't count. But that is a most peculiar response. It is true that it is only a psychological question in the sense that psychologists may be interested in it, and have something to say about it. But that is also the only sense in which it is a sociological question. What it actually is, as we've said, is an empirical question in which anybody may be interested. It is profoundly misleading and incoherent to assume that this is a matter that sociology might have proved single-handed, and that those ignorant of sociology might be unable to appreciate this. What might be the case at best, is that a mass of empirical inquiries launched or carried out by sociologists consistently suggest this. But, and this is of crucial importance, the question of whether each or any of the pieces of research carried out were adequate, the question of what they established, and the question of whether taken together (with or without reference to other research carried out by people who were not sociologists) they present conclusive evidence, are none of them sociological questions. So it cannot be legitimate for a sociologist to take cover behind his expertise, to insist that only he and his fellow sociologists can judge such issues.

The possibility that preoccupation with sociology may seriously hamper one's understanding in a wider sense, even while it increases one's knowledge of particular matters, being only a contingent point, cannot be used as the sole argument for excluding the subject from the core curriculum. It is after all comparable in its logic to the point that philosophy can be misunderstood and abused, and as such do as much harm as good. The essential reason for not including sociology in a core curriculum is rather that there is no positive argument for doing so, once its findings are being introduced separately. It is not a logically unique type or form of understanding, so it cannot increase breadth of understanding in the requisite way, and it has no distinctive contribution to make that is logically necessary to the educated man, or the intelligent or critical thinker. One may be educated and unversed in sociology or steeped in sociology and uneducated. Nor is there any obvious argument relating to other functions of schooling that would make any of the social sciences a vital part of the core curriculum. It is only given that, that it becomes pertinent to add reference to some of the attendant dangers that uncritical adherence to sociology may bring.

7 SUMMARY

To summarise: the core curriculum should involve the study of the following elements: English, history, philosophy, natural sciences, vocational courses, social study, physical training and aesthetics. The first three are the vital elements in relation to educating people. I need say no more about them, except to point out that by the study of English language and literature is meant such literature as is available in English and this would therefore include translations. Study of the natural sciences is relevant to education, but its inclusion is based more on the wider concern of schooling to prepare people to understand and cope with the world we live in. It has been argued that it is a mistake to actually prepare people for particular types of jobs at school, since that is to shape the future as much as prepare for it and, inevitably, rather disadvantageously for some. It also risks allowing industry and economic forces to dominate schooling at the expense of, most notably, education. Vocational guidance is therefore seen as informative rather than preparatory. Social study, justified by reference to the socialising function of schooling, is likewise presumed to be essentially informative. Physical training, meaning both engaging in activities for keeping fit and healthy, and acquiring some understanding of how to remain that way in later life, has its own justification. So-called preparation for leisure is catered for by a curriculum that successfully serves the other functions of educating, socialising, contributing to physical health and emotional maturity.

In this chapter I have not drawn any curriculum conclusions relating to moral or aesthetic matters. The former will be examined thoroughly in the next chapter. As to the latter, it follows both from the claim that schooling (rather than education) should concern itself with the various dimensions of man and not just his intellect, and from the observation that aesthetics represents one of the fundamental disciplines in the domain of knowledge, and therefore constitutes a significant element in true breadth of knowledge, such as is a necessity for the educated mind, that schools may reasonably seek to provide children with some understanding of aesthetic matters.

5 Morality and Religion

1 THE RELATIONSHIP BETWEEN MORALITY AND RELIGION

The grip of both morality and religion on schools in the Western world is strong. There are a considerable number of religious schools and colleges; there is a widespread assumption that it is the school's proper function to combat decline in moral standards and manners, and to resist any increase in crime statistics. In Britain there is still a statutory requirement that schools should provide some form of religious education, while in America, where that is not generally the case, a minor industry in moral education has arisen, as if to compensate. For the most common belief of all is that morality and religion are very closely connected.

In this chapter I shall show that in fact morality and religion are logically independent of one another. (They are autonomous or discrete areas, as it is sometimes put.) I shall then argue against the inclusion of religious study as an essential element in the curriculum and against formal religious assemblies at institutional level. The nature and problems of the moral sphere will be explained, and a distinction drawn between moral training and moral upbringing. Finally the place of moral study in the curriculum will be considered. (I shall define a religion as any set of beliefs involving a supernatural being who has influence over our lives and a code of conduct.)

Historically, morality and religion have been inextricably interwoven. In some societies no distinction between moral duties and religious duties has been conceived of, whilst in almost all there has been a very close connection, so that moral duties and religious duties generally at least coincided. Even today, for many people the two go hand in hand. So our first question is, what is the nature of the relationship between the two? Are they logically connected, are they contingently connected, or is there no real connection except in popular belief?

A *contingent connection* would be a connection that exists as a matter of fact, but which conceivably might not have done, without distorting the nature of either of the two things connected. There is a contingent link between being human and having two legs, or between being a child and going to school. These connections do exist, but they might not have done or they might cease to do so. People without two legs are still human, and children who don't go to school are still children. A *logical connection* would be one that could not conceivably be broken without distorting the nature of one or other of the elements. Thus triangularity and three-sidedness, or fatherhood and having had at least one child, or murder and wrongness are logically connected. It is not a mere matter of fact that all triangles do have three sides. A triangle must have three sides, or else it is not a triangle. If you haven't had at least one child you are not a father. Similarly, murder is wrong by definition: it must be wrong, because of what the word means and if we don't think that it is wrong, we call it something different like justified homicide (although we may argue about whether a particular killing should or should not be classified as murder).

The question for us, therefore, is whether moral duties are necessarily religious ones, as triangles are necessarily three-sided, whether they are as a matter of fact more or less coextensive, as human beings as a matter of fact generally have two legs, or whether there is no real connection of any sort and they just happen to coincide sometimes. To put the question more graphically: does God require us to do good things because they are good (contingent), are good things good in that they are required of us by God (logical), or does God sometimes require us to do good things and sometimes not (no connection)?

It is clear on reflection that we cannot plausibly maintain that there is a logical connection. To say that good things are good in that they are required of us by God is to say that what "goodness" means is "required of us by God". Things are good iff [if, and only if] they are required of us by God. If we take this view, we will face a number of problems about determining what we ought to do, since in order to know what is good, we will have to know that God exists and what he requires us to do. But the devastating objection to this view is that, if "good" means "required of us by God", then there is no apparent reason why we should do or feel obliged to do good things. Our normal understanding is that good things are things that ought to be done for their own sakes, and not just because we are under orders to do them. But if "good" simply means "required of us by God", then the only apparent motive for doing good is to obey God. But why should I obey God? It is not open to us to answer that question by saying "Because God is good", for that of course does not make sense on the view under consideration, being equivalent to "Because God is required of us by God". Certainly reasons can be produced that make it seem sensible to obey God (he will destroy you, if you don't; he will love you, if you do). But any such move reduces moral behaviour to a form of self-interest, whereas one thing that is clear about truly moral behaviour is that it is the sort of behaviour one should engage in for its own sake, rather than out of fear or self-interest. It is, then, quite contrary to common-sense, and leaves us with no particular reason to do the good, to define good in terms of God's requirements.

Quite different is the suggestion that there is a contingent connection between religion and morality, in that as a matter of fact God only requires good things of us. But to take this view, which is surely the view that any sensible religious believer would take, carries with it the implication that God and goodness, religion and morality, are in logic quite distinct or autonomous units. For if God commends the good to us rather than the bad, this must mean that the good is good independently of God. How could God commend the good, if the good did not already exist independently of his commendation?

It is clear then that "good" does not mean "required of us by God", and that rather God is presumed by those who believe in him to support moral goodness. The ten commandments, to use a Christian example, are not good because and in that God issues them; he issued these rather than other commandments, because he saw them as morally good. So as far as logic goes morality does not depend for its existence on religion.

But what of the practical argument that, though the two are logically distinct, they should be treated as inseparable, because as a matter of fact the only successful way of getting people to do good is to fill them with the fear of God? This view raises a number of important and interesting questions such as whether doing something good because you fear the wrath of God would count as truly moral behaviour; whether coercing people into moral behaviour in this sort of way is not both contradictory and itself immoral; whether the particular moral views of any given sect are our moral views. But the immediate point to make is that such a claim is an empirical one and, at any rate in the form I've presented it, it is certainly false. Some people may indeed act morally only for fear or love of God. But some people clearly act morally without any belief in God, which shows that religion is *not* the only means of promoting moral behviour. (It might conceivably be the case that instilling religion into people is generally the most effective way of bringing them up to do good, but in the absence of any evidence to support that view, it seems reasonable to ignore it.)

In short, there are no apparent grounds for maintaining that moral upbringing entails a religious upbringing or vice versa, and consequently no grounds for justifying religious study in schools on moral grounds or vice versa. We therefore need to examine the claims for time devoted to either study independently.

2 The Nature of Religious Discourse

The central philosophical problems in the religious domain are: what can a claim such as "God exists" possibly mean, and how can it possibly be known to be true or false? Antony Flew tells a parable of two explorers in a jungle who come across a clearing containing flowers.[1] One explorer thinks that there must be a gardener, the other thinks not. They remain there but never see a gardener, so the first explorer adds the qualification that "He must be an invisible gardener." A barbed wire fence is put up, bloodhounds set to patrol the clearing. Still no sign of the gardener, who is now thought to be "invisible, intangible, insensible and eternally elusive" by the first explorer. How long, wonders Flew (and his second explorer), can this addition of qualifications sensibly go on? Surely we are reaching the point where the force of the original assertion has been entirely dissipated. It is suffering "death by a thousand qualifications". Nowadays everybody recognises that "God exists" is not supposed to mean "There is a being, flesh and blood, like you and me, by name of God, who exists a long way away, just as you and I exist here." On many occasions the qualifications have been made explicit. God is not flesh and blood, he is intangible, he is omnipotent, etc., etc. The question is: what, if anything, is left? Are we actually talking about anything comprehensible?

Let the reader at this point ask himself: "What do I mean by God?" Now clearly various verbal answers can be given to that question. For example, one might say "By 'God' I mean 'a supreme, invisible, omniscient being'". But the question that needs pressing is, can you really conceptualise this being, or does it remain merely a matter of words? Conceptualising, incidentally, does not necessarily mean picturing; it means grasping the idea of something, and that might take various forms. I cannot picture something called love, but I can conceptualise it, because I can give an account of it that has practical application; I could recognise instances of love if I came across any. Because I can conceptualise love, I can sensibly enough value it, have faith in it or believe in it. The question is: can you conceptualise God? Behind the words is this a notion or idea such that you would recognise God if you saw him (or sensed him)? If not, what exactly are you talking about? Does the notion of "an invisible, intangible, omnipotent being" have any more meaning than "everywhereness"?

Assuming some sort of satisfactory answer to the question of whether one can really conceptualise God, turn now to the question of existence. On the face of it the one thing that omnipresent, omniscient, intangible, invisible beings don't do is exist! For in everyday language "existence" has implications of "having life", which will naturally be understood in conventional biological terms, and of "occurrence" or "being found". Yet this God is not found; he does not occur; he does not have life—at any rate as these expressions are normally understood. So, whatever "God exists" means, it is fairly clear that it does not mean what an ordinary language user would presume it did. That being the case, may we not legitimately raise the question of what it does mean? And indeed, is not some answer to that question necessary before we could meaningfully make any claim to believe or not believe in the existence of God?

Speaking for myself, I cannot see that talk of God's existence or the existence of some transcendental (i.e. beyond the sphere of experience) being can have any descriptive meaning at all. It can have other kinds of meaning; for instance, religious language obviously does have emotive meaning. But given the meaning of "existence" and the apparent descriptive meaninglessness of "God", it seems impossible to classify "God exists" as a descriptive utterance, whether true or false.

However we do not need to pursue that particular matter here. For what seems quite clear is that, if an utterance such as "God exists" expresses a meaningful proposition at all, it is an unprovable proposition. [The notion of an unprovable proposition, it will be recalled, should be distinguished from that of an unproven one. There are many propositions that have been or might be stated which are in fact unproven, but are not in principle unprovable. Thus it was not proven that Richard III murdered the princes in the tower, or that there is a planet with a race of green men on it in the universe. But in either case we know and agree on the sort of evidence that would constitute proof or refutation of the claim, and conceivably it might turn up one day. By an unprovable proposition is meant one such that it is not known what would count as evidence for or against it. Here the full significance of Flew's parable comes out, for, even assuming "God exists" really does mean something descriptively, it seems that believers and non-believers are divided not so much by different views of what is going on, but by different estimates of what what is agreed to be going on signifies. Both explorers are in the jungle, both see the flowers in the clearing. One attributes this to a gardener, the other doesn't. From that point on their views of what is and what is not evidence pertaining to the matter grow wider and wider apart; the fact that he is not seen is evidence against there being a gardener for one, but not for the other and so on. In exactly the same way it seems to the non-believer, not that the believer is ignorant of evidence, but that nothing for him is going to be allowed to count against the truth of the proposition that God exists; the phenomenon of evil, the fact that this being is not apparent to the senses and such like is not ignored or denied. It is just that it is not treated as relevant. In the complete absence of agreement as to what would count as relevant evidence, we have the reason why religious utterances have to be classified as prime examples of unprovable propositions.]

It may at this point be suggested that even if it is granted that religious propositions are unprovable, which is to say not demonstrably true, there are nonetheless arguments for believing in God. There are, for example, the so-called arguments from design and revelation, the ontological argument and the view that religious truths can be intuitively perceived. But none of these prove very convincing on close scrutiny.

The argument from design suggests that the existence of a grand designer can be inferred from the observation of a certain kind of regularity in nature, just as the existence of some watchmaker could be inferred from looking at something so obviously purpose-built as a watch. But, even if the analogy were accepted, it is hard to see how it could justify belief in any religion embodying a particular kind of God with specific attributes, such as benevolence, and particular forms of worship. All that one could reasonably surmise on coming across a watch for the first time is that it was the product of conscious design; one could not reasonably start listing attributes belonging to the putative watchmaker. In the same way, the most one could legitimately infer from a sense of design in the world is a designing force behind it; all further inferences relating to characteristics such as benevolence, omnipotence and a being worthy to be venerated would be quite illegitimate. And then, why should we accept the analogy? In the first place it is not clear that there is design in the universe in the sense of conscious imposition of pattern for a purpose. Certainly we may detect what we are pleased to call design, but all that we are strictly speaking entitled to do is say that we are capable of superimposing a pattern of purpose on what we see. In the same way an observer seeing what is in fact the random result of somebody spilling a pot of paint on canvas, may see a design in it and wrongly assume it was consciously designed. In the second place it will not be universally agreed that there is design even in the limited sense of a coherent and consistent pattern. Perhaps it is difficult, when confronted with what we know of the world, to deny a sense of vast mystery and a feeling that there is some kind of pattern to it all. But it is a very long way from that feeling to any conclusions about a particular kind of God, and the inference and other steps along the way are not compelling.

The argument from revelation, which says that the truth of religion has been revealed to us through wise men or prophets and holy books, obviously won't do. This is a straightforward appeal to authority which can never yield sufficient cause for belief. Even when individuals are acknowledged to be authorities in a field, and therefore deserving of some respect on matters in that field, it is no good, when we have reason to question their pronouncement, appealing to the fact that they are authorities. The fact that I am an authority on philosophy may make it sensible for you to listen to me, but it can never be what makes what I say true, assuming it to be true. Besides, in this particular case, the presumption that certain individuals or written records are authoritative is circular. It is obviously absurd to cite the testimony of Christ or the Bible as proof of the validity of the Christian faith, for they could only be authoritative on the assumption that what is being questioned was true.

The ontological argument is based upon the assumption that God, if he exists, is a being than which no greater being can be conceived. But, it is then said, an actually existing instance of anything is bound to be greater than the mere idea of the same thing. Therefore existence is a necessary feature of the concept of God (because an actual being would be greater than an imaginary being, and God is supposed to be the greatest conceivable being). Therefore, it is concluded, God exists. There are those who still believe that some variant of this argument can be made to hold water. I think it probably fair to say that the majority of those who have considered it carefully doubt if it can even be made to make sense. One might question what is meant here by "being greater", and one might argue that existence is not a property of people or

things and therefore cannot be predicated of them in the way the
argument demands. One might also question whether, even
ignoring those telling objections, the argument shows what it is
supposed to show. Does it show that God exists or that those who
entertain the idea of God or believe in him must presume he
exists, if they believe him to be the greatest of beings? In my view
it shows only the latter.

There is the argument that *everything must have a cause* and that
therefore there must be a first cause of everything, which is to say
God, but this is vulnerable on three counts. Firstly, it is questionable whether the premise that everything must have a cause is
true. Secondly, if we assume it is and therefore seek a first cause,
we are being inconsistent, for what would be meant by a first cause
here is an uncaused cause, which there cannot be according to our
premises. Thirdly, as with the argument from design, at best this
argument would give us a first principle without any attributes. To
establish a first cause, if one could, is light years away from
establishing a first cause that should be worshipped.

There is, finally, the possibility of saying that recognition that
God exists is not a matter to be proven or demonstrated, but a
matter of personal insight or private *intuition*. It is something that
one just senses or sees with one's mind's eye, analogously to the
way in which some people just do scent the roses or see yellow,
while others do not. It is certainly possible that this is so, nonetheless the cases are not analogous in one vital respect. It is not the
fact that some people scent roses or see yellow that alone
establishes the truth of the matter. On the contrary, it is because
the experience of most people and more rigorous tests show that
roses have a scent and that some things are yellow, that we trust
people's sight and sense of smell. We classify as colour-blind those
who fail to meet the requirements of those other tests and
experiences. In the same way, if "God exists" does have a clear
descriptive meaning, it is conceivable that it is true that he exists
and that certain people are able to sense this. But the fact that
some people sense it cannot itself be used as evidence or proof.
After all, plenty of people sense or intuit things that can be shown
to be meaningless or false. So, if it is the case that the existence of
God is a matter for personal revelation, that is tantamount to
conceding the point that there are not in fact any arguments that
establish the truth of the claim that God exists.

The above paragraphs merely sketch points and arguments that
deserve considerably more attention. Even if valid, they would not
in any case establish that there is no God, or that religious
discourse is meaningless. One might, for instance, argue very

plausibly, with A. J. Ayer, that though fundamental religious utterances (such as "God exists") lack any descriptive meaning, and are therefore in one sense of the word literally nonsensical, they nonetheless have emotive meaning and may serve a variety of purposes.[2] One particular point, well-made by Ayer, is that his account of the nature of religious language coincides with the view of many believers, for they say that the nature of God is a mystery which transcends human understanding. "But to say that something transcends the human understanding is to say that it is unintelligible."[3] To say that belief in God is a matter of faith is to say that it is not a demonstrable truth. What the above paragraphs do establish is that religions (of the sort we are concerned with) are based upon utterances which, if they are propositions with intelligible meaning at all, are unprovable.

3 RELIGIOUS EDUCATION

It follows directly from the nature of religious discourse that, if schools attempt to initiate children into a particular religion, if, that is to say, they take particular steps with the intention of committing children to a set of beliefs, they are guilty of indoctrination. For we have defined indoctrination as the intentional implanting of belief so that it will stick, by non-rational means. [See above Chapter Two.] Since the basic propositions of religion are unprovable, there are no rational means of establishing their truth, and any success in evoking permanent commitment to them must rely on non-rational means. To demand that children should take part in religious services and assemblies as many schools do, though this is not in itself to indoctrinate, is to introduce non-rational means of persuasion which may contribute to indoctrination. Similarly, to conduct bible classes or religious instruction lessons, even if they do not overtly assert the religious truths in question, may serve as a means to indoctrination, by taking it for granted that the religious subject matter is straightforwardly factual. Whereas the only certain fact in all this is that, if schools attempt to send their children out into the world with religious commitment, they are indoctrinating, and that, being anti-educational, is quite unacceptable.

This firm conclusion, which incidentally means that many schools are in fact guilty of indoctrination, does not mean that there can be no place for religion in schools. It is entirely in order to study religions or a particular religion, perhaps historically or merely with a view to learning more about them, considered in isolation. But important as the phenomenon of religion has been and is, it is not self-evident that this study should be guaranteed core curriculum time (as it alone has enjoyed, by legal statute, in Britain up to this time). It might for instance be regarded as quite satisfactory to include reference to religious matters in the wider context of historical study. But whatever the precise details (and I really don't think they matter very much), the important point is that imposing a long-overdue ban on the practice of teaching religion, should not be confused with an attempt to prevent teaching about religion.

Parents of a religious persuasion may feel that the argument puts them in a difficult position. Perhaps it does, but not in an impossible one. Obviously, they too would be guilty of indoctrination, if they attempted to commit their children to belief in their religion. But the objections to indoctrination cannot be taken so far as to impose restrictions on people's own beliefs and practices. Religious parents will, and have every right to, live their own lives according to their religious beliefs. Their example is bound to have some influence on their children (though only a fool would predict what direction such influence will have). But here we see the importance both of clear conceptions and of using words with a degree of specificity and consistency. Influence, which in this case happens to be unavoidable, is to be distinguished from indoctrination, which is not. And the difference lies in the fact that the latter involves a deliberate attempt to ensure commitment to beliefs.

A final question worth raising in this context, and one that usefully looks forward to the second half of this chapter, is whether practices such as saluting the flag at school assembly and other patriotic rituals, or even activities designed to foster school spirit and loyalty, are open to the same objection as religious assemblies as a part of schooling. If such activities are designed as part of a deliberate attempt to foster commitment to a set of beliefs based on propositions such as "America is the best country in the world" or "Australia can do no wrong", then it is at least arguable that they too should be banned from schools, on the same grounds that they are being used as a means to indoctrination. For, as we shall see, it is at least arguable that moral and political utterances such as these are, like religious utterances, unprovable propositions. In which case the only conceivable defence for patriotic rather than religious rituals would have to be one based on claims about the greater utility or practical importance of the former. (We have already suggested that there are no grounds for asserting that people need religious belief in order to be good. One might rather more convincingly argue that people have to have some moral beliefs, if society is going to survive.) But in fact it is doubtful that flag-saluting ceremonies and the like are designed to function quite like that. It is not so much belief in particular propositions that is being fostered, as attitudes. The important thing is not that citizens shall subscribe to the belief that Britain can do no wrong, but that they will stand loyal to Britain's way of life. Whatever is to be said for or against the cultivation of patriotic feelings such as this, it does seem to be distinct from the cultivation of belief that is an integral part of religious worship.

4 MORALITY AND NATURE

So far I have argued that there is no good reason to teach morality through religion and that there is good reason for not teaching religion, unless we mean by that teaching about religion. In this section I want to examine the long tradition that sees nature and morality as inextricably interwoven, and which therefore sees moral upbringing as in one sense or another a natural business. On this view morality is not something that you could or should inculcate into children, nor something to be taught as one might teach the ten commandments or biblical lessons. Rather the child should be free to develop naturally. Rules of conduct and values that the child is to adopt must be discovered and decided by him in a natural environment.

One species of the "according to nature" genus is what I shall term the *naturalistic view*. This itself may take different forms depending on what sense of the word "natural" is intended, but what characterises any naturalistic view is the assumption that what is good is whatever is natural. That is to say, this kind of view argues that by definition it is naturalness that makes things good, just as it is the lack of wives that makes men bachelors. There is one sense of "natural" that makes this thesis undeniably true. Sometimes the word "natural" is used to mean "fitting" or "right and proper", and obviously, in that sense of the word, it is true that whatever is natural is good. It is in fact a tautology. But it isn't of much use, for it takes us no nearer to determining what conduct is good or natural in this sense. To argue that homosexuality is unnatural and therefore bad, for example, would in this case be to beg the question. More informative would be a naturalistic theory that took "natural" to mean something like "spontaneous", so that the claim would be "whatever happens spontaneously is good". But this is immediately seen to be implausible. Beating somebody up spontaneously isn't good. Aggression and competitiveness, if good at all, are not good because they are spontaneous. So, whatever value spontaneity may have, it is clear that it is not a necessary and sufficient condition of moral goodness, and people are not being good whenever they do their own thing. Similarly, the view that natural behaviour in the sense of a pre-civilised non-urban kind of behaviour is the hallmark of goodness is to be rejected. Here we have the additional problem of determining what such behaviour would be like. John Locke pictured natural man, in this sense, as being gentle and cooperative, while Thomas Hobbes imagined that such a life would be brutish, nasty and short.[4] But even supposing we could settle that problem, there is no plausibility in the claim that, being natural, such a way of life is *ipso facto* good.

Here we hit upon the fundamental weakness of any naturalistic theory. A naturalistic theory is one that proceeds by identifying some actual fact about the world, some natural phenomenon (in one sense of "natural" or another) and promotes it as the standard or the defining characteristic of goodness and right. It is a game as old as the hills, and typically (but not invariably) it has been used to defend the thesis that might is right. As long ago as the fifth century BC a character named Callicles was arguing that the fact that some men are stronger than others by nature justifies them in controlling the world—an argument subsequently used explicitly by Hitler and implicitly by numerous other thugs and tyrants.[5] But it might be used in respect of any values; all that is required is that somebody should see them as natural. Some have presumed that the course of evolution, being natural, must be regarded as progress towards perfection. Many people, consciously or otherwise, assume that since man is by nature rational, rationality must be a good thing. The fundamental trouble with all such views is not that the argument is weak or fallacious, so much as that there doesn't appear to be an argument at all! One moment we are talking about what is the case (*x* is natural) and the next about what ought to be the case (*x* is good). But this simply will not do. As David Hume so excellently put it:

In every system of morality which I have hitherto met with, I have always remarked that the author proceeds for some time in the ordinary way of reasoning . . . and makes observations concerning human affairs; when of a sudden I am surprised to find that instead of the usual copulation of propositions, is and is not, I meet with no proposition that is not connected with an ought or ought not. The change is imperceptible; but it is however of the last consequence. For as this ought or ought not expresses some new relation or affirmation, 'tis necessary that it should be observed and explained—and at the same time that a reason should be given for what seems altogether inconceivable, how this new relation can be a deduction from others which are entirely different from it.

To put it less elegantly but more directly: what is the link between the is and the ought? How is the move made from one kind of utterance (descriptive) to another (evaluative)? And to answer that question equally directly: there can be no ought from an is, meaning that the mere fact that something is the case cannot alone determine that it ought to be the case. That is obviously correct. The important questions to ask of any version of the naturalistic theory (apart from the tautological one) are: what sense of natural is intended here? Why pick out this aspect of natural behaviour, in your sense, rather than any other? (Or, how do you know that this behaviour is the only natural behaviour?) But above all, how does one move from the admission that *x* is natural, in any sense, to the conclusion that it ought to persist and is good?

It is clear, I think, that naturalistic theories give us no help. What about what I term *the optimistic thesis*? According to this, there is no problem of moral upbringing for us to worry about; there is no need for us to determine what is good and steer children towards it, because children will of their own accord adopt morally acceptable values and patterns of behaviour. Morality is not to be defined in terms of nature, but it does come naturally to people. A. S. Neill was a proponent of this view, as can be seen from this quotation:

> One should not attempt to hasten the development of a youngster's moral sense. The parent must exercise patience, secure in the thought that the child has been born good, and that he will inevitably turn out to be a good human being, if he is not crippled and thwarted in his natural development by interference. There is no need whatsoever to teach children how to behave. A child will learn what is right and what is wrong in good time—provided he is not pressured.[7]

This passage gives rise to a number of points of interest. First, how Neill or anyone else can be certain that the child is born good is a bit of a mystery. Indeed it is not clear what it means, since it is not clear what is involved in being born good, and what kind of evidence would be appropriate to determining the matter one way or the other. But there are certain observations that we can make. There is no obvious reason to accept an analogy with plant life, such that, as the acorn's natural course of development is into the oak tree, so the human baby has a natural course of development into a particular kind of adult. There is no obvious reason to accept that within the new-born baby is the potentiality of being a particular end product. The analogy between plant life and human physical development is one thing, but the idea that there must be a similar spiritual progression is quite gratuitous. Then there are, in any case, certain contradictions in Neill's claim. If the child is born good, why is it said that, given the right conditions, he will learn what is right? More seriously, if people are born good, it is logically impossible that evil should ever have arisen in the world. For, on this theory, evil arises out of corruption by others, but, if the theory is correct, there is no explanation of how corruption ever originated.

It has often been said that Neill didn't mean "born good" so much as "not born bad", and that his concern was to combat the effects of the doctrine of original sin. Thus what he really meant was that the child is not born in sin, but in a neutral state. This is probably what he did mean, but in that case there is no argument here at all, for to say that the child is born neither one thing nor the other is precisely to say that it depends upon what happens to it and how it reacts to its environment as it grows up, and it is therefore not true that a child will "inevitably" become one thing or another. Unless, that is to say, the thesis is quite specifically that as a matter of empirical fact all children unpressured in any way become good, while all others do not. But now that we have a clear thesis, its vulnerability is surely plain.

Firstly, there is a severe problem involved in what counts as pressure. Is setting an example to count as putting on pressure or interfering? Does reprimanding or giving encouragement constitute pressure? We would need to have a precise idea of how to interpret "interference" and "pressure" in order to put the policy into effect or to test it. Secondly, although it looks like a straight-forward empirical thesis, there is a large assumption built into it, namely that we agree on what constitutes good behaviour, for obviously the claim couldn't be made, let alone proved, without a clear idea of what good behaviour is, yet we know that people disagree on this matter. One would like at least to know what kind of behaviour Neill has in mind. And in the absence of that knowledge we can't judge the plausibility of his claims at all. Thirdly, even if we stipulate a meaning for "good behaviour", the sad truth is that we lack evidence, partly because there has been little or no research into the effects of this type of schooling on moral behaviour, and partly, which helps to account for the last point, because, as Neill recognises, there are no completely free children, and therefore the thesis could never be properly tested. (It would be fallacious to assume that it follows from Neill's premise that complete absence of interference is good, even if true, that little interference is better than more interference. For from the fact that no restraint has a certain effect, it obviously doesn't follow that a little restraint has nearly the same effect.)

We have varying views as to what constitutes good behaviour. We have next to no evidence about what would happen if we took Neill seriously, even if we knew what taking him seriously would involve and could do it. As far as I know, we have no evidence that a large lack of active interest (which reading both the lines and between the lines of his published statements seems to be what Neill means by "no interference") is necessarily more likely to produce any particular type of good behaviour than a fair amount of active interest (interference). We do, on the other hand, certainly have some evidence that interference can produce what some would regard as good behaviour—namely several generations of traditional upbringing. All in all, the optimistic theory seems to boil down to little more than a hunch to the effect that left more to their own devices, children would be more likely to develop in certain ways that are unspecified but seem good to Neill. It is a hunch no more and no less inspired, plausible or verifiable, than William Golding's contrary hunch in *Lord of the Flies* to the effect that, left alone, children will turn into savages.

This leaves us with the *individualistic thesis*. This is the view not that, if I spontaneously choose to do something, it is *ipso facto* good (a species of the naturalistic view), not that, if left alone, I am bound to choose good (the optimistic view), but that it is morally right in itself that the child, as he grows, should be free to make up his own mind on what is good. The view that he should do what comes naturally to him, rather than be taught, influenced or cajoled, not because what comes naturally is necessarily right, but because it is a necessary condition of being right, and because for us to interfere with others must in itself be morally wrong. This thesis opens up a completely new range of questions, and, before we examine it, a detour is needed to look into the question of whether moral knowledge is a possibility.

5 Can there be Moral Knowledge?

Can we know what is morally good? The question is not intended as an empirical one ("Do you think there's any chance we might know by the end of the year?"), but as a logical one ("Does it make sense to talk in terms of knowing in this domain?"). The answer therefore depends on a view of what constitutes knowing and a view of what constitutes morality.

What is involved in knowing something? What does it mean to say that somebody knows that *x*, rather than that he believes, claims or guesses that *x*? There seem to be three necessary and, taken together, sufficient conditions: one must believe that *x*, it must be true that *x* and one must have adequate evidence that *x*.

It is very important to appreciate that we are here talking about meaning and meaning only. We are not for instance talking about possible sources of knowledge (e.g. can I trust my eyes?), nor about whether one can be sure that one does in fact know something. We are asking only whether, if somebody does know something, it would be the same thing to say that he believes and has adequate evidence for a particular true proposition. Clearly, one must believe. "I know he's at home, but I don't believe he's at home" is contradictory. Equally obviously that is not enough. Belief and knowledge need to be distinguished; to know is not simply to believe. A crucial difference is that what you know must be true, which is not the case with belief. I can believe that Richard Nixon is President but, precisely because he is not, I cannot know it. Once again we have an obviously necessary condition. But then, surely to believe what happens to be true is not in itself to know. If I, sitting in Leicester, England, guess or believe that Michigan State University have won the Rose Bowl, and then it is announced on the BBC that they have, we don't assume that I knew it. What converts true belief into knowledge is the third criterion of adequate evidence. At the time I first said it, I did not know Michigan State University had won, even though they had. Now that the BBC (that paragon of reliable evidence!) has announced it, I have adequate evidence and I know it. We say a person knows that Jack the Ripper was a member of the Royal household or that Sacco and Vanzetti were innocent, iff he believes it and has adequate evidence to support or reveal its truth. Otherwise we have to say something like "he conjectures", "he believes it" or, perhaps, "it's true, but he can't be sure of it."

That is what to know means. Now it is at once apparent that if that is what it means, people often make claims to know something which strictly speaking they do not know, because they lack adequate evidence. I may, for example, talk of knowing that my best friend didn't commit a particular crime, when I might more accurately have said I simply do not believe it. [The sense of know outlined here is sometimes called a weak sense, to contrast it with a strong sense in which knowing means believing what is true and having sufficient rather than merely adequate evidence. But the weak sense will suffice for our purposes in this chapter, despite the fact that philosophers are traditionally interested in gaining knowledge in the strong sense, i.e. in the sense of acquiring beliefs which without a shadow of a doubt will not prove false.] Nonetheless, equally clearly, we can reasonably claim to know quite a lot: two times two equals four, I am scratching away with my pen, my neighbour is mowing his grass, the sun is more than ninety million miles away, Henry II was king of England, etc. We may conceivably be mistaken in some claims to knowledge like these, but it is not an obvious misuse of language to make the claims. To say "I know that two times two equals four" is to talk sense. And the reason why it obviously makes sense is that there is no dispute about the nature of the sort of evidence appropriate to the claim. Conceivably, I may be mistaken in my claim to know that Elvis Presley died on August 16th 1977, but it is nonetheless correct to talk of knowledge rather than opinion or guessing, because I have the sort of evidence that would be agreed to be relevant and adequate. (Newspaper clippings of the time, memory of the event, agreement of others, notes on record sleeves released subsequently, references in books, official records, etc.)

Everybody is familiar with the quite frequent need to check out claims to knowledge in the sense of checking that the evidence somebody appeals to is indeed adequate. (e.g. Do we know that Lamarckian evolutionary theory about inherited characteristics is false? is the evidence adequate to invalidate the hypothesis? Do we know that the roof is secure or are we just assuming it is?) But what is of importance to us, in the context of this chapter, is the fact that in some areas we do not merely have to check that the evidence is adequate—we have no agreement as to what kind of evidence would be appropriate. One example of such an area we have already met in religion. The point is not that believers say there is design in the world or there isn't any evil, while nonbelievers say the opposite; usually all are agreed on the facts of the matter, but are in considerable disagreement as to which are relevant. When you say to me "You are incorrect in saying that religion is dead in this town, there are eight thousand regular worshippers", on the face of it the evidence forces me to change my view. I can hardly claim not to see the relevance of the point you make. But when you say "The fact that there is no sickness in this town of believers shows that God exists", it is quite open to argument as to whether I should accept the evidence alluded to as relevant.

It is fairly clear that morality is in much the same boat as religion. Moral disagreements do not only arise out of different accounts of the evidence (e.g. disagreement about whether a particular policy will or will not make people happy), but also out of wildly different views as to what constitutes the relevant sort of evidence. Take, for example, an issue like abortion. There are some matters of fact here that may be disputed, but it would be quite conceivable that twenty people should agree to all the following claims: legalising abortion will increase the number of abortions, will bring foreigners into the country for the sake of having abortions, will diminish the number of unwanted children, involves taking human life, gives the mother a right to decide and will minimise suffering. But even if they did accept all those points, the problem remains; for they may all disagree as to which of those points counts as relevant to determining what ought to happen.

The problem in a nutshell is this. If moral knowledge (as opposed to moral opinion, moral belief, etc.) is to be possible, then, given what "to know" means, it must be possible to discern adequate evidence for moral claims. But it seems that it is not possible to discern adequate evidence for fundamental or basic moral principles (if it were we would not have the disagreements we do), and that suggests that moral knowledge is not possible. What is the true state of affairs here? Is it possible to know what is good?

Let us now look at the various attempts that have been made to answer that question. Firstly, there are three views that seek to reduce the matter from its apparent mystery to simple fact. The *naïve conventionalist view*, according to which what is good is a matter of what the majority believe; *the subjectivist view*, according to which good is to be identified with the preferences of the agent; and the *cultural-relativist view* which identifies it with the *mores* of a society. It should be admitted at once that each of these views may contain a grain of truth at the level of incidental comment. It is, for instance, obviously true that very often we regard things as good, if we approve of them. But that is different from suggesting that "a good act" simply means, or is, "one that I approve of", which is plainly false. What is wrong with each of these views is that, being over-simple, it flies in the face of crucial aspects of what we understand by moral goodness. You and I may flatly disagree about what behaviour is good, but we both know perfectly well that it is not something to be determined solely by majority opinion. Capital punishment doesn't become morally right as soon as an opinion poll shows a majority in favour of it. "Goodness" just doesn't mean "what the majority approves". So even if the majority in our society had a coherent non-contradictory view, which manifestly it doesn't, the naïve conventionalist view would be untenable.

The subjectivist is one who says that moral terms like "good" mean "approved of by me". A moment's reflection shows that this too is not true. It may be the case that I am only prepared to rate what I approve of as good, but, even were that so, that clearly wouldn't be what I meant by calling something "good". If I did simply mean that, argument with others would be senseless, for there is no real disagreement involved in your saying "War is approved of by me" (i.e. "War is good") and my saying "War is not approved of by me" (i.e. "War is bad"). Another consequence of this view is that there would be no appreciable difference between "I approve of girls in short dresses" and "Kindness is good" (which would be equivalent to "I approve of kindness"), but that kind of distinction is an integral part of our moral understanding. Thirdly, it would be self-contradictory to say "I approve of cheating the tax-man, but I know it's wrong", but, whatever our views about making such a remark may be, it is not self-contradictory. All these conclusions are unacceptable to common sense and therefore the subjectivist view has to be rejected as providing an inadequate account of our moral sense.

The same arguments count against the cultural-relativist position. Of course different cultures have different values, but that does not show that a moral value is just a cultural value, and in fact our normal presumption is the very opposite. The fact that Frenchmen tend to drink a lot of wine with their meals is a cultural difference between them and us, and as such is quite distinct from a moral difference, such as would arise if they started putting people in concentration camps. So the suggestion that moral utterances are really just ways of saying "My country does this", and are hence straightforwardly factual, won't do at all. The truth is that, whether we are correct or incorrect, and whether or not we can prove it, we mean by the remark "It's morally good" something about it independent of subjective or cultural conditions. A more coherent position would be that of the *nihilist*, who does not misleadingly say that we mean by moral utterances things we patently do not mean, but who says "Never mind what you mean, I can't take this moral business seriously. I'm just not moved to try and be moral." The trouble with that view for most of us (perhaps fortunately) is that, however feebly, we *are* moved to try and be moral. We do believe in it.

Another attempt to explain what is going on when we make moral utterances worth noting is the *emotivist view*, which sidesteps the problem of whether we can know moral truths or not by asserting that moral utterances are not capable of being true or false, but are literally nonsense, and therefore the question of knowledge does not arise. In saying they are nonsense, it is not denied that they have a function or serve a purpose, but it is suggested that there is no content, no message, no proposition that can be true or false. [See above, for a similar account of religious discourse, Section 2.] Rather, utterances of the form "Kindness is good", though they look like descriptive statements attributing some property to something (on the model of "John is black"), are in fact merely ways of evincing the speaker's attitude. Thus "Kindness is good" should be construed as equivalent to "Kindness, hurrah!". Note that this is distinct from subjectivism, which claims that "This is good" means "I approve of this", for emotivism claims that to say it is to express one's enthusiasm or approval for *x*. The former leaves some room for questions about truth or falsehood (e.g. are you sincere when you say "I approve of this" or is it a lie?), while the latter does not. This is a neat and tidy theory that would certainly settle the problem of moral knowledge. Unfortunately, at any rate in this stark form, it won't do. For once again the account doesn't square with what you and I actually understand by morality. When I say that torture is wrong I do not just mean "Torture, ugh!". In particular, saying "Torture is wrong" is quite different from saying "Fish, ugh!" when served fish at a dinner party; yet on the simplistic account of emotivism given these very different utterances would have to be regarded as logically indistinguishable, so that my comments on torture and fish would be the same in kind, which they are obviously not. In the second place, on this view (just as on the subjectivist view) it would make no sense to say "I like committing adultery, but it is morally wrong", for that would mean "I like committing adultery; committing adultery, ugh!", which looks as near to a contradictory utterance as one could get. But the remark is not contradictory and it does make sense.

More promising is the *intuitionist view*. According to this view goodness is something that you intuitively recognise when you come across it, just as yellowness is something you see when you come face to face with it. There are no tests employable to prove that it is there; you either see it or you don't. Those who don't see it are morally blind, just as those who can't see yellow are colour blind. According to some intuitionist philosophers goodness alone is intuited and the rightness or wrongness of acts must then be calculated. Thus one intuits that, say, friendship and beauty are good, and one works out that it would be right to behave in certain ways and do certain things because they promote or enhance friendship or beauty. According to others, one has to intuit rights as well. W. D. Ross posits a network of what he calls *prima facie* duties (such as helping people in trouble or keeping promises), which is to say things one intuitively recognises as one's duties, other things being equal.[8] When these *prima facie* duties clash, as they frequently may, what one should then do is known as one's actual duty, and that too has to be intuitively recognised. This view asserts in effect that there are moral truths and that they can be known, but suggests that they are of a unique kind and have to be discerned by intuition, rather than by sifting empirical evidence.

The trouble with the intuitionist view, though it may be correct, is that there is no way of showing that it is. *Ex hypothesi* the only way of knowing whether something is good is by intuition, so there is no way of checking the hypothesis that what is intuited is really a property of the thing in question rather than just a fancy of the agent. Furthermore intuitions notoriously differ. How are we to determine whose intuition to trust? Strictly speaking you cannot know something by intuition, for "intuition" is little more than a dignified term for an accurate guess. One may hit upon the truth by intuition, but that accurate guess only becomes knowledge, as opposed to true belief, when supporting evidence is produced. So there may be moral truths, we may have to rely on intuition to discern them, but, if that is so, we must concede the impossibility of moral knowledge.

At this point let us concede that we are no nearer establishing that moral knowledge is possible, and return to the individualistic thesis we left hanging in the air at the end of the previous section.

6 The Individualistic Thesis

The essence of the *individualistic thesis* is that each individual ought to be free to make up his own mind on moral matters, regardless of who or what he is, and that the matter must therefore be left to nature rather than schooling.

The view gains whatever plausibility it has from the prior claim we have just considered, that moral utterances are not as other statements in that they cannot be known to be true or false. A proposition like "Stealing is wrong" is crucially different from a proposition like "George Gissing wrote *New Grub Street*." So, while nobody in his right mind would suggest that every individual should decide for himself whether or not Gissing wrote *New Grub Street*, it is rather different in the other case. (It might be suggested that the child should find out for himself or be given relevant evidence rather than be told that Gissing wrote *New Grub Street*. It is also conceivable that someone might look into the evidence and discover that he didn't write it. But such suggestions are quite different. Finding out for oneself is not the same thing as deciding for oneself. To come to a conclusion about the authorship of *New Grub Street* would only count or be regarded as acceptable, if the individual established the conclusion via evidence agreed to be relevant. Just to think that Gissing didn't write it isn't good enough. With regard to such a statement, then, it is simply grotesque to suggest that people should make up their own minds as to its truth or falsity, if that means that they should ignore arguments and evidence that just are relevant to determining the matter.) What needs to be considered here is whether the admission that "Stealing is wrong" does not parallel "George Gissing wrote *New Grub Street*", and the admission that it is not known to be true and that there is not full agreement on what would count as evidence, leads to the conclusion that we ought to take the individualistic view.

The argument appears to be as follows. It must be wrong to teach as true, propositions, such as moral propositions, which are not known to be true. It must be wrong to get people to believe that one ought to be kind and suchlike, since it is not known to be true that one ought, and indeed it is conceivable that it is not true. The matter therefore exactly parallels religion.

Two points strike one. The first is that in principle the argument is a good one. We cannot approve of a situation where people falsely assume that what is in fact not known to be true is unquestionably true. There is something repugnant about people unquestioningly assuming the rectitude of their moral beliefs (whatever they are) and looking down on or deploring those who do not share them. This is different from scientists deploring those who make ignorant and mistaken scientific claims. To seek to impose unquestioning belief in the moral domain would be to indoctrinate, and those who value truth cannot approve of the manifest error involved in assuming that one's moral position is unquestionably correct. But the second point is that what is demanded, if we follow the logic of the argument, is not that people should make up their own minds as chance will have it or circumstances (nature) randomly dictate, but that they should come to have a proper understanding of the status of moral utterances. It is not, for instance, any better that people should come to assume unquestionably that the basic moral axioms of their society are untrue, or that they are just emotive utterances, or that they are just cultural norms, for, as we have seen in the previous section, none of these doctrines are known to be true either (and in fact they look very unconvincing). The argument demands that people should appreciate what in fact appears to be the case—namely that we do not know whether propositions such as "One ought to be kind" are true or false in some objective sense, or whether they ought to be regarded as meaningful propositions at all. All that the apparent impossibility of moral knowledge implies is that to teach people that such and such is unquestionably good would be to teach them to parrot falsehood. It does not imply that it is necessarily objectionable to guide and influence children in a variety of ways, provided that they ultimately come to understand the nature of moral discourse, the topic to which we must now turn. [On the question of guidance and influence, see below Section 8.]

7 THE NATURE OF MORAL DISCOURSE

It follows from what has been said that gaining understanding of the moral sphere will not consist in learning a list of truths. Rather it will involve coming to appreciate something of the way in which moral discourse works, and something of the nature of the moral sphere.

Let us look first at the meaning of key terms such as "good" and the way in which moral talk functions, picking up some of the points already made in this chapter. There is a tendency to assume that goodness must be some kind of definable property or quality, and that it must in principle be possible to explain what goodness consists in, as one can explain that triangularity consists in having three sides. But this might not be the case. One cannot offer that kind of a definition of yellow, for instance. You can say things about it (e.g. give a scientific account of light rays or point out examples), but you cannot give a verbal equivalent or a synonymous phrase. Yellow is yellow, and the only way to introduce somebody to the idea of yellow for the first time is to show him something yellow. In point of fact it is far more plausible to suggest that good is like yellow than that it is like triangularity, and to argue that it is, as G. E. Moore put it, a unique unanalysable quality.[9] Certainly, attempts to define it in terms of some other quality or qualities, such as pleasure or God, are not convincing. If "good" meant "conducive to pleasure", then it would not make sense to say "I think that this is conducive to pleasure, but it is not good", or, if it meant "pleasing to God", it would not make sense to say "Vengeance is pleasing to God, but in my view immoral", yet these kinds of remark do seem to make sense, and indeed, of any proposed definition of goodness (call it x), it always seems to make sense to say "I know that this is x, but is it good?"

[The above form of argument is known as the *open-question argument*, and the mistake of attempting to define goodness in terms of some other quality is known as the *naturalistic fallacy*. It should perhaps be said that the argument is not as much of a knock-out as is often supposed. It is conceivable that it is our prejudice and ignorance that makes us think it makes sense to say "I know that this is X, but is it good?" in all cases, whereas in fact there might be one case in which it does not hold, and that case would give us the true definition. The open-question argument relies heavily on ordinary language as the arbiter of sense, and as such I mistrust it. But I do believe it to be the case that goodness is a unique unanalysable quality, and that to say that something is good is not a way of saying something that we could say in another way such as "This tickles me", "This pleases me" or "This pleases God". While we are in parentheses, I should also point out that we are arguing about whether good could be said to mean something like "conducive to pleasure", which is quite different from arguing about whether being conducive to pleasure is a good thing. This is important to me, since I believe that pleasure and pleasure alone is good in itself, but that does not mean that I think goodness is to be defined in terms of pleasure. In exactly the same way a man might say "As far as I'm concerned golf is the only likeable thing in the world", but that would not mean that he defined "likeable" in terms of "golf".]

Good cannot be defined or identified with anything. It has no synonym. As Moore put it: ". . . if I am asked how is good to be defined, my answer is that it cannot be defined and that is all I have to say about it."[10] So in one sense of "meaning", it has no meaning, but of course it has meaning in other senses. In particular it has a function. Its most obvious function is *to commend*, and to this extent the subjectivist was correct, for part of what is going on when someone says "This is good" is that he commends or indicates approval, but only part. What we need to consider is what else is involved in calling something "morally good". Well, surely the emotivists also had a point: saying "This is good" is not only a way of saying that I approve, but also in itself a way of expressing or *evincing* that *approval*. If I really think kindness is good (in other words provided I am being sincere and am not just saying it or meaning to say that it is generally thought to be good) then part of what you know about me is that I'm for it. I've given myself away; I've evinced my attitude. Subsequent

166 The Philosophy of Schooling

developments in emotivism, particularly through the work of Stevenson, put stress on another feature of moral language, namely its *persuasive force*.[11] This too seems an important point. When I say "Ice-cream, hurrah!" I evince my attitude, but when I say "Kindness is morally good" I do more; I clearly hope thereby to enlist you on my side. Here, it must be repeated, we are not dealing with empirical claims or generalisations. We are not saying that generally people use moral terms in this way for these purposes (though that might be true), but arguing that such is the logic of moral terms that it has to be this way; it doesn't make sense to think that kindness is good and yet not to care what other people think about it. Wanting other people to share one's views is part of the logic of moral, as opposed to other kinds of, views.

Similar to persuasive meaning is *prescriptive meaning*, a feature of moral language most notably advertised by R. M. Hare.[12] While Stevenson had argued that moral discourse is essentially designed in its logic to persuade, Hare sees it as being to prescribe or to demand something of one. He argues that all moral utterances are disguised imperatives. "You ought to do this" is a way of saying "Do this". "This is good" is a way of saying "This is a must be done thing. Do it." It follows that, if one sincerely thinks that a particular course of action is good, and if one is in a position to carry it out, one will. Conversely, failure to act in accordance with one's stated moral beliefs, where one could, indicates a degree of insincerity. Now to say that moral utterances merely persuade won't do. If that were true, successful propaganda would be a fine instance of moral discourse, which it is not, and discussion between people whose views are known to be similar would be pointless, which it certainly isn't. Similarly it cannot be that moral discourse is just prescriptive, for then moral utterances would be indistinguishable from any command to which one was sincerely committed. My willingness to act on the maxim "Jews should be killed" would make it moral, which is surely ridiculous. Nonetheless these surely are amongst the features belonging to moral discourse: it is inherently concerned to persuade and prescribe.

One other feature of moral discourse is recognised by Hare himself. This is that even particular judgements (e.g. "You ought to do this now"), if they are moral, imply a *universal judgement*. That is to say that, if it is your moral duty to do this now, then it must be that anyone else placed in a similar situation ought likewise to do it. "Love thy neighbour" issued as a one-off command akin to "Close the door" carries no implications what-soever for anyone other than the person addressed. But "Love thy neighbour" intended as a moral injunction must carry the implication that everyone, the speaker included, should exhibit such love. As with all the other features we have uncovered, this is not in itself a sufficient condition of morality (and it isn't unique to morality), but it surely is a necessary feature. If you say that abortion is wrong, and are then seen acting as if you believed otherwise when it comes to your own daughter, then you are inconsistent and hence failing in moral good faith or integrity. (What you do may be explicable, what you said may have been sincerely intended, but the fact is that, if in the event you act as if abortion is all right for your family but not for others, without further explanation, your position cannot be a truly moral one.)

Moral discourse then has certain essential features that mark it out from other kinds of discourse, particularly descriptive discourse, and talking moral sense presupposes understanding those features. If we compare the descriptive proposition "Adultery is on the increase" with the moral utterance "Adultery is wrong", we see firstly, that the latter evinces the speaker's attitude, which the former does not (I can state the former fact without revealing anything of what I think about it; whereas if I opine that it is wrong, you know that I don't glory in it, even if, through weakness of will, I do it.) Secondly and thirdly the latter necessarily both seeks to persuade and prescribes, while the former does not. It simply doesn't make sense to assume that in saying "Adultery is wrong" I care nothing about whether others share my view and see myself as laying no obligations on anybody. Fourthly, the latter implies obligation not just for me or whomsoever I'm addressing, but for anyone in like circumstances. Clearly this factor of universality does not even have application to the descriptive statement.

But although these features distinguish moral from descriptive statements and undoubtedly tell us something about what it is to say that something is good or to make a moral judgement, there is clearly something else going on as well; for, although we have agreed that it cannot be verbally defined, there can be no doubt that when we say that something is good we are saying something about it. We are attributing some quality, feature or property to it. If that is not admitted, quite apart from offending our common sense, we shall not have distinguished moral utterances from other kinds of value judgements, such as aesthetic ones. For to say that Picasso is frightful likewise involves evincing attitude, persuasion, prescription and universality. Wherein, then, lies the difference between "Picasso is frightful" and "Concentration camps are objectionable"? The answer is that, though the logic of the discourse in either case is the same, they are about different kinds of thing. Moral quality is distinct from aesthetic quality. Our final task therefore is to locate the particular nature of moral quality.

Morality, like football, art or indeed anything else, is something to be distinguished from other things, and that fact alone sets a limit to what can sensibly be done or said in its name. Even though we have conceded that there is not a set of known moral qualities that enable us to state categorically whether an act is moral or not, nonetheless there are limits set on what might conceivably count as morally good by the nature of the enterprise itself, by the name of the game. Thus, to illustrate first by an appropriate sporting analogy: football being what it is, though we may argue till late in the night about the advisability of changing a rule or the rival merits of one team over another, with no apparent way of settling our differences rationally, the question of whether the centre back was right to use a bat simply doesn't arise. Football being what it is, such a practice simply isn't permissible. Again, art being what it is (although this may be a more difficult matter to reach agreement on), the popularity of a painting is not in itself relevant to determining aesthetic merit. That is not just an opinion of mine. It is a matter of fact, and to suggest that popularity does make a painting good would be to redefine art. In exactly the same way, although morality is a complex and disputable concept to some extent, we can say straightaway, without fear of contradiction, that there are things that it, too, is clearly not about. Morality being what it is (even though sharpening up this concept is the very task we are engaged in), considerations of aesthetic merit are not directly relevant. The aesthetic improvement achieved by a policy of mass murder and slum clearance cannot be relevant to the question of its moral acceptability.

We could proceed at once with an attempt to define morality negatively (e.g. morality is not about aesthetics, popularity or success), and that might not be a bad exercise to perform when depressed by the seeming intractability of moral problems. But I shall try to give some indications of the nature of morality in positive terms.

What is morality about? [Note that the question pertains to morality as such, or to morality as a concept, rather than to particular moral codes or views. We are not asking, what do we thing should be done, but what makes a code a moral code as opposed to just a code of living.] First and fundamentally, morality is surely concerned with conduct amongst, and in relation to, sentient beings. Only beings with some degree of responsibility for their actions can behave on the moral plane, and questions of whether one has behaved morally to others can only arise in respect of animate beings. One may have moral responsibility to those who are not able to exercise moral choice themselves, such as children, the sick or certain animals.[13] But morality is not concerned with the behaviour of floods or behaviour towards bricks and mortar. The issue of the morality of an act only arises when sentient beings are affected by it. No moral problem arises directly from my planting a tree, but if the tree gets in your way there is the possibility of a moral dimension intruding. Any action that may affect other people to their advantage or disadvantage, may thereby give rise to moral questions. What that reveals is the important point that morality is fundamentally concerned with people's advantage or, as I prefer to term it, well-being. In and of itself, science has nothing to do with morality, but as soon as questions arise about its use and effects to the advantage or disadvantage of sentient beings, moral questions arise.

I am not trying to argue that one moral principle we should support is that of promoting people's well-being. I am saying something at once more far-reaching and simpler than that. I am saying that, although people may disagree and argue about what well-being is, about what does promote it, about whose well-being counts for most in a clash, about whether some people don't forfeit their right to it, and so on, morality is nonetheless about people's well-being as certainly as baseball is about making home runs. We would say of somebody from another planet or another culture who remarked "In our community we have no thought for anyone's well-being. We just have rules of conduct relating to the quality of grade people get in school, the number of children they have and the size of their bank balance", not that he holds different moral views to us, but that he doesn't hold a *moral* view at all. This code of conduct is not recognisably a moral code.

Secondly, there is an important point that the individualistic thesis may have recognised. Morality is logically tied up with some degree of freedom of choice. Truly moral conduct is not possible where there is no freedom (that is why it makes no sense to talk of sticks and stones being moral). If you do what you do, solely because you have a gun sticking in your back, or because you have been indoctrinated, or because it is all that you physically can do, then though what you do may be good, or right in our judgement, your behaviour is not truly moral behaviour, and you deserve no moral credit.

Thirdly, anything recognisable as moral behaviour, whether to be praised or condemned, would have to be impartial behaviour. [See above Chapter Three.] This follows directly from the point that moral discourse is universalisable; it is entailed by that consideration. For to say that truly moral maxims should apply equally to all persons in exactly similar circumstances, involves saying that relevant differences alone can justify different treatment or different responsibilities.

To summarise: although there will continue to be disagreement about specific moral claims (e.g. about the acceptability or otherwise of adultery, civil disobedience, abortion), it can be said firmly that anything that deserves to be taken seriously as a moral claim or demand must relate to welfare and freedom. To understand morality involves at least recognising that it is a domain characterised by prescriptive, persuasive, universalisable utterances ultimately related to choice, impartiality and well-being. We may disagree with the man who thinks that capital punishment ought to be practised, but provided he recognises that his position entails that he too should suffer the death penalty in certain circumstances, and provided he has a reason for believing such a practice to be in the interests of human well-being, his position is at least recognisable as a moral one. He is playing the same game. Furthermore and finally, any truly moral code would, by definition, have to involve reference to the principles of well-being, freedom and impartiality.

8 MORAL UPBRINGING

Now we can revert to the question of moral upbringing. Consider the options that appear to be closed to us. The use of religion as a means of moral instruction is unwarranted. Leaving the whole thing to chance, flatteringly renamed nature, is without justification. Implanting unquestioning allegiance to a set of fixed and specific rules (e.g. do this, don't do that) is also unacceptable, for that would amount to indoctrination. What is left open to us? Fortunately, the path that common sense has always insisted we should tread. For we can seek to habituate young children to certain ways of behaving and then, when they are older, try to provide them with the sort of understanding that has been delineated above. The former constitutes *moral training*, the latter *moral education*. But it is important that we should envisage both as taking place and together constituting moral upbringing, for the subsequent provision of moral education is our best guarantee that moral training will not degenerate into moral indoctrination.

It is noteworthy that most of the literature in the field of moral upbringing refers to "moral education" rather than "moral training". To some extent that may just reflect an inability to think of the distinction, but it may also reflect a quite widespread feeling that training is something to be embarrassed about. Education, as was pointed out above, is almost universally thought of as a good thing, even in situations such as that of the third world, where in fact other priorities might be considerably more important, while training is seen as inherently unattractive, belonging more to the Victorian era than to today. No doubt there is a relationship of some sort between this belief and recent fads for methods of bringing up babies that eschew all routine or anything that could be called toilet-training or feeding patterns. Whatever the merits of such particular practices, it is plainly wrong to treat training in all its manifestations as inherently objectionable. Training has an important part to play in schooling generally, sometimes as an end in itself, as with aspects of physical training, and sometimes as a means to further ends, as training in reading and writing skills is a necessary preliminary to further education. In the sphere of moral upbringing training is important both for its own sake and as a means to moral education. Socialisation demands a degree of moral training, which is to say familiarising children with the moral demands and expectations of society and habituating them to various practices, and moral education would be impossible with people who had no moral sense and no moral beliefs or attitudes in the first place.

As was hinted at the end of the last paragraph but one, some people seem to fear moral training on the grounds that it is tantamount to indoctrination. Stated like that the fear is misplaced. It is true that behaviour and beliefs are in practice bound to be related, and therefore getting young children to behave and act in certain ways must give rise to certain assumptions and beliefs on their part. But it is not the mere cultivation of beliefs, even by non-rational means, that constitutes indoctrination. It is the deliberate attempt to implant unquestioning commitment to beliefs, which need not have any part in early moral training, that is indoctrination. There is nothing wrong in itself with cultivating certain types of behaviour and thereby fostering certain assumptions. Indeed it is quite unavoidable, for children just do develop patterns of behaviour and assumptions in response to their surroundings (including the behaviour of adults). The only choice is between providing a planned and coherent environment and leaving it to chance. We have already seen that there is no reason to support the optimistic thesis (that things will turn out for the best, if we leave it to chance). Here I would only add that there is good reason to take positive steps and plan for the moral development of our children, because half the point of moral behaviour lies in its reciprocity. The exact nature of a rule is quite often less important from the moral point of view than that there should be a rule and a uniformity of expectation and behaviour. One culture's code of sexual practice is seldom, if ever, less moral than another's, but the interests of morality may well be served by a society having some kind of code universally accepted and acted on.

There is the problem here of whose moral values we should introduce children to, for within the parameters outlined, which limit the range of possible values, there is still room for divergence of opinion, and this will be all the more acutely felt in open and multi-cultural societies. Should this be a matter for individual parents to decide perhaps? Or for schools or individual teachers? Or should it be a matter for the state to decide? Surely, for reasons that mirror those given in arguing for a core curriculum, the answer must be that, whatever parents choose to do, schools should be expected to impart the broad assumptions and values of our society or the state as a whole. There is then the further question of whether a particular state has got it right; but the important point to recognise is that the objection to Soviet Russia, for example, is not that she initially develops a set of moral and political beliefs in the child, but that she does it in such a way and with such rigour as hopefully to ensure unquestioning commitment to those beliefs through later life (i.e. indoctrinates), and/or that what she implants may in some respects be objectionable. And we *are* entitled to make the latter claim, despite the relative openness of the moral domain, for certain values (impartiality, freedom and concern for all sentient beings' well-being) are, as we've seen, implicit in the nature of morality. Naturally, too, we would expect our own society to require only behaviour in accordance with such principles.

One important consequence of distinguishing firmly between moral training and moral education is that it enables us to appreciate that the practical difficulties in moral upbringing belong almost entirely to moral education. If one thinks of the wider business of moral upbringing, encompassing both training and education, there are indeed problems about how to be successful, how to avoid proceeding in a manner logically incompatible with the nature of morality, and how to organise whatever material is being used. But these problems are problems for moral education. Moral training, by which we mean causing children to adopt particular attitudes and types of behaviour such as telling the truth, being kind and keeping promises, is not a mysterious business. It does not require any fervid theorising, any large-scale empirical inquiry or any special programmes. We are already perfectly well aware that the way to carry out such training is to bring children up in an environment that exhibits such behaviour, expects such behaviour and praises such behaviour. This is not to say that success is guaranteed, or that more general considerations such as the desirability of a consistent and loving environment are not important. But it is to say that there is no mystery about the correct way in which to approach the matter. It is noteworthy that it is in this respect that comparative research such as that of Bronfenbrenner shows totalitarian states to be more effective than liberal democracies.[14] His study of groups of American and Russian children does not necessarily show that the latter were more successfully morally educated or even more moral in the full sense of the term. But it does show that the more uniform and persistent demand for certain types of behaviour results in better moral training, measured essentially in terms of social rather than anti-social behaviour.

Kohlberg and his associates have for many years now been refining a classificatory system of the stages through which individuals may pass on the path of moral development.[15] They pinpoint six stages, beginning with one classified as one of "obedience and punishment orientation", during which the individual can only see moral goodness in terms of consequences to himself. Stage two involves "naïvely egotistic orientation", which, as its name implies, means that the individual sees right actions in terms of self gratification. Stage three is classified as "good boy orientation", when the individual is moved by the desire to gain approval, and stage four, "authority and social-order maintaining orientation", marks a switch to concern for duty for duty's sake. Stage five, one of "contracted legalistic orientation", represents the tendency to view morality in terms of a set of mutual agreements, and stage six, "conscience or principle orientation", involves autonomous moral behaviour. The main points that Kohlberg wants to make are: that firstly, though no individual anywhere necessarily advances through all these stages, insofar as an individual does change his orientation then, in any culture, he will go through as many stages as he does in that order. (In other words, to be at stage four one must have passed through stages one, two and three, for example.) Secondly, that in order to encourage an individual to move from one stage to another, it is important to talk to him in terms of the stage immediately following his present one. Faced with a child who is intent on seeking approval, if you want to change his orientation, you must recognise the fact that he must next proceed to the stage of being authority orientated, and communicate with him in those terms rather than in terms of stage six or stage two.

The main value of Kohlberg's work (if we ignore possible criticisms is that it offers empirical confirmation in a particular sphere of the general point that, when bringing children up, it is important neither to talk above their heads nor to insult their intelligence, but rather to stop just slightly ahead of them, and that it offers, in the stages, some sort of guide as to what one step ahead involves in any particular case. Moral training will inevitably give rise to questions about why we should do this or that on the part of the children, and it will obviously be important to pitch one's answers at the right level.

As we move from training to education, the prime question becomes whether a particular programme of moral education is required (and if so what sort) to help encourage the understanding that is the object of the exercise. Opinions diverge widely on this issue, ranging from the view that we shouldn't do anything in particular, since opportunities for dealing with moral issues arise in a multitude of ways in the school as it is, to the view that we need a carefully designed programme of education lasting many years. It is quite true that moral issues may arise all the time either at first hand ("What ought we to do about the bullying in the school?"), or second-hand in, say, the context of history or English lessons. The trouble with this approach, however, is that it is extremely random and uneven in its effects as a programme of moral education, and it may, if it is carried out conscientiously, become a major irritation and hindrance to other lessons and activities. Maybe the English teacher has other things to do besides discussing the moral implications of *Hard Times*. There is also another, more fundamental, criticism which might apply to this approach which will be considered in a moment.

More systematic, and therefore more appealing, if we are convinced that ideally all children should become morally educated, are programmes such as the Lifeline Project arising out of the work of McPhail.[16] McPhail started his research by surveying the attitudes of a number of teenage children, as a result of which he discovered that consideration for others seemed to be widely regarded as a pivotal moral value. On the basis of that he sought to devise a programme liable to foster the value of consideration and to increase children's ability to see the advantage to all concerned of living with some consideration for each other. To that end he proposed a democratic organisation of the school, in order to institutionalise a setting in which the need for and advantages of such consideration would become apparent, and he and his team produced loosely graded materials, largely in the form of moral dilemmas for students to discuss, act out or respond to in a variety of other possible ways. A couple of criticisms must be made at once: firstly, although it might not be difficult to argue that consideration for others is an important value, McPhail's assumption that it is, or that it should serve as the centre-piece of morality because a small group of people say they think it is, is blatantly fallacious. (It incidentally also requires rather more work on the quetion of what constitutes consideration for others.) Secondly, there is a clear implication, running through both the rationale behind the materials and the programme material itself, that what needs to be understood is what good sense it makes for us all to co-operate and be considerate towards each other. I'm sure that that is true, but teaching people that moral behaviour is actually a matter of self-interest is not quite the same thing as providing moral education. On the other hand, an approach such as McPhail advocates does at least recognise that part of what is necessary for moral education is an understanding and appreciation of the way in which moral questions are embedded in real everyday problems. For it is possible to have a theoretical knowledge, not which one simply lacks the will to put into practice, but which one fails to recognise in its practical manifestations.

My main criticism of McPhail's programme is one which also applies to many of the "values clarification" exercises quite common in North America and, possibly, to a policy of leaving the matter to be dealt with through other subjects and activities. It is that there is a distinction between appreciating the moral dimension to a problem (including perhaps having a view on it), and understanding the logic and nature of morality. Both are essential to the educated moral mind, but all the approaches so far considered think only in terms of the first. The fact is that to think long and hard about a specific moral problem ("Should a man steal a drug he can't afford, because it has been overpriced by an unscrupulous chemist, to save his sick wife?") is a useful and necessary exercise, but it is not sufficient as an exercise for developing understanding of the moral sphere. For full moral understanding must include understanding of the kind of philosophical points discussed above, and they do not come into a typical values clarification exercise.

One person who has recognised this dimension is John Wilson, who, in his work for the Farmington Trust, outlined a programme designed precisely to meet such a need.[17] My only criticisms of his proposals are that he goes to the other extreme in putting all the emphasis on the philosophical understanding, and that he proposes a new jargon (including terms like Phil, Gig and Krat) which seems to me quite unnecessary and extremely offputting.

There is not, I think, any need to pursue the details of any further programmes of moral education. It is evident that if we wish children to be morally educated we have to do two things: provide philosophical understanding of the moral sphere and practical appreciation of the moral dimensions to particular situations. Neither of these will be picked up from the individual's surroundings in the way that attitudes and habits of behaviour will be in the training stage. Both could be treated through other subjects and activities, but that seems to impose an unnecessary burden on those subjects and activities, and there seems no good reason why there should not be lessons in moral philosophy supplemented by or including reference to and exploration of actual moral dilemmas.

[It used to be an axiom of colleges of education in Britain that the particular moral stance of the teacher, meaning by that the ethical theory to which he subscribed, would naturally make a difference to his view of moral upbringing. It therefore was important for the would-be teacher to determine whether he was a utilitarian, an intuitionist or whatever. But this argument seems rather curious. As I have argued, whether you are a relativist, a utilitarian, an intuitionist or an emotivist, cannot be allowed to obscure the essential nature of morality, and it follows from that essential nature that certain things such as keeping promises, freedom of speech, promoting people's happiness, telling the truth, and treating people impartially, just are good. Those are the sort of basic assumptions we should be habituating people to. Now when it comes to complex issues like abortion or direct clashes of principle, it is not so easy, and different ethical views may lead to different answers. But moral training should not be concerning itself with beliefs about complex matters like these. These are matters that require moral understanding, and again the teacher's personal convictions as to the truth of, say, utilitarianism, should not have any effect on his lessons in moral philosophy.]

This leaves us with one question: ought everybody to be morally educated? In particular, if we want to reply to that question in the affirmative, how are we going to distinguish between the need for moral education and the need for religious education? For it has already been pointed out that the logic of both religion and morality is similar, and we have argued against the provision of religious education as a necessary part of schooling. The difference is simple but important (and worth contemplating, for it is quite conceivable that in twenty years' time we will regard morality as we now regard religion). The difference is that, as things are, many of us don't believe in religion at all, and many religious people appear to be quite capable of understanding the possibility of having no religious sense at all, but we all believe in morality and cannot conceive of not doing so. (Remember what that means: it means that we cannot take seriously the idea that absolutely nothing matters in a moral sense.) We can contemplate life without religion, and therefore we take seriously the question of whether we should initiate children into it. We cannot contemplate life without morality, and therefore we cannot take seriously the suggestion that moral education is not important or might be set aside.

6   Methodological Questions

1 LIMITATIONS IN EMPIRICAL RESEARCH

So far very little has been said about methods of teaching. This is partly the result of a straightforward decision to bring all questions to do with methodology together in this one chapter. But it is also partly due to my belief that despite the emphasis on method in most courses, it is not the most important nor the most profitable aspect of teacher preparation. Whether that view can be substantiated must be judged by the reader after he has read and considered this chapter.

A more common view, that some would invoke to justify a lack of emphasis on methodological questions in a book like this, is that methodological matters are not philosophical. But this view may be seriously misleading. In the end, no doubt, methodological questions are not philosophical. In the end, most things are not. In the end, establishing whether a particular method does or does not have certain results is usually a matter for empirical testing. But there is a great deal that needs doing before we can hope to get to the end. There are also some important qualifications to be made to the concessions granted in respect of the end.

(a) I have said that "usually, in the end" the viability of a proposed method is a matter for empirical tests. But every so often it is not. Every so often there is no cause and no place for empirical observation, because a point of logic is involved. We have in fact already met some examples of logically derived methodological propositions. You don't, for instance, carry out empirical tests to see whether indoctrination leads to better education. It cannot do so, being by definition anti-educational. You don't look in classrooms to see whether it is true that concentrating on composition exercises aids thinking. You consider what is meant and you see that it is bound to be so. You consider intelligence tests or creativity tests in the abstract, and you recognise at once that they cannot measure creativity or intelligence as popularly (and admittedly hazily) understood. You distinguish moral training and moral education, and you appreciate therewith that the way to achieve one is not in itself going to achieve the other. You consider what education is, and realise that you must teach in ways that, taken as a whole, lead to understanding rather than mere memorisation.

(*b*) Secondly, it must be remembered that empirical testing or research does not make things right or wrong. Empirical findings are not a criterion of success and truth. This is a very obvious point, too often forgotten. Empirical testing either tentatively confirms or invalidates a hypothesis. Lack of successful testing or the impossibility of testing does not necessarily take us beyond the realm of truth and falsehood. It may, for example, be true that the most important factor in successful teaching is the personality of the teacher, and the fact tht no adequate research programme has been devised to look into this has nothing to do with its truth or falsity. It does, however, have the consequence that all observation of teaching strategies must be imperfect, in as much as this variable at least is not under control. It is therefore a regrettable tendency in many branches of study, but particularly in education, that focusses on the empirically researched, which means in effect on the measurable or quantifiable. It is regrettable because there is no reason whatsoever to assume that things have to be quantifiable to be significant, and every reason to assume that in the interests of quantification a great deal of distortion unavoidably goes on. It is reasonable that certain psychologists should adopt behaviourism as a methodology; indeed there is not much you can study systematically about man's psyche or personality beyond its outward manifestations. But it is unreasonable, in fact it is absurd, that some people should assume that things like love and jealousy are no more than behavioural patterns, or that anybody should assume that what the psychologist tells us about jealousy, based on the use of behaviourist methods, is either all there is to be said or indeed sacrosanct, provided only that his studies are not confused. His studies, as far as they go, might conceivably be entirely in order, but simply fail to tell us anything about the essence of whatever it is he is looking at through the filter of observable behaviour.

(*c*) Implicit in the previous point is reference to the wider point, worth listing separately as here, that empirical research into teaching methods and such like is not, and can never be, truly scientific. This has been well summarised by Ruth Barwood in her very sensible paper on "Empirical Research and Educational Theory", arising out of work on teaching methods with which she was associated.[1]

"Looking at what happens in classrooms," she writes, "is not analogous to looking at what happens in test tubes, and to suggest that we should proceed as if it were, since science is the norm of all our thinking, is to radically misunderstand science. Science is the study of matter, and matter is all that test tubes contain. Classrooms also contain minds. When molecules collide, they do not do so either unintentionally or deliberately, they simply collide. When people interact, they do not simply interact; there is meaning in their interaction. If we ask why molecules collide, we are asking for reasons, all of which will be causal. If we ask why a particular human interaction took place, some but not all of the reasons asked for, will be causal. There are reasons, which we can search for and find, why molecules collide: but the molecules themselves do not collide *for a reason*. There are reasons, similarly, why people interact in given ways, but they themselves have reasons for their actions which are not co-extensive with causal explanations. If we observe a child's arm rise in a classroom, a scientific explanation for this can be offered in terms of electrical impulses in the brain, neural messages to the muscles in the arm and biochemical changes in these contracting muscles. This is an explanation of how and why *his arm rises*. To understand why *he raises his arm* we can only speculate about shared social conventions and their application to this particular incident. The answer to 'why did his arm rise?' can be fully given in physiological terms. The answer to 'why did he raise his arm?' is quite other: he is requesting permission to visit the lavatory —but he might be just fooling. Any description or explanation of an action which fails to take account of its purposiveness is an incomplete description: to suppose otherwise is to overlook the fundamental difference between actions and happenings, between people and things."[2]

Mrs Barwood goes on to add that no observation techniques can get around the assumptions and presuppositions of the observers or the viewpoint and interests of the research designer, with the consequence that no reasearch of this kind can lay claim to an undistorted image of what is going on.

(*d*) But the most important qualification of all is not that some claims do not ultimately require empirical investigation, nor that some things, perhaps the most important, are in many of their aspects not empirically testable, and that therefore any purely empirical research distorts, nor even 'that the notion of research into human activity being analogous to scientific research is suspect. It is that even *bona fide* empirical testing is only as good as its conceptual base and logical build up, and is therefore, in one sense, in the end, not empirical at all. This fourth point also explains why much of it is in the event rather poor. At the heart of the trouble here lies the failure of most people to appreciate the difference between a verbal definition and conceptual analysis, and their total inability to grasp and perform the latter. For it is no good presuming that provided you offer a verbal definition of what you are inquiring into (and all attendant items of interest), all must be straightforward and plain sailing. It will only be so if your verbal definition happens to amount to a coherent, clear, measurable concept, and, in addition, your research will only be illuminating if the conception is also relatively specific. [See above Chapter One.] Announcing that you are going to research into intelligence, without stopping to think what it is, is ridiculous. But pausing just long enough to say "What I mean by 'intelligence' is 'mental agility'" is scarcely better. Only when you understand what constitutes this mental agility you refer to, can you *hope* to proceed, only if and when what it is clearly involves quantifiable elements, *can* you proceed, and only if it is a reasonably specific concept is it *worth* proceeding.

This means, what there is no disputing, that what we call psychology and sociology, or any other kind of empirical research, is blind without what we call philosophy. That is not intended as a point scored in the tedious game of subject politics. My point is not that philosophers are superior *tout court* nor that an academic study of philosophy is necessary (neither of which follows from what has been said), but that good empirical research is entirely dependent on good conceptualisation and logical procedures, and, as a matter of fact, for whatever reason, a great deal of it is not so based. Take for example some research conducted by Bradburn and Caplovitz into the question of whether positive and negative feelings relating to happiness and unhappiness correlate.[3] They wanted to know whether or not there is a negative correlation between people's response to questions about logical opposites in terms of happiness and unhappiness. They found, unexpectedly, a statistically insignificant positive correlation. But, as Wilson has pointed out, their findings are meaningless, since they failed to construct items that were true polar opposites, and that is a philosophical rather than an empirical shortcoming.[4]

Having made these general points about the qualifications to be made to the crude claim that methodological matters are not philosophical, I shall illustrate them, particularly the last, in more detail, by a slightly closer look at some recent research on teaching methods themselves, namely the research conducted by Neville Bennett and his associates at Lancaster University.[5]

At the time of the first publication of Bennett's findings some criticised the research on statistical grounds, but I shall ignore those criticisms here. Nor do I want to make too much of the fact that a very small sample was used (thirty-seven teachers) or that there is an extraordinary list of variables that were not apparently controlled, critical though such inadequacies may be. (Variables not controlled include: the type of background of different children, attitudes of parents, differences of social class, different qualities of schools, differences in quality and experience of teachers, different schemes of teaching maths and reading employed in different schools, different reactions of children to the fact that they were being tested, the differing aims of teachers.) But I must make the general point that a great deal of empirical research in education is, like this, both conducted on so small a scale that its significance is inevitably minimised, and beset by glaring weaknesses such as a failure to control variables, and yet its findings are broadcast abroad, without any reference to such devastating distortions or crucial qualifications as may be involved. No doubt in many cases brother academics spit and growl in various obscure journals, but I am thinking of the damage that may be done by the wide publicity given to isolated pieces of poor research, and the extent to which national policy may be affected by this kind of research, notwithstanding its limitations.

However, what really needs pointing out and sorting out is the clumsy conceptualisation that lies behind this research. This is, incidentally, rather remarkable, since Bennett rightly criticises other research into such matters for the gross oversimplification involved in using broad categories like progressive and traditional teachers. Let there be no doubt about this—a point on which Bennett and I formally agree, as we must, for it is so—research based on such broad categories cannot be particularly illuminating, though naturally it will furnish some "results". It cannot be illuminating because the generality of the categories, besides making it difficult to know how to classify subjects (which in itself may obviously distort the whole inquiry), means that one necessarily knows very little about the causes or reasons for any differences in outcome observed. It is as if you were to divide teachers into those with blue eyes and those with brown eyes. You would no doubt find some differences between the behaviour of children taught by the blue-eyed teachers and those taught by the brown-eyed teachers. What you wouldn't get is any good reason to suppose that these differences are the result of the difference between having a blue-eyed and having a brown-eyed teacher, still less any explanation of these differences. Exactly the same would be true of research that simply divided people into progressive and traditional teachers.

Having appreciated that point, Bennett accordingly introduced twelve categories or twelve distinguishable teaching styles. I have criticisms to make of his categories, because some of them are themselves inadequately conceptualised, but that turns out to be neither here nor there, for when it came to the point Bennett astonishingly collapsed the twelve into three categories: teachers with a formal style, those with an informal style and those with a mixed style. In other words, he did the equivalent of dividing them into blue, brown and hazel-eyed teachers, and effectively ignored the important and correct observation he had made.

Bennett's "results" suggested that over a given period children taught reading by teachers using a mixed style made most progress, followed by those taught formally and then those taught informally. In maths the order was formal, informal, mixed, and in English formal, mixed, informal. The children who made most progress overall, however, were taught by an informal style.

Of course, many people tried to claim that these "results" proved their case—most notably advocates of formal teaching methods (perhaps understandably, if you just read them off). More responsible commentators countered by saying that it didn't prove the traditionalist case. But the trap, into which practically all sophisticated critics fell, was that of denying that it proved the superiority of any one style, and saying that it showed there was little to choose between them. Alas, no. This research was not inconclusive, so much as a non-starter. It shows and proves nothing. It just wasn't good enough. Its conclusions may by chance be correct, but it is no more reliable support for any conclusion than my intuitive feelings based on limited experience in a few schools.

It is a little unkind to single out individual pieces of research, even when they are, as here, related to our central concern, so I want to make it quite clear that I do not single Bennett's work out as particularly deserving of criticism. Sadly, I have to suggest that this kind of weakness, crippling as it undoubtedly is, even if people find ways of ignoring it, is typical of much empirical research in education. It is poor because it lacks a solid conceptual base, which means an armoury of precise and specific concepts. To this it may be replied that, if you take account of all the subtleties, you limit what you can sensibly research into. You can research into a broad issue such as what kind of children learn Latin rather more easily than into more specific issues like what is the most effective way to teach Latin to fifteen-year-old girls, because the latter would demand too much in the way of specificity, precision and control. But that just makes my point: many of the serious issues in education are so complex, that the crude and happy-go-lucky way we research into them is an intellectual disgrace. When I hear that some researcher with little experience of schools, no grasp of conceptual subtlety, no concern for logic and no experience of

2‌84 *The Philosophy of Schooling*

trying to control variables with human subjects, is researching into
the effects of social class on schooling, I am embarrassed for us all.

2 TEACHING OBJECTIVES AND MODELS

A slightly different example of interest in teaching methods comes
from the United States. I refer to the attempt to reduce teaching to
a technology on the ground that teaching is (or in order to make
sure that teaching is) fundamentally a repertoire of stratagems. It
is, on the face of it, curious that anybody should hold that view,
when one considers that all the famous and supposedly successful
teachers from Socrates, through Jesus Christ to Mortimer Adler
and one's own most admired teachers, seem clearly to have done it
largely on personality. Nonetheless the development of teaching
techniques is a recent phenomenon that has to be given some
consideration.

What is it that causes people to confuse truth with certainty,
systematisation with accuracy, and the quantifiable or measurable
with the real? For consider: a thing may be true, but not certainly
known to be. An observation may be accurate but not systematised
and vice versa. A thousand and one things are really the case, but
are not measurable. That I love my wife is certain, but I cannot
demonstrably prove that I do. Conversely much that is backed by
systematic measurement may turn out to be far from the case. On
the face of it nothing could be more odd than the idea that
schooling in general and education in particular can be assessed in
terms of input/output.

The argument for behavioural objectives, pioneered during the
sixties in North America, was, in outline, that teachers needed to
replace aims, which were said to be general and vague, with
objectives, which were said to be specific and clear, and also
measurable. As a consequence it would be possible to check on
success. Whereupon there began to appear such volumes as
Bloom's *Taxonomy of Educational Objectives*, a handbook for
aspiring teachers who might plan their day down to the last minute
with objectives such as engineering "a willingness to respond" or
"satisfaction in response" amongst their students.[6] The flaws and
begged questions in this approach are surely self-evident once one
considers it carefully. There is an assumption, common in schooling circles, that aims are inherently vague and distant, whilst
objectives are necessarily attainable and precise. But any such
assumption is nonsense. Ultimate aims, precisely because being
ultimate they are distant, are quite often broad and general (e.g.

"We should educate for citizenship"). But in the first place being general is not the same thing as being vague or imprecise. In the second place there is no such thing as an inherently vague aim or a vague anything else in nature; there are only vague ideas about things in people's heads. In the third place people may just as easily entertain vague ideas of more immediate aims or objectives. If we ignore semantic differences between aims and objectives, we are left with a straightforward demand that teachers should think not in terms of ultimate, distant objectives, but in terms of immediate and measurable objectives. But this is both incoherent and dangerous. It is incoherent because, though you can concentrate on immediate objectives, if you are going to select them, you need to do so in the light of more distant objectives. It is dangerous because it suggests that what is of value in schooling must be measurable. But this is surely to be aggressively resisted. It is as if one were to assess an artist's calibre as an artist, by testing various observable details of his technique as he goes along, or to test a successful marriage by reference to a check list of daily do's and don't's. Not only in this not necessarily a good guide, it may also seriously get in the way of the enterprise. One final irony should be noted: many of the objectives listed by Bloom are about as vague and difficult to grasp as any general statement of aims has ever been. Educating people is a long-lived process which is the more successful in the extent to which people gain a surer grasp of a breadth of understanding and discriminatory power. It cannot be measured. It has to be estimated. You can only take stock. Schooling too, though some aspects are more measurable than others, is predominantly something that demands the informed judgement of those who understand the nature of the enterprise.

Let us now turn to teaching models. Bruce Joyce and Marsha Weil in such books as their *Models of Teaching* have pioneered the way, and have given us encapsulated accounts of the educational views of such diverse figures as Thalen, Bruner, Taba, Piaget and Skinner.[7] Their approach is in effect a modern variant of the *Ideas of the Great Educators* approach, with the main difference lying in the tone of the presentation.[8] Whereas the ideas deriving from various individuals used to be thought of as part of the speculative, ruminative side of educational study, the models derived from them present more or less the same material as part of methodological work. One feature of this approach is that the writer (or tutor) presents his models uncritically—deliberately so, because the idea is that they should serve as interchangeable models, suitable to different people on different occasions. This lack of dogmatism is in principle welcome. But to refuse to be dogmatic about the overall superiority of one teaching style is one thing. To introduce the ideas of Piaget, Skinner and Schultz, as if there were no question about the coherence, sense or quality of any of what they say, is quite another. The disturbing thing here (which could of course be remedied) is not the refusal to rank order the models, but the lack of critical onslaught on each individual model. (One might add a specific criticism about the way in which educators and educationalists with very different kinds of interest are lumped together as providing models of teaching.) But the major objection to this approach remains that, although it is more flexible than the behavioural objectives approach, and blessedly concentrates on input rather than output, it still must serve, if used as intended, as a straightjacket. To say, as these authors do, that the teacher may want to employ a different model with different classes just isn't good enough. Teaching is not like that. The good teacher does not select his programme for the lesson, as if he were a washing machine, not even had he twenty programmes to choose from. He may need to change programmes, if we must think in these kind of terms, every minute or with every child. It is not a question of there being a time for the Piagetian way and a time for the Platonic way. Piaget and Plato, or the valuable parts of what they have to say need to be understood, so that they become part of the teacher's thinking, not adopted wholesale as models. Then the teacher must be himself at all times, responding, not programmatically, but directly and sensitively to every nuance of the situation. What it boils down to is this: *contra* Joyce's view, teaching cannot "be reasonably analysed into specific, even minute behavioural components without doing violence to the essential nature of the act",[9] not at any rate so long as the teaching is seen as part of a general programme of schooling and educating. Good teachers have to rely heavily on sensitive handling of human relationships, and on making good use of their own personalities, in conjunction with handling subject matter in ways that render it clear and articulate. Their concern should be with that, rather than with sticking by a list of previously determined models, methods or objectives.

One final example of the danger of this advance towards mechanistic totalitarianism and technological teachers is provided by the (again largely North American) drift towards a quantitative system of teacher assessment. [See above Chapter Three.] In many colleges students are required to fill in questionnaires relating to their instructor at the end of a course. Questions such as the following might be asked: "Is this course relevant?" "Does the instructor know his material?" "Does he easily build rapport with his class?" "Does he make learning more interesting than you expected?" "Have you made progress through this course?" "Are students in this class interested in getting to know one another?"

I draw attention to this phenomenon, although what needs to be said about it is much the same as needs to be said about the use of behavioural teaching objectives and models of teaching, partly because it is a very serious one, since people's jobs can quite literally depend on the kind of response their students provide to such questionnaires, and partly because the limitations conspicuously involved in this practice may be felt to apply no less to that vast mass of educational research, which is likewise no more than consumer response assessed by imperfect questioning. Everybody knows that the value of such information gathering depends upon the quality of the questions in the first instance. What few seem to realise is how poor it often is. The above questions are all taken from actual questionnaires at hazard. Yet look at the problems raised even by some of this arbitrary handful of examples. There is the problem of whether specific questions are worth asking or appropriate in this context. Should the teacher's success and security, for instance, be measured in terms of factors such as whether his students get to know each other? Secondly, there is the problem of whether all these questions actually mean anything. What, for instance, is the class supposed to be relevant to? Thirdly, there is the problem that many responses are bound to be subjective, in the sense of more revealing about the student than the instructor on whom he is commenting. Fourthly, there is the problem of ensuring that or determining whether those filling in the responses interpret and understand the items in the way that was intended. Interpretations of progress, for example, might vary considerably, while different people might have different understandings of what constitutes knowing one's material. Those straightforward problems alone seem to me to be sufficient to discredit this kind of approach to this kind of a situation (and there are of course other objections, such as those referred to above in the wider context of empirical research).

But the major danger to be guarded against is the assumption that since this is an empirical test of teacher performance, it must be objective in a way that peer group opinion informally sounded, or a head of department's judgement, could not be. Those heavily engaged in research of this type do tend to think this, and indeed, if they did not, there would be no point in their proceeding. Why take time and trouble to do it this way, if sounding people's opinions informally, or waiting for specific student complaints, or listening to the grapevine, or scrutinising exam results, or observing one's colleagues and forming one's own judgement, were as effective and reliable? But once again the assumption that that is so seems to arise out of confusing system with certainty. For the only objectivity involved here comes at the stage of sorting, classifying and working out percentages from the responses. It is in some sense, if you like, an objective ordering of responses. But those responses themselves were classic instances of subjective opinion. The objective ordering of hundreds of disparate subjective reactions does not necessarily approximate to truth.

3 THE MEDIUM IS NOT THE MESSAGE

It may be thought that I wish to suggest that there is nothing that can profitably be said about teaching methods and that we cannot or should not seek to take objective measures of the effectiveness of our teachers. That is not quite the case. I do suggest that much research into teaching methods has been severely flawed and that there is a danger (both indicated by and possibly intensified by such research) of methodology becoming a great pseudo-science. Teaching methods are not clear and uncontentious, autonomous and readily identifiable items to be picked out and observed by experts under isolated laboratory conditions. Interpretations of what "instruction" is may vary considerably, and it is worth noting that even such an innocuous term as that is unlikely to be used in a value-free way. Besides, even if teaching methods and strategies were easily and uncontentiously locatable and classifiable (e.g. so that at this moment there could be no doubt that the teacher is instructing and only instructing his class), it would not follow that claims about their efficacy and value could be settled decisively by experts. For such claims would require an overall context, embodying a view of what schooling and education are all about. It is, therefore, a great mistake to think that methodological issues fall into the realm of hard empirical fact and that empirical research into methodology is somehow more reliable, more objective or more scientific than, say, inquiries into what is worthwhile or the nature of education. We must explode that myth of our time; empirical research does *not* necessarily furnish more facts than pure reflection may. Not all facts are empirical (it is a fact that bachelors are unmarried), and not all empirical findings are facts. And, in line with some of the points that have emerged in this book, we can say with a fair degree of certainty that time spent clarifying one's concept of education would be more useful for a practising teacher than time spent studying behavioural objectives or observation research into teaching methods.

One view that this flouts is one noted in a previous chapter, to the effect that the medium is the message, or, slightly more explicitly, that what you teach is the way you teach, from which, presumably, one is expected to draw the general conclusion that we should devote our time to considering the implications of various teaching styles rather than to considering what we want to teach. As is usually the case, the strengths and weaknesses of this claim fluctuate according to the way in which it is interpreted.

If we take it literally, assuming that it means what it says rather than that it is deliberately overstated, then it is simply false. For what it literally claims is that there is no message other than what is conveyed by the manner of presentation — that there is no content to a lesson other than the style of the teaching. This may be paralleled by claims in a number of other contexts, such as the extreme view that there is nothing in the world except private perceptions and points of view, or the view that in literature form and content are one, so that there is no content other than the form. It can easily be shown that each of these extreme interpretations, of a similar logical kind, is absurd. In a quite straightforward sense there is a desk at which I am now writing, which is distinct from, and not dependent for its existence on, my partial perception of it. Similarly, H. G. Wells' *History of Mr. Polly* tells a particular story which is not identical to the way in which it is told and which might, indeed, be told in several other ways. (There are those who say, unkindly, that Wells found some of them.) In like manner, if I teach a lesson about the Greeks, then, however I teach it, it is about the Greeks rather than the Romans. There is a content or message that is not one with the manner of putting it across or the medium. [If, in the first example, someone were to raise the rather interesting philosophical puzzle of how I know that my desk has any further existence than that vouchsafed by my perception, I would for the moment fend it off, by pointing out that by a number of criteria you will accept — sight, touch, smell — there is a difference between the desk I perceive and my perception, which latter is a merely-perceived partial desk.]

In other words, nobody could seriously maintain, after a moment's honest reflection, that there is no world other than a mass of individual perceptions. And nobody could seriously maintain that what we do or may teach is coextensive with and to be defined by our manner of teaching. The second law of thermodynamics and the origin of the Second World War are two distinct subjects, no matter how they are taught. So, if this claim is going to make any sense at all, it will have to be interpreted less dramatically. What it could be taken to mean (despite the fact that this is not quite what it says), and what obviously is true and important, is that the manner in which we teach may to a greater or lesser extent modify the nature of what we are teaching. This, as I say, is obviously true; to put it at its crudest, the overbearing manner of a teacher may itself add a new dimension of content to whatever is being taught by making it seem objectionable. An authoritative type of instruction may add a further lesson and have consequences that are distinct from, say, a discussion group on the same topic. Tell the story another way and it may become a different version (but even then it is less misleading to put it this way than to say that it becomes a different story. The latter phrasing perpetuates the ambiguity. In one sense two books on the Boston Strangler are telling the same story, in another they are not.) Certainly the room in which I am sitting is very different to me than it is to my wife or than it can be to you. But still we are talking about the same room.

This slogan, then, may be a timely reminder for some. How one teaches matters, regardless of effectiveness, because it may have consequences either in terms of implying its own message or in terms of modifying the meaning or force of what is being said so far as student perception goes. This is worth remembering and may contribute towards explaining why students sometimes appear to learn other than what we think we have taught them. But it is not, by itself, a very useful reminder, because the practical thing we would need to know is exactly what effect our instruction, sarcasm, precision, discussion-groups, free and easy classes, disciplined material, disciplined demands on behaviour, humour, kindness, appearance, age, compassion, fear, etc., etc., have on this child today, this child tomorrow, that child yesterday, Henry on his own, Henry in the company of Jane, etc., etc., in the context of a school like this, a school like that, parents of one sort, headmasters of another and so forth and so on. Here we return to where we were, and I fear that the truth is we probably know very little for certain, and that further research is in the nature of things not likely to be any more illuminating than a combination of clear-headedness, experience and judgement.

I say "I fear", but why, on reflection, be fearful? Why do I let myself, despite all that I've said, fall in with the superstition that we must have clearly and empirically demonstrated answers to every question? Why should we fear to acknowledge that there are not many precise, hard-and-fast rules about teaching and that, as with bringing up young babies or possibly even running countries, more damage is done by those who stick by a book of rules at any price than by those who do not believe there are very many certain rules? I beg your pardon, I do not "fear". Unperturbed, I venture to suggest that there are really only five undoubted truths about teaching method, none of these very exciting, but all at any rate of importance. The first is that there is no known best way to teach, no best style nor model of teaching. Far more important than specific drills, techniques, games, strategies and such like are general common-sense points (though not so commonly found) such as know what you are talking about, think out what you say or do clearly, articulate it audibly, write legibly, keep even-tempered, try and look at things from the child's point of view as well. Secondly, the fact that an approach works well in one subject is no reason for supposing that it should do or will in another. I can think of some very good reasons for teaching introductory philosophy in a rather different way from teaching physics to advanced students. Thirdly, different ages and different personalities amongst students may respond in different ways to different styles and techniques of teaching. It is worth bearing in mind, obvious though it is, that even if we had overwhelming evidence that a particular teaching style was generally far more effective with a certain type of student in relation to a particular subject (and I cannot over-emphasise how far we are from that, and must to some extent forever remain), there is still the question of whether the particular class before you isn't predominantly part of the minority. To estimate that, you have to have the kind of judgement which could act as your sole and adequate guide. Fourthly, different teachers, because of their personal idiosyncrasies, strengths and weaknesses may be better employed using different approaches, even where every other variable remains constant (again an unrealistic scenario). It is quite feasible that even with a group of students known to prefer and profit more from seminars, my conducting of seminars should be so poor as to make it better for the students concerned that I lecture, if I'm going to teach them at all. Finally, different purposes may require different approaches; a sensible way to get the multiplication tables learnt, if that is what you want done, is not necessarily a sensible way to develop literary appreciation. A useful way of building rapport in the class may not be the best way of getting a point across.

If we bear those five points in mind and think back over the necessary limitations and the contingent weaknesses to be found in research into teaching methods, one is tempted to come to the amazing conclusion that it is best to have no preconceived ideas about the best way to teach and best not to try to acquire a

repertoire of models and skills. Better to get a thorough understanding of what you want to achieve, both in the long and in the
short term, to take critical stock of such information as may be
gleaned from sociology, psychology and classroom studies, and to
adapt as seems intuitively sensible to the situation you find
yourself in, in the light of your understanding and knowledge.
Certainly any pre-emptive prescriptive attitude towards instruction, rote-learning, discovery, play, integrated courses or group-
learning would seem to be sheer simple-mindedness, and any
attempt to balance them, giving due and equal weight to each in
turn, or to consciously shift from one technique to another at
regular intervals, extraordinarily imperceptive. For once a mech-
anical analogy may be legitimate: of course it's not good to drive a
car at 100 kph all the time, nor yet at 5 kph. But sensible people
don't swing from one to the other at regular intervals, nor do they
drive at a steady 50 kph. They do what is appropriate to the
occasion. The question the teacher should be asking is not "Isn't it
time I switched to discovery?" but "What am I trying to do at the
moment?" If the answer is that I'm trying to tell some children
something, then it is not time to switch. If you are referring to the
Kings and Queens of England and you want them to know their
names, tell them their names, ask them to learn them or whatever
else seems suitable. But if you want them to practice using books
and libraries, tell them to find out for themselves. If your students
are bored, try something else. But if you know you can't be
amusing, don't try and make it funny.

4 Assessment

The two final issues to be considered are too complex to admit of a
straightforward solution, particularly in the context of a philosophical book. But in this they are typical of many educational
problems and it would be as well to draw this book to a close with a
reminder that though the nature of philosophy means there are
very few issues where there is not a crucial philosophical dimension (hence its practical utility), there are quite a number where
there are other dimensions too (hence the need to harness
philosophy to other disciplines in the context of schooling). When
I say that these issues are complex, I do not necessarily mean that
they are deep and require great intellect and insight to unravel
them. I mean that there are many interwoven threads: it may be
time, patience and information that are needed rather than the
mind of a genius. But anyway, for the reason given, they will not

be solved here. Instead I shall draw attention to some of the important factors and distinctions relating to the issues of *assessment* and *class-organisation* within the school and leave the reader to take the matter further on his own account.

It has already been argued in a previous chapter that teachers should be accountable for their overall success as teachers, but that because of the nature of the activity, monitoring of such success should be informal rather than formal, and accountability should be to a body representing all interested parties. What remains to be considered is the assessment of pupil progress. (The distinction, incidentally, is theoretical. In practice there is a tight interrelationship between pupil progress and teacher success, though not an absolute one, since a teacher might be doing the best that could be done without response, or doing a very poor job, but getting away with it thanks to the initiative of the pupils. But it is legitimate to separate the two for theoretical purposes and indeed vital to do so, otherwise we shall not know what is interrelated with what.)

Though it may have some more particular meaning for experts in "assessment and evaluation" courses (courses generally less concerned with a rationale for such activity than with systematising procedures), for most of us "assessment" is a broad generic term covering the whole business of exams, qualifications, tests, grades, personal judgement and such like. As always, provided we understand one another, the terminology is less important than noting distinctions. In this case in particular we need to distinguish between monitoring the progress of pupils, which may itself take many forms, the use of the findings of such monitoring as guidance and/or qualification in respect of pursuing similar work, the private use of such findings as a more general guide to individual ability or quality, and the public use of such findings for similar purposes. I suggest that these four practices have been introduced in ascending order of dubiousness.

Assessing the progress of pupils, or monitoring it, is in itself an entirely acceptable practice, despite the fact that some deny it. Not only is it acceptable, it is logically unavoidable.[10] For schools are designed to serve certain ends rather than others. Since educationalists and teachers alike are presumably concerned about and sincerely committed to trying to achieve those ends, they must want to know and be able to know what progress, if any, is being made. Part of what it is to be concerned about something is to take it seriously enough to expect to have a true picture of what is going on. We doubt whether a man who claims to be interested in cricket, but who shows no curiosity as to who won the Test Match, is entirely sincere. We question the genuineness of the art-lover who indiscriminately embraces everything. In the same way a teacher who does not want to know, and does not intend to find out, whether his pupils are making any progress of any sort, besides being a curious individual, would not be committed to playing his part in schooling in any serious way. The best that could be said for him would be that he might be presuming that his benign influence was bound to have some good effect on children, so it was worth his while being around, but unnecessary to check whether things were in fact going well. Apart from the absurdity and arrogance of such a claim in general, this approach would be inappropriate in relation to any specific conceptions of schooling and education, which entail particular goals and not just any consequence of benign influences.

In principle, then, there can be no serious objection to the monitoring aspect of assessment. What there can be is a great deal of empirical argument about the advantages and disadvantages of various different methods of monitoring, ranging from very formal patterns such as examinations, through to the more informal judgement of class teachers on yearly work. Intertwined with the question of what type of monitoring is the question of by whom it should be carried out. Should monitoring be carried out in a uniform way by national agencies, or should it be left to individual schools? What other possible combinations are there? Some of the strengths and weakneses of competing proposals are reasonably straightforward; standardised exams may impose great stresses on individuals and hazard a great deal of time and work on the chance of the moment. On the other hand, at least in some areas, they represent a not inappropriate test of the ability of the individual to deal with a particular issue in a succinct, coherent and telling manner, and they give some indication of the point the student has finally reached. They may function as a ruinous restriction on teaching syllabi: on the other hand they may serve to lend purpose and structure to the teaching programme. If they are nationally or state administered they allow of some degree of comparison and hence ease of mobility, and they are relatively impersonal, and consequently avoid the dangers of individual teachers' preconceptions. On the other hand more flexibility and attuning to particular situations is possible, if more emphasis is placed on the role of individual schools in the examining process. A programme of continuous assessment takes away the strain imposed by thought of the fateful examination day. On the other hand it makes more continual demands and inevitably loses something of the impersonal element of examinations. It is also likely to turn out to be pinpointing and monitoring different things (some no doubt equally or more important than those tested by examinations, some less so).

The above list is incomplete. That is because it is at this point that the issue passes beyond our immediate concerns. Features of various forms of monitoring, such as those mentioned, can be listed, but even a complete list will not solve the problem of what best to do. Nor even would empirical verification of all the claims made (e.g. Just how many children typically do feel strain at the onset of examinations? Does it materially effect their performance?), which would in turn require some careful conceptualisation (What is going to count as strain and effect on performance? Can we adequately conceive such concepts in observable terms?), be enough to settle the issue. For quite apart from the possibility that different schooling aims might quite properly lead different people to advocate different methods of monitoring, there is always at the end of the day the vexed problem of weighing up pluses and minuses. That is a business which does not have regular procedures. Estimating whether the anxiety induced by examinations is or is not offset by the degree of impersonal monitoring, or whether the limitations imposed by an examination are compensated for by having some degree of uniformity in our monitoring procedures, is like estimating whether the ugliness of a new factory is outweighed by its usefulness, or the lack of safety of a car by its speed. There is no proper way of weighing such incommeasurables; things can only be compared in respect of like attributes. Consequently, it is not, in the end, a matter of determining whether beauty does or does not outweigh use, as one determines which of two crates is heavier, but of deciding or arguing for putting more weight on one or the other. There is, that is to say, no way of calculating or demonstrating that one system of monitoring progress is better than another. We must be content to consider clear and detailed alternatives, gather what information we can about their consequences and implicit demands, and then reason towards a tentative conclusion in the light of the information and the aims we have.

My initial point was that any teacher must want to know whether his students are making progress, which does not in itself necessitate a public system, whether it be an examination system or anything else. But one further, perfectly reasonable, use of assessments made of progress is as a guide to the suitability of carrying on working in a field, which would be greatly facilitated by a national system. It is undeniably useful, both within the schooling system, particularly at points such as the transition to college or university, and in respect of jobs and careers, for people to be able to point to qualifications they have, if those qualifications consist in statements or certificates to the effect that they have been monitored and found to have attained a certain standard. Anybody with any sense remains sceptical of the sanctity of such certificates; not everybody who has "O" level mathematics or Grade Eight physics is equally competent, not everybody who lacks them is necessarily ignorant in these subjects. But, if what is required for a university degree course in engineering, or a job in the bank, is a certain level of mathematical competency, the system of requiring some national qualification directly related to the purpose, for all its obvious potential weaknesses, seems clearly efficient and sensible.

The point at which such a policy becomes markedly more suspect is when qualifications of some sort or another are demanded even for jobs where they seem to have no particular relevance. Quite often qualifications, which certainly do have relevance to some pursuits and activities, are laid down as prerequisites for those to which they don't have relevance. There are many jobs where it is very understandable that only candidates with a qualification in mathematics should be given consideration. But when park attendants are also expected to have that qualification, and when garbage collectors are expected to have a certificate or diploma of some kind, things are getting out of hand. There is no intrinsic merit in having qualifications or in glorifying experience by awarding it a diploma, which is one reason why the idea of awarding an attendance certificate to some university students who don't want a degree is faintly ridiculous.[11] If park attendants or garbage collectors need certain skills and abilities which they cannot readily pick up on the job, as one might say a student entering medical school needs to know some chemistry, or a teller entering a bank needs to be basically competent at mathematics, then it is reasonable to demand evidence of such skills and abilities. If that is not the case, then neither demanding irrelevant existing qualifications nor inventing new ones has any justification.

This brings us to the fourth and perhaps most flagrantly absurd aspect of assessment, namely the use of results on monitored tests or exercises to represent a profile of the person. I refer to the tendency to convert specific information ("He has attained such and such a standard in this and that") into an overall character judgement ("He's a double-first." "Nine 'A' levels, don't you know." "He reached Grade 17"). Not only is this kind of shift unwarranted, since the man with eight specific qualifications might be otherwise and in spite of those rather dumb, but it must also be partly responsible for the current increase in dissatisfaction with assessment in any shape or form. As it gradually dawns on one and all that even noted Harvard and Oxford men, let alone people with nine "O" levels or those who reached Grade 13, can look pretty stupid, the whole business of qualifications and assessments takes a knocking. But, as I have tried to suggest, it is not the business of assessment that is inherently dubious (though it is inherently complex); it is abuses and misuses of assessment that cause most of the trouble. The fact that a man with a first class degree in physics may be uneducated, does not necessarily make it unreasonable to publicly label him a first-class physicist. The fact that we don't need diplomas in garbage collecting of any sort, and that garbage collectors of any sort don't need to be mathematicians, does not necessarily make it unreasonable to award diplomas in mathematics to some noteworthy mathematics students. The fact that it is confused to see well-qualified people (in terms of examinations, diplomas etc.) as necessarily educated people, or to see the number of diplomas attained as the mark of a good school, constitutes, not an argument for doing away with assessment, but for doing away with confused thinking.

There are, then, risks and drawbacks attached to the general business of assessment. Nonetheless, the idea that we can just do away with it is childishly unrealistic. What we can do is remain alert to the fact that any assessment procedures will be fallible and that procedures are not necessarily preferable in proportion to the degree to which they eliminate room for human judgement. (A multiple choice examination, for instance, may sometimes involve less room for human judgement than other types of examination, but that doesn't necessarily make it a better examination.) And we can be more cautious about what we take a particular qualification as evidence of: after all, whether a degree in English is evidence of any more than the ability to satisfy the examiners of your competence in particular areas, depends upon the nature of the examination, the nature of the work being examined and one's view of the nature of things like intelligence, the educated mind and human understanding. It is not perhaps that we need to do away with assessment, so much as that we need to become less hypnotised by the results of assessment.

5 STREAMING, BANDING AND SETTING

There is a certain amount of evidence to suggest that the results of
assessment generally bear some kind of correlation to the expectations of teachers. One possible contributory factor to such
correlation, but obviously only one, could be the way in which
teachers deal with pupils of whom they have different expectations.
And one marked way of distinguishing one's dealings with different
groups of children is to separate them physically. This brings me to
the other matter to do with methods of teaching in the widest sense
that I want briefly to mention: the merits and demerits of
streaming, setting, banding and mixed-ability grouping.

There are at bottom three kinds of argument that may be
advanced for *mixed-ability grouping*, by which is meant grouping
according to some criterion such as age, without reference to merit
or experience (though presumably in a fully mixed-ability system
there would not be discrepancies in experience as distinct from
ability; one could in any case argue that mixed ability should not
be taken to include mixed experience). Teaching arguments, to
the effect that this is a more effective way of teaching students;
social arguments, to the effect that this is better for children than
bringing them up to think in terms of stratified groups; and
arguments concerning fairness, to the effect that selection procedures of various sorts are unfair.

As with the issue of assessment, I have no intention of trying to
solve a problem which is complex and in the end involves matching
incommeasurables against each other. All I want to do is unravel
some elements and make some broad observations, so that
subsequent thinking on the matter can proceed across clear
ground. In response to the three kinds of argument noted, it must
be said at once that there is no conclusive evidence that mixed
ability teaching is necessarily in general a more effective way of
teaching; assuming that social concerns should take priority, it is
arguable that that can be catered for by seeing and presenting
academic groupings in a different way to that in which we do at
present, rather than by refusing to tolerate any stratifications; the
fact that any selection procedure yet devised has undoubtedly
involved some unfairness in terms of misclassification or making
people what you classify them as, rather than what they might
have been, is not in itself an argument for refusing to select.
Especially is that the case when refusal to select equally obviously
involves some unfairness. If anything is clear, therefore, it is that
there is no incontestable case for mixed-ability teaching, and any
argument for it is likely to have to rely heavily on social con-

siderations and the judgement that those should count for more than other kinds of consideration.

However, the practice of *streaming*, by which is meant the practice of putting children into various ability groupings and keeping them in those groups for everything, seems scarcely more convincing. For it is, on the face of it, quite contrary to our experience to assume that an individual who is good at one thing will be similarly good at all things, even when the things in question are all academic, let alone when we extend the arrangement to cover the whole school curriculum. No doubt this policy seems less absurd than it might because a number of people, once classified as A streamers, D streamers or whatever, consciously or unconsciously act out the part until they become what they were judged to be. Possibly also there are a reasonable number of people who, by the time the school wants to classify them, are generally A or C or D all round. The fact remains that the presumption that people are more or less inevitably all round As, Ds or what have you (by the time classification takes place) is certainly false.

Setting, on the other hand, whereby individuals are grouped separately with respect to their ability for each different subject, seems quite reasonable so far as considerations of teaching and learning go. There is still the risk of misclassifying pupils and thereby either making them what they need not have been or in some way disappointing them, but it must be appreciated that in this context (as opposed to the streaming context) that is a difficulty about doing the job well rather than an inherent problem in the enterprise. We do make mistakes and are, sadly, likely to go on doing so. But it is not inevitable that we should, as it is with a system of streaming, so long as people remain much as they are. All the evidence in the world telling us that individuals might have displayed different talents and interests had they grown up and lived in different circumstances, even if it finally discredited any notion of inherent genetic determinants (which, important and revealing as such evidence is, it does not), would not alter the truth that when children enter a given stage, they have developed different talents, interests and abilities. Some are now ready to take on a certain level of mathematics or English study and some are not. Some (a different but related point) have studied certain periods of history, others have not. Some find foreign languages easier to master than others. There is also the point that teachers too are different; some are better at teaching in certain kinds of ways that might be more suited to certain kinds of children than others. For these reasons, I find it difficult to resist the view that setting, whether in football or Greek, is certainly an acceptable, and possibly a desirable, practice for schools to engage in.

Banding, whereby students are placed in quite large groups and then further subdivided into ability groups for certain subjects, seems to be a typical administrative compromise that has little to recommend it in logic. The initial large groups are merely a slightly diluted form of streaming, the smaller groups are of course settings, but settings chosen only from a limited number of individuals. The child with a flair for physics and nothing else is set for physics with the best physicists from the group of children judged least generally able, which might be wholly inappropriate.

Let me conclude by observing that there are no obvious grounds for objecting that setting or any other form of differential treatment offends against the *principle of equality*. It would, of course, if we were to take the principle of equality to be the principle that all persons should in all circumstances be treated exactly the same, or that all persons should end up in exactly the same condition. But in neither of those senses does the principle of equality seem worth defending. Nobody in their right mind believes that everybody should be treated exactly the same in all circumstances without qualification, so that scarce food supplies are measured out in equal proportions to the big and the small, the hungry and the well-fed, and so that, for every canvas the painter is allowed, you and I have to have one too. And though the view that everybody ought to end up in the same position is considerably less ridiculous, it is not very plausible. One important clarification that would be needed is in respect of what counts as "the end". The end of the world? The end of the week? The end of the individual's life? But in any case, even believers in equality of material wealth, such as myself, do not thereby feel driven to advocate sameness in how that wealth is subsequently spent or in all other matters. What is particularly moral about insisting that if you play golf, I must play golf, or that if you become proficient at Sanskrit I must be made or allowed the chance to become similarly proficient?

What we should understand by the principle of equality is rather, as we saw above, the principle that everybody's interests should count equally, or that people should be treated impartially, which is to say that differential treatment needs to be justified. In suggesting that setting might well be justified in schools I am not offending against or ignoring the principle of equality, for my claim is precisely that differences in ability can be the good reasons that justify different learning situations. What would offend against the principle of equality would be to treat all children, different as they are, as if they were alike.[12]

6 CONCLUSION

Many readers may be surprised, if not disappointed, by the fact that a chapter entitled "Methodological Questions" should have had so little to say about the nitty gritty of teaching practice. I hope that recapitulating the argument or reasons for this will serve as a suitable epilogue to the book as a whole.

I do not believe and I have not argued that there is nothing to teaching. I have not said that skills of teaching cannot be taught, or that useful dialogue cannot take place about ways of proceeding in the classroom. I know, as an experienced teacher, that these things can be taught and furthermore I believe they should be. But teaching people to teach, in this sense, should, it seems to me, be a matter of inducting people into it, by means of discussion, example and opportunity for practice at a relatively informal and personal level. (That is, of course, the way it is very often done.)

What I have been rather sceptical of is the idea of what might be called a science of teaching, and what I have been critical of is some research into teaching methods which is both weak in itself (partly inescapably, but partly not) and mistakenly suggests that what is needed is more empirical inquiry. There's certainly nothing wrong with empirical inquiry in itself, but in the study of education the emphasis on it, at any rate in its present state, causes gross distortion. There are no firm guidelines as to teaching methods or techniques in this chapter, because whatever particular protagonists of particular bits of empirical research may say to the contrary, there is no clear evidence in the light of which to lay down specific rules. No hard-and-fast conclusions are warranted.

One of the points I have tried to make is that, particular criticisms of specific research apart, to be effective and illuminating any empirical research is going to have to be conducted with a better conceptual and logical grasp than is often evident in educational research. In my own self-interests I must repeat for the last time that it is not empirical research as such that I have attacked. I have merely done something to redress the very dangerous and misleading assumption that the only path to any kind of truth or fact is through empirical inquiry, and that this can somehow proceed without interest in non-empirical disciplines, by pointing out that both parts of the assumption are plain false. In particular, neither empirical work in general nor educational studies in particular can possibly be worthwhile until or unless they are conducted by those with a proper grasp of philosophy (whether they recognise it as philosophy or not).

More positively I have pointed out that coherent schooling

policy and sensible educational views, which are not necessary attributes of the good teacher in a narrow sense, but which one could convincingly argue the teaching profession should seek to have, depend upon clear ideas about what schooling is for, clear and rational argument, and clear conceptions of education, morality, intelligence and other ideas that are central to the enterprise. It is also necessary to understand and to be able to distinguish between logically distinct kinds of question, so that one does not simple-mindedly reduce, say, the moral dimension to just one more thing for empirical inquiry.

All the above relates to what might be termed the formal content of this book. Since this is designed as an introductory text, I have been very concerned throughout to convey a thorough understanding of what philosophy is and of how it fits in to the broader picture. In doing so I have used many illustrations, and in doing that I hope to have made some substantive points and to have laid the foundations of a philosophy of schooling in that other sense of a co-ordinated and reasoned theory of what schooling is all about.

Notes

(For publishing details see bibliography)

CHAPTER 1

1. R. St. C. Barrow and R. G. Woods *Introduction to Philosophy of Education*. The review in question appeared in The Times Higher Education Supplement.

CHAPTER 2

1. See, for example, Ivan Illich *Deschooling Society* and *Celebration of Awareness*: Everett Reimer *School is Dead*. Also Ian Lister *Deschooling*.
2. For a critical examination of deschooling arguments see my *Radical Education*.
3. For a detailed examination of the many meanings of "natural" see *Radical Education*.
4. See especially R. S. Peters *Ethics and Education* part 1.
5. The initial presentation of the "forms of knowledge" thesis was in P. H. Hirst "Liberal education and the nature of knowledge". A slightly modified presentation, to which I refer in the text, is to be found in P. H. Hirst and R. S. Peters *The Logic of Education*.
6. P. H. Hirst "The forms of knowledge revisited".
7. P. H. Hirst and R. S. Peters *The Logic of Education*.
8. Ibid.
9. P. H. Hirst "Literature and the Fine Arts as a form of knowledge".
10. For a comprehensive study of Critical Thinking see John McPeck *Critical Thinking*.
11. On indoctrination see 1. Snook (ed) *Concepts of Indoctrination*.
12. Everett Reimer *School is Dead*.
13. My *Radical Education*.
14. Juvenal Satire 10.356.
15. An excellent book exploring some of the claims typically made in the context of movement studies is David Best *Philosophy and Human Movement*.
16. D. Anthony "Is there a future for P.E.?"
17. I follow R. W. Hepburn "The arts and the education of feeling and emotion" fairly closely.
18. I say "possibly", because in section 9 I discount the importance of the creative dimension of man's nature in schooling.
19. J. S. Bruner "The conditions of creativity."
20. See Hugh Lytton *Creativity and Education* for a useful summary of the research.

21. James Gribble *Introduction to Philosophy of Education.*
22. Liam Hudson *Contrary Imaginations.*
23. W. S. Gilbert *The Gondoliers.*

CHAPTER 3

1. P. S. Wilson "Child Centred Education."
2. Ibid.
3. Ibid.
4. For a fuller discussion of arguments for free schools see my *Moral Philosophy for Education* and *Radical Education.*
5. See, for example, John Gretton and Mark Jackson *William Tyndale Collapse of a School—or a System?*
6. Hugh Sockett (ed) *Accountability in the English Educational System.*
7. See R. S. Peters (ed) *The Role of the Head.*
8. Ibid.

CHAPTER 4

1. Since writing the above I have modified my views slightly on the importance of spelling, thanks in part to the arguments of Ann Dubbs in Michael Marland (ed) *Language Across the Curriculum.* She points out the close connection between spelling and meaning, such that to be ignorant of the spelling of a word may often signify ignorance of the constituent parts and hence sense of a word.
2. Plato's objection to introducing the young to philosophy is to be found at *Republic* 539.
3. See N. Postman and C. Weingartner *Teaching as a Subversive activity.* Marshall McLuhan *Understanding Media.* Berkeley *Essay Towards a New Theory of Vision.*
4. See M. R. F. Young (ed) *Knowledge and Control.* For a criticism of radical sociology see A. Flew *Sociology, Equality and Education.*
5. See, for example, *Journal of Pre-College Philosophy, Teaching Philosophy* and *Thinking: Journal of Philosophy for Children.*

CHAPTER 5

1. A. Flew "Theology and falsification: a symposium."
2. A. J. Ayer *Language, Truth and Logic.*
3. Ibid.
4. John Locke on *Politics and Education.* Thomas Hobbes *Leviathan.*
5. Plato *Gorgias.*
6. David Hume *A Treatise of Human Nature.*
7. A. S. Neill *Summerhill.*
8. W. D. Ross *The Right and the Good.*
9. G. E. Moore *Principia Ethica.*
10. Ibid.
11. C. L. Stevenson *Ethics and Language.*

12. R. M. Hare *The Language of Morals*.
13. On the extension of the moral domain to include man's relationship with other animals see Peter Singer *Animal Liberation*.
14. Urie Bronfenbrenner *Two Worlds of Childhood*.
15. See, for example, L. Kohlberg "Stage and Sequence: the Cognitive-Developmental Approach to Socialisation" and "Education for Justice: a Modern Statement of the Platonic View."
16. Peter McPhail *Moral Education in the Secondary School*.
17. John Wilson *Moral Thinking*.

CHAPTER 6

1. Ruth Barwood in a forthcoming paper. Mrs Barwood worked on the ORACLE project with my colleagues from the University of Leicester, Paul Croll, Maurice Galton and Brian Simon. At the time of writing their research findings are about to be published. I am hopeful and confident that they will have avoided all the avoidable pitfalls in this kind of empirical research.
2. Ruth Barwood unpublished paper.
3. N. Bradburn and D. Caplovitz *Reports on Happiness*.
4. W. Wilson "Correlates of Avowed Happiness."
5. Neville Bennett *Teaching Styles and Pupil Progress*.
6. B. S. Bloom *A Taxonomy of Educational Objectives*.
7. Bruce Joyce and Marsha Weil *Models of Teaching*.
8. Rusk *The Doctrines of the Great Educators*.
9. Bruce Joyce *Preservice Teacher Education*.
10. For the logical connection between teaching and evaluation see A. Flew *Sociology, Equality and Education*.
11. Again see Flew on this proposal for "A certificate of no known achievement."
12. On equality see David E. Cooper's excellent book *Illusions of Equality*.

Bibliography

David B. Annis (1974) *Techniques of Critical Reasoning*, Charles E. Merrill Publishing Company, Columbus.

D. Anthony (1971) "Is there a future for P.E.?" in The Times Educational Supplement 16th February 1971.

A. J. Ayer (1971) *Language, Truth and Logic*, Penguin, Harmondsworth.

Robin Barrow (1975) *Moral Philosophy for Education*, Allen and Unwin, London.

Robin Barrow (1976) *Common Sense and Curriculum*, Allen and Unwin, London.

Robin Barrow (1979) *The Canadian Curriculum*, University of Western Ontario, London. Canada.

Robin Barrow (1978) *Radical Education*, Martin Robertson, Oxford.

Robin Barrow (1980) *Happiness*, Martin Robertson, Oxford.

Neville Bennett (1976) *Teaching Styles and Pupil Progress*, Open Books, London.

Berkeley (1934) *Essay Towards a New Theory of Vision*. J. M. Dent and Sons, Everyman's Library, London.

David Best (1978) *Philosophy and Human Movement*, Allen and Unwin, London.

B. S. Bloom (ed) (1956) *Taxonomy of Educational Objectives*, David McKay, N. Bradburn and D. Caplovitz (1965) *Reports on Happiness*, Aldine, Chicago.

David Bridges and Peter Scrimshaw (eds) (1975) *Values and Authority in Schools*, Hodder and Stoughton, London.

David Bridges (1979) *Education, Democracy and Discussion* N.F.E.R. Publishing Company, London.

James Britton (1972) *Language and Learning*, Penguin, Harmondsworth.

Urie Bronfenbrenner (1971) *Two Worlds of Childhood: US and USSR*, Allen and Unwin, London.

J. S. Bruner (1962) "The Conditions of Creativity" in H. E. Gruber, G. Terrell, M. Wertheimer (eds) *Contemporary Approaches to Creative Thinking*, Atherton Press, New York.

Lewis Carroll (1962) "The Hunting of the Snark" in Martin Gardner (ed) *The Annotated Snark*, Penguin, Harmondsworth.

David E. Cooper (1980) *Illusions of Equality*, Routledge & Kegan Paul, London.

Maurice Cranston (ed) (1965) *Locke on Politics, Religion and Education*, Collier-Macmillan, London.

S. J. Curtis and M. E. A. Boultwood (1953) *A Short History of Educational Ideas*, University Tutorial Press, London.

Antony Flew, R. M. Hare, B. Mitchell (1971) "Theology and falsification: a symposium," in B. Mitchell (ed) *The Philosophy of Religion*, Oxford.

Antony Flew (1975) *Thinking about Thinking*, Fontana/Collins, Glasgow.

Antony Flew (1976) *Sociology, Equality and Education*, Macmillan, London.

G. N. Garmonsway (ed) (1965) *The Penguin English Dictionary*, Penguin, Harmondsworth.

Keith Graham (1977) *J. L. Austin, A Critique of Ordinary Language Philosophy*, Harvester, Hassocks.

James Gribble (1969) *Introduction to Philosophy of Education*, Allyn and Bacon, Boston.

R. M. Hare (1952) *The Language of Morals*, Oxford.

R. W. Hepburn (1972) "The arts and the education of feeling and emotion" in R. F. Dearden, P. H. Hirst and R. S. Peters (eds) *Education and the Development of Reason*, Routledge & Kegan Paul, London.

P. H. Hirst and R. S. Peters (1970) *The Logic of Education*, Routledge & Kegan Paul, London.

P. H. Hirst (1974) "Liberal Education and the nature of knowledge", "The forms of knowledge revisited" and "Literature and the fine arts as a form of knowledge" in *Knowledge and the Curriculum*, Routledge & Kegan Paul, London.

John Hospers (1970) *Human conduct*, Hart-Davis, London.

Liam Hudson (1967) *Contrary Imaginations*, Penguin, Harmondsworth.

David Hume (1955) *A Treatise of Human Nature*, Regnery, Chicago.

Ivan Illich (1973) *Celebration of Awareness*, Penguin, Harmondsworth.

Ivan Illich (1973) *Deschooling Society*, Penguin, Harmondsworth.

Bruce Joyce and Marsha Weil (1972) *Models of Teaching*, Prentice-Hall, New Jersey.

Bruce Joyce (1977) *Preservice Teacher Education*, Palo Alto, California.

L. Kohlberg (1968) "Stage and Sequence: The Cognitive-Developmental Approach to Socialisation" in D. Goslin (ed) *Handbook of Socialisation*, Rand McNally, New York.

L. Kohlberg (1970) "Education for Justice" in N. F. and T. R. Sizer (eds) *Moral Education*, Harvard University Press, Cambridge, Mass.

Ian Lister (1975) *Deschooling*, Cambridge.

John Locke (1947) (ed H. R. Penniman) on *Politics and Education*, Van Nostrand, New York.

Hugh Lytton (1971) *Creativity and Education*, Routledge & Kegan Paul, London.

M. McLuhan (1965) *Understanding Media*, McGraw-Hill, New York.

J. McPeck (1981) *Critical Thinking*, Martin Robertson, Oxford.

Peter McPhail (1972) *Moral Education in the Secondary School*, Longman, London.

Michael Marland (ed) (1977) *Language Across the Curriculum*, Heinemann, London.

Alex C. Michalos (1970) *Improving your reasoning*, Prentice-Hall, New Jersey.

G. E. Moore (1962) *Principia Ethica*, Cambridge.

D. J. O'Connor (1957) *An Introduction to the Philosophy of Education*, Routledge and Kegan Paul, London.

R. S. Peters (1966) *Ethics and Education*, Allen and Unwin, London.

R. S. Peters (1973) *Authority, Responsibility and Education*, 3rd edition, Allen and Unwin, London.

R. S. Peters (ed) (1976) *Role of the Head*, Routledge & Kegan Paul, London.

Plato (1974) *The Republic* (trs Desmond Lee), Penguin, Harmondsworth.

Plato (1954) *The Last Days of Socrates* (trs Hugh Tredennick), Penguin, Harmondsworth.

L. A. Reid (1962) *Philosophy and Education*, Heinemann, London.

Everett Reimer (1971) *School is Dead*, Penguin, Harmondsworth.

W. D. Ross (1930) *The Right and the Good*, Oxford.

R. Rusk (1969) *The Doctrines of the Great Educators*, Macmillan, London.

I. Scheffler (1973) *Reason and Teaching,* Routledge & Kegan Paul, London.

Michael Scriven (1976) *Reasoning*, McGraw Hill, New York.

Peter Singer (1977) *Animal Liberation*, Paladin, London.

Peter Singer (1979) *Practical Ethics*, Cambridge.

I. Snook (1972) *Concepts of Indoctrination*, Routledge & Kegan Paul, London.

Hugh Sockett (ed) (1980) *Accountability in the English Educational System*, Hodder and Stoughton, London.

C. L. Stevenson (1944) *Ethics and Language.* Yale University Press, New Haven.

Frederick Vivian (1969) *Thinking Philosophically*, Chatto and Windus, London.

D. Warwick (ed) (1974) *Integrated Studies in the Secondary School*, University of London Press.

John Wilson (1963) *Thinking with Concepts*, Cambridge.

John Wilson (1970) *Moral Thinking*, Heinemann, London.

P. S. Wilson (1969) "Child centred education" in Proceedings of the Annual Conference of the Philosophy of Education Society of Great Britain, January, 1969.

W. Wilson (1967) "Correlates of Avowed Happiness" *Psychological Bulletin*, 1967.

Nigel Wright (1977) *Progress in Education*, Croom Helm, London.

Index